CONTENTS

LIST OF MAPS

About the Author
Lee Atkinson is a freelance travel writer and guidebook author. Her stories regularly appear in the travel sections of various newspapers and glossy travel magazines in both Australia and internationally. She is the author of six books about travelling in and around Australia, including *Frommer's Sydney Day by Day*, and a contributor to *Frommer's Australia*.

Acknowledgements

Thank you to my fellow cheapskates Anna Maguire, Kris Madden, Kim McKay, Kerry Lorimer, Derek Holt, John Fraser and Alex McKinnon for all their suggestions, and company, while researching this first edition. Thanks also to Katherine Drew and Brooke Lyons at Wiley for all their help and encouragement, and to Bella Hindle for being such a great editor to work with. Special thanks, though, to Bill McKinnon, for never complaining about all the cheap dates.

—Lee Atkinson

An Invitation to the Reader

In researching this book, we discovered many wonderful places—hotels, restaurants, shops, and more. We're sure you'll find others. Please tell us about them, so we can share the information with your fellow travellers in upcoming editions. If you were disappointed with a recommendation, we'd love to know that, too. Please write to:

Frommer's Sydney Free & Dirt Cheap, 1st Edition
John Wiley & Sons Australia, Inc. ● 42 McDougall Street ● Milton Qld
Australia 4064

An Additional Note

Please be advised that travel information is subject to change at any time—and this is especially true of prices. We therefore suggest that you write or call ahead for confirmation when making your travel plans. The authors, editors and publisher cannot be held responsible for the experiences of readers while travelling. Your safety is important to us, however, so we encourage you to stay alert and be aware of your surroundings. Keep a close eye on cameras, purses and wallets, all favourite targets of thieves and pickpockets.

Other Great Guides for Your Trip:

Frommer's Sydney Day by Day

Frommer's Australia

Free & Dirt Cheap Icons & Abbreviations

We also use **feature icons** that point you to the great deals, in-the-know advice and unique experiences that separate urban adventurers from tourists. Throughout the book, look for:

FREE   Events, attractions or experiences that cost no more than your time.

FINE PRINT   The unspoken conditions or necessary preparations to experience certain free and dirt cheap events.

★   The best free and dirt cheap events, dining, shopping, living and exploring in the city.

OVERRATED   Places or experiences not worth your time or money.

Frommers.com

Now that you have this guidebook to help you plan a great trip, visit our website at **www.frommers.com** for additional travel information on more than 4,000 destinations. We update features regularly to give you instant access to the most current trip-planning information available. At Frommers.com, you'll find information on the best airfares, accommodation rates and car rental bargains. You can even book your travel online through our reliable travel booking partners. Other popular features include:

- Online updates of our most popular guidebooks

- Holiday sweepstakes and contest giveaways

- Newsletters highlighting the hottest travel trends

- Podcasts, interactive maps and up-to-the-minute events listings

- Opinionated blog entries by Arthur Frommer himself

- Online travel message boards with featured travel discussions

The view of that famous bridge from Observatory Park (p. 114) is both free and spectacular.

THE BEST THINGS IN LIFE ARE FREE

Sydney has an image problem. Seen as a millionaire's playground, the city has a bad reputation for being wickedly expensive and there's no denying that it is the capital of conspicuous consumption. But I'll let you in on a well-kept secret: it's all just for show. Sure, waterfront real estate is the stuff of fantasy and it might be home to $1,000-per-head dinners at restaurants such as Astral, $50 cocktails at the Beresford Hotel and $7,000-a-night suites at Ivy, but there's absolutely no reason why you can't have the time of your life in Sydney without spending a fortune. I do it all the time!

My idea of the perfect Sydney day starts at Bronte Beach. I try to make it all the way to Bondi along the cliff-top walk before I succumb to breakfast, which I eat alfresco overlooking the surf. Then, if the weather's kind (it most often is) I keep strolling all the way to South Head, stopping for a swim along the way, followed by fish and chips on the beach at Watson's Bay.

When it's dark I head into the inner west or city fringe to catch a band or see a free movie at a pub, or maybe eat a few steamed dumplings from a tiny hole-in-the-wall noodle house in Chinatown.

By the end of the day I've explored some of the city's best neighbourhoods, seen some of the world's most breathtaking views, marvelled at how good it is to be alive and hardly spent a cent.

Call me biased, but not many other cities can boast such consistently glorious weather as Sydney; few capitals have so much wild national parkland so close to the city; hardly any other urban centres have beaches better than ours; and no other metropolis has a natural wonder than can match Sydney Harbour. One of the biggest on the planet, the harbour is not only one of the world's most beautiful waterways, it's also the spiritual, historical and cultural heart of the city. So it's only natural that many of the city's best only-in-Sydney experiences are on, in or beside the water.

But living it up in Sydney is not just about the great outdoors. Egalitarian to its core, Sydney has a flourishing arts scene, but just like the city itself, it's far from stuffy or pretentious and most of the galleries are free. The same goes for our history—it's out there on the streets, literally a living open-air museum where you can almost hear the clanking of the convicts' chains and smell the fear of criminals past as you wander the alleys of The Rocks.

And while we might well enjoy stripping off our clothes at the beach, when we do dress up it's always in style. Many of the country's best designers cut their fashion teeth in the weekend markets across the city; if you want to be on-trend before it's even become one, Sydney's markets are the place to shop.

It's the same story when it comes to music and theatre. Some of the best musical and theatrical performances are to be found for free (or a nominal fee) in the pubs and back-street theatres. Sydney's inner-city pubs have always been incubators for some of the hottest rocks bands ever to have hit the airways, and some of the world's best actors learnt their craft on Sydney's stages.

And when it comes to feeding the body rather than the mind, Sydney is brimming with cheap eateries of every flavour, home to one of the most diverse cuisine pools on the planet. Dine out on authentic Vietnamese noodle soup for not much more than it would cost in Saigon, fill up with a seemingly never-ending stream of steaming dim sum at yum cha for less than $20 a head or tuck into a super-sized steak at your local pub for $10. In Sydney, you can eat like a king, but pay like a pauper.

It doesn't matter whether you're a visitor or a local, you'll find hundreds of ways to enjoy the harbour city for free, or dirt cheap.

Sydney may come across as a town for the moneyed few, but the good news is that you don't have to be rich to see the best of it.

The majestic sails of the Sydney Opera House provide a classic photo op.

THE BEST OF FREE & DIRT-CHEAP SYDNEY

E ver heard of the saying 'you get what you pay for'? It is usually proven true—unless you're lucky enough to be in Sydney, where you can get a whole lot for not very much at all. But here's the really good news: here in sunny Sydney, you'll often find that the very best things on offer—the types of things you just can't find anywhere else, and that are worth crossing the country (or indeed the world) for—are all free or dirt cheap. From mouth-watering food to knock-your-socks-off harbour views, fantastic beaches, great shopping finds and the hottest live acts—you can find them all in Sydney and at pocket-pleasing prices, to boot.

To save you having to search for them yourself, we've put together a list of the city's best of the best.

1 The Best Free Only-in-Sydney Experiences

● **Watching the Sun Go Down Behind the Sydney Harbour Bridge.** Nothing ends a perfect Sydney day in more style than watching the sun set behind the Harbour Bridge from **Mrs Macquarie's Chair,** a convict-carved rock-ledge chair in the Botanic Gardens. It was made for the wife of Governor Macquarie, who also enjoyed the same stunning sunset views (without the Harbour Bridge or Opera House, of course) in 1810. See p. 94.

● **Watching the Sun Rise Out of the Sea.** Take an early morning stroll along the **Bronte to Bondi Coastal Walk** for one of the best sunrise shows in Sydney. See p. 127.

● **Bringing in the New Year with the World's Best Fireworks Show.** Sydney puts on one of the world's most awe-inspiring displays of pyrotechnics on New Year's Eve. And the best thing about it is that it's free. See p. 20.

● **Walking Along the Cliff Edges.** Sydney is home to some of the world's best urban cliff-top walks. My favourite is the **Federation Cliff Walk** (p. 127), which extends the more famous **Bronte to Bondi Coastal Walk** (p. 127) from Dover Heights to Watsons Bay and South Head. It's not nearly as popular or crowded as the Bronte to Bondi section, but it's every bit as scenic.

● **Crossing the Coathanger For Free.** Save yourself a couple of hundred dollars and walk across the **Sydney Harbour Bridge** at road level for free. The view is breathtaking! See p. 240.

● **Strutting Your Stuff on Bondi Beach.** Sydney has more than 40 beaches and they all offer a perfect combination of sun, sand and sea, but if you only have time to visit one, make it **Bondi Beach.** More than three million visitors a year can't be wrong. See p. 134.

● **Unpacking a Picnic.** Head to one of the harbourside parks and watch the world sail by. Trust me, it's the thing to do any sunny Sunday. With more than 240km of foreshore in

Sydney Harbour, there are dozens of parks to choose from. If you have to pick just one it should be **Nielsen Park** for its unbeatable combination of sun, sand, sea, shade and proximity to decent coffee. See p. 136.

- **Doing Laps.** Swim some laps in one of Sydney's harbour- or beachside pools. They're cold, old and crumbling, there are no fancy change rooms and there are often small sea creatures lurking in the depths, but these outdoor rock pools are almost always free to swim in and all have five-star views. See p. 137.

- **Watching a Surf Lifesaving Carnival.** The burly, toned and tanned surf lifesavers are Sydney's home-grown guardian angels, and you can watch them compete in any number of surf carnivals during summer for free. Now that's what I call perfect people-watching! See p. 145.

- **Watching the Sydney Gay & Lesbian Mardi Gras.** The world's most glamorous civil rights demonstration started as a protest rally back in 1978 and has grown into one of the world's great gay and lesbian festivals. It draws thousands of fabulously and extravagantly costumed marchers to Sydney each February, as well as huge crowds of all sexual persuasions. See p. 17.

- **Visiting the Brett Whiteley Studio.** The late Brett Whiteley painted some of the most iconic images of Sydney and produced those love-'em-or-hate-'em giant matches behind the Art Gallery of New South Wales. Visit his studio in Surry Hills to find out what made this brilliant artist tick, and to see work you won't find anywhere else. See p. 117.

- **Watching Whales.** See if you can spot the beautiful white whale, Migaloo, from one of the many cliff-top whale-watching vantage points in Sydney during his annual winter migration. See p. 141.

2 The Best Dirt-Cheap Only-in-Sydney Experiences

- **Taking a Ferry Ride.** The half-hour trip across the harbour on the **Manly Ferry** is one of the best-value harbour cruises in the world. It's an experience not to be missed. See p. 249.

- **Finding a Designer Bargain.** Saturday's Paddington Markets is one of the best places to find a hot new fashion label before it becomes famous—or expensive. See p. 182.

● **Going Barefoot Bowling.** What's not to love about an outdoor team sport that you can play with bare feet and a cold schooner in your hand? See p. 142.

● **Watching the Passing Street Parade from a Newtown Coffee Shop.** You'll never know who or what you'll see in this colourful, unconventional inner-city suburb. It's people-watching at its best and it costs only the price of a cup of coffee.

● **Having a Beer in one of Sydney's Oldest Pubs.** Both the **Fortune of War** (p. 206) and **The Lord Nelson** (p. 27) like to boast that they are the oldest pubs in Sydney (the detail's in the fine print).

● **Racing a Yacht.** Get your life jacket on and sail the harbour for the price of a couple of post-race beers. There are a number of sailing clubs that are always looking for crew on race days. The catch is that

you'll need to know what you're doing. See p. 102.

● **Walking in World-Heritage-Listed Wilderness.** There aren't many cities in the world where you can find yourself in World-Heritage-Listed wilderness just an hour or so from the city centre. The **Blue Mountains** (p. 262) are practically on the city's doorstep and it's a speedy train ride away.

● **Exploring Sydney Harbour at Sea Level in a Hired Kayak.** Get away from the tourist throng and discover a different aspect of Sydney as you paddle around the deep water frontages of the city's rich and famous in the sheltered bays of Middle Harbour. It's a view of Sydney that few people ever get to see. See p. 102.

● **Partaking of a Cheap Night Out at the Sydney Opera House.** You don't have to be loaded to enjoy a show at one of the world's most instantly recognisable entertainment venues. Most shows in **The Studio** cost less than $30. See p. 219.

3 The Best Cheap Sleeps

● **Best Place to Make Like a Rock Star.** This tiny boutique hotel gets my vote as the best place

to stay in Sydney for less than $150. There might not be many rooms at the **Hotel Altamont**

(207 Darlinghurst Rd.; ℭ **(02) 9360 6000**), but it punches way above its weight when it comes to style and value. See p. 33.

- **Best (Affordable) Room with a View.** Almost all of the rooms at **The Macleay Serviced Apartments** (28 Macleay St.; ℭ **(02) 9357 7755)** have sensational harbour views at a price that won't send you bankrupt. See p. 37.

- **Best Middle-of-the-Harbour Sleep-Out.** Pitch a tent on **Cockatoo Island**; ℭ **(02) 8898 9774**) and enjoy an unimpeded harbour view from your sleeping bag. If you don't have your own tent, you can hire all the equipment you need on the island. Kids love it! See p. 30.

- **Best Bush Getaway in the Middle of the City.** Get back to nature in **Lane Cove National Park.** Pitch a tent, park the caravan or stay in one of the self-contained cabins at **Lane Cove River Tourist Park** (Plassey Rd.; ℭ **(02) 9888 9133**). See p. 46.

- **Best Backpackers. Sydney Central YHA** (cnr Pitt St. and Rawson Place; ℭ **(02) 9218 9000**; p. 31) and **Sydney Harbour YHA** (110 Cumberland St.; ℭ **(02) 8272 0900**; p. 31) are neck and neck when it comes to the best backpackers in town. If I had to pick it would be Sydney Harbour, which is brand spanking new and has views of the Opera House.

- **Best Night on the Rails.** Spend the night in a converted railway carriage at **Railway Square YHA** (8–10 Lee St.; ℭ **(02) 9281 9666**). See p. 31.

- **Best Value Beachside Rooms.** The rooms aren't super stylish at the **Manly Paradise Motel & Apartments** (54 North Steyne; ℭ **(02) 9977 5799**), but they have everything you need and they are directly opposite Manly Beach. See p. 42.

- **Best Pet-Friendly Hotel.** The **Hotel Altamont** (207 Darlinghurst Rd.; ℭ **(02) 9360 6000**) is one of the few hotels in the city that will welcome your pet, but only if it is well behaved. See p. 33.

4 The Best Cheap Eats

- **Best Lunch on the Run.** Roll up for some brilliant Vietnamese finger food from the hole-in-the-wall cafe in Darlinghurst,

MISSCHU (cnr. Bourke and William sts.; ✆ **(02) 8356 9988**). See p. 67.

● **Best Burger.** It's hard to find a better burger than the melt-in-your-mouth grain-fed Wagyu beef burger at **Plan B** (204 Clarence St.; ✆ **(02) 9283 3450**). See p. 61.

● **Best Snack Under $2.** The scrumptious little savoury pastry pillows from the **Maltese Pastizzi Cafe** (310 Crown St.; ✆ **(02) 9361 6942**) in Surry Hills are addictive, and at just $1.50 each you can have half a dozen and still get change from a $10 note. See p. 71.

● **Best Dinner with a View.** Cross the bridge for stunning Opera House views at **Ripples** (Olympic Dr.; ✆ **(02) 9929 7722**), without the hefty pay-for-view price tag. Equally fabulous for breakfast, lunch and dinner. See p. 81.

● **Best Dumplings.** The piping hot soup-filled dumplings at **Din Tai Fung** (Level 1, World Square Shopping Centre, 644 George St.; ✆ **(02) 9264 6010**) are bursting with eye-popping flavour. Just one is enough to send you to dumpling heaven, but go all out and order a dozen. See p. 56.

● **Best Fish and Chips.** During the '70s and '80s **Doyles on the Wharf** (Fishermans Wharf; ✆ **(02) 9337 6214**) was Sydney's most famous place to eat fish. The kiosk next door sells pretty much the same food at takeaway prices, making it some of the best fish and chips in Sydney. See p. 74.

● **Most Meaty Meal.** It's a vegetarian's nightmare, but **Churrasco** (240 Coogee Bay Rd.; ✆ **(02) 9665 6535**) in Coogee will serve you all the meat you can eat for just $35. See p. 78.

● **Best Salt-and-Pepper Squid.** It's a tough call to make in a city that is obsessed with spicy deep-fried tentacles, but the salt-and-pepper squid at Coogee's **Banana Palm** (260 Arden St.; ✆ **(02) 9665 1212**) is pretty close to perfect. See p. 73.

● **Best Comfort Food.** Savour hearty, old-fashioned favourites that warm your tummy and your soul at **Betty's Soup Kitchen** (84 Oxford St.; ✆ **(02) 9360 9698**). See p. 68.

● **Best Dirt-Cheap Meal at a Very Expensive Restaurant.** The three-course lunch on Friday at **Marque** (355 Crown St.; ✆ **(02) 9332 2225**) is unbelievable value, giving you a taste of

THE BEST FREE & DIRT CHEAP WAYS TO EXPLORE SYDNEY **11**

some of the best food cooked up by one of the country's most highly awarded chefs in town for less than $50. Not bad, when you consider that mains alone are usually $48. See p. 72.

- **Best Dessert Cocktail.** Who needs cake when you can have a chili chocolate margarita at **Wet Paint** (56–60 Macpherson St.; ℂ **(02) 9369 4634**)? Chocolate liqueur, crème de cacao, espresso and chili-infused tequila combine to make the perfect alcoholic dessert. See p. 79.

5 The Best Free & Dirt Cheap Ways to Explore Sydney

- **Best Dirt-Cheap Harbour Cruise.** Ride the **RiverCat** (Circular Quay; ℂ **131 500**) to Rydalmere and back for a two-hour harbour cruise that costs less than $15. Take the family on a Sunday and it will cost just $2.50 each. See p. 94.

- **Best Free Aquarium.** Forget about paying $10 or $15 to look at marine life through a glass wall; grab a mask and snorkel and see the real thing at **Cabbage Tree Bay Aquatic Reserve** (Marine Pde.). See p. 140.

- **Best Free Local History Museum.** The Rocks is one of Sydney's most fascinating (and oldest) suburbs. **The Rocks Discovery Museum** (Kendall Lane; ℂ **(02) 9251 8804**) will help you put 220 or so years of history into context. See p. 113.

- **Best Free Mummies.** Nothing delights kids more than ancient dead people. There are Egyptian mummies on display at the free **Nicholson Museum** (University of Sydney; ℂ **(02) 9351 2812**), as well as Australia's largest collection of antiquities. See p. 111.

- **Best Free Art.** There's always something new on show at the **Art Gallery of New South Wales** (Art Gallery Rd.; ℂ **(02) 9225 1700**) and it's also home to an impressive collection of Australian art. See p. 115.

- **Best Free Walk in the Park.** Join a free 90-minute tour through the **Royal Botanic Gardens** (Mrs Macquaries Rd.; ℂ **(02) 9231 8134**) to receive a crash course in Australian botany. See p. 131.

- **Best Free Tour.** Not only is it the only working **Government House** (Macquarie St., Royal Botanic Gardens; ℂ **(02) 9931 5222**) in Australia that is open to the public, it has an excellent free tour every half hour that brings the history and people of the house alive. See p. 106.

- **Best Pool with a View.** Brush up on your backstroke—the views of the Harbour Bridge from **North Sydney Olympic Pool** (4 Alfred St. South; ✆ **(02) 9955 2309**) are too good to ignore. See p. 139.

- **Most Icky Exhibits.** Not one for those with a weak stomach or hypochondriacs—or maybe it

is? If you like looking at weird body bits and the effects of unmentionable diseases, you'll love the **Museum of Human Disease** (Samuels Building, University of NSW, cnr. High and Botany sts.; ✆ **(02) 9385 1522**). See p. 110.

- **Best Beach for Swimming.** Clovelly Beach's unique cigar shape and rock ledges make it a great place for some serious saltwater swimming. Find it at the end of Clovelly Rd. See p. 137.

6 The Best Free & Dirt Cheap Local Living

- **Best Dirt-Cheap Day Spa.** There's a full range of feel-good beauty treatments of offer at bargain basement prices at **Fuss Beauty College** (161 New South Head Rd.; ✆ **(02) 9326 2204**). See p. 158.

- **Best Cheap Shrink.** Students give adult, child and family therapy sessions for just $10 at the **University of Sydney Psychology Clinic** (Transient Building F12, Fisher Rd.; ✆ **(02) 9351 2629**). See p. 163.

- **Best Dirt-Cheap Haircut.** Save hundreds of dollars on a cut and colour when you sign up to be a model at the **Toni&Guy Academy** (255C Oxford St.; ✆ **(02) 9380 2299**). See p. 160.

- **Best Free Cooking Class.** Learn how to cook Italian food from the experts at **Fratelli Fresh** (7 Danks St.; ✆ **(02) 9699 3161**). See p. 153.

- **Best Free Dance Classes.** The summertime salsa and waltzing lessons on **The Corso** (outside Manly Town Hall, The Corso; ✆ **(02) 9976 1721**) will have you dancing in the streets—literally. See p. 164.

- **Best Library for Lounging.** The ground floor 'magazine salon' at **Customs House Library** (31 Alfred St.; ✆ **(02) 9242 8595**) has an inexhaustible range of international newspapers and magazines, free for the reading. See p. 154.

- **Best Dirt-Cheap Gym.** Get fit for small change without having to sign up for a costly membership at **Pyrmont Community Centre** (cnr. John and Mount sts.; ℂ **(02) 9298 3130**). See p. 161.

- **Funniest Free Yoga Class.** There's a free **Laughter Yoga** (Memorial Park, cnr. Federation Rd. and Australia St.; no phone) class at Bondi Beach every Sunday morning. See p. 165.

7 The Best Free & Dirt Cheap Shopping

- **Best Markets for Designer Clothing.** Many of Australia's best fashion designers cut their fashion teeth at the Saturday **Paddington Markets** (Paddington Uniting Church, Oxford St.; ℂ **(02) 9331 2923**) and it's the best place to find the next fashion icon before their work becomes expensive. See p. 182.

- **Best Markets for Second-Hand Clothes.** It's all second-hand and handmade at the **Surry Hills Market** (cnr. Crown and Little Collins sts.). See p. 183.

- **Best Place to Drink and Shop.** The Marlborough Hotel is home to the **Marly Markets** (145 King St.; ℂ **(02) 9519 1222**), where you can browse boho, vintage and soon-to-be fashionable threads. See p. 183.

- **Best Street for Retro Shopping.** Wander down the western end of **King Street** in Newtown to find all things recycled, reused and retro. See p. 173.

- **Best Second-Hand Books.** Gould's Book Arcade (32 King St.; ℂ **(02) 9519 8947**) is a multi-level temple to second-hand and out-of-print books. See p. 186.

- **Best Pre-Loved Furniture.** Furnish your house with second-hand furniture from **Recycling Works** (45 Parramatta Rd.; ℂ **(02) 9517 2711**). You can feel good about it, knowing that a portion of the profits is donated to a range of charities. See p. 179.

- **Best Factory Outlet Centre.** Homebush's **DFO** (cnr. Homebush Bay Dr. and Underwood Rd.; ℂ **(02) 9748 9800**) has 90 stores selling pretty much everything at up to 70% off recommended retail prices. See p. 180.

- **Best Thrift Shop.** Ferret through huge piles of unsorted clothing and uncover some real gems. Pay by the kilo at the **Anglicare Depot** (105 Carlton Cr.; ℂ **(02) 9798 8206**). See p. 173.

8 The Best Free & Dirt Cheap Entertainment

- **Best Spot for Free Jazz.** Drink in one of the most spectacular views in Sydney while imbibing some fine food and wine and listening to live jazz on a Sunday afternoon at the **Opera Bar** (Lower Concourse, Sydney Opera House; ℂ **(02) 9247 1666**). See p. 206.

- **Best Place to See New Rock Superstars for Free.** Catch the Next Big Thing on stage every night except Tuesday at the **Annandale Hotel** (17–19 Parramatta Rd.; ℂ **(02) 9550 1078**). See p. 84.

- **Best Cheap Laughs.** Seeing three comics for $10 at **The Fringe Bar** (106 Oxford St.; ℂ **(02) 9360 5443**) is a deal not to be laughed at—or maybe it is? See p. 224.

- **Best Beer, Laksa and Show Deal.** It might look like yet another of Sydney's 100-year-old pubs from the outside, but don't be fooled: the **Old Fitzroy Theatre** (129 Dowling St.; ℂ **1300 438 849**) is the place to see the work of some of the best emerging playwrights. See p. 217.

- **Best Free Flicks.** Monday night is movie night, when free cult and classic films are shown in the beer garden of **The Beresford Hotel** (354 Bourke St.; ℂ **(02) 9357 1111**), as long as it's not raining. While you're there, check out the best loos in the city. See p. 220.

- **Best Place for a Cheap First Date.** Dine out on the gourmet vegetarian buffet then retire upstairs and lay back on the cushions at the most comfy movie house in town: **Govinda's** (112 Darlinghurst Rd.; ℂ **(02) 9380 5155**). See p. 66.

- **Best Free Outdoor Concerts. The Domain Concert Series** comprises two of the city's largest and most popular free outdoor concerts each January: one for classical music lovers with the Sydney Symphony, and the other for jazz fans. See p. 212.

- **Best Gay Bingo.** A version of the old folks' favourite pastime that will have you in stitches at **The Sly Fox** (199 Enmore Rd.; ℂ **(02) 9557 1016**), whatever your sexual persuasion. See p. 215.

9 The Best Free & Dirt Cheap Nightlife

- **Best Place to Meet Prince Charming.** Girl-next-door Mary Donaldson met her prince charming (Frederik, Crown Prince of Denmark) at the **Slip Inn** (111 Sussex St.; ✆ **(02) 8295 9999**). European royals may be a bit thin on the ground, but it's a great spot for a drink after work on Friday. See p. 232.

- **Best Two-for-One Cocktails.** The cocktails are always good at **Kuleto's** (157 King St.; ✆ **(02) 9519 6369**), but they're doubly so during the nightly happy hour, when you can get two freshly mixed, shaken or stirred concoctions for the price of one. See p. 232.

- **Best Free Pool.** Rack 'em up for nix at **Jacksons on George** (200 George St.; ✆ **(02) 9247 2727**). It's even better when the jukebox is also free on Monday. See p. 168.

- **Best Free Bubbles.** Who says you can't enjoy champagne on a beer budget? The sparkling is free every Thursday between 5pm and 8pm at the **Brooklyn Hotel** (cnr. George and Grosvenor sts.; ✆ **(02) 9247 6744**; p. 229) and bubbly is $3 all day on Friday at Paddo's **Bellevue Hotel** (159 Hargrave St.; ✆ **(02) 9363 2293**; p. 229).

- **Best Place to Dance Until Dawn.** Entry to **Pontoon** (201 Sussex St.; ✆ **(02) 9267 7099**) is free on Friday night. See p. 214.

- **Best Backpackers Party Bar.** There's something fun and cheap on every night at the sub-terranean **Scubar** (cnr. George St. and Rawson Place; ✆ **(02) 9212 4244**). See p. 232.

- **Best Happy Hour with a View.** Gazing out at Bondi Beach from the balcony at **Bondi Social** (Level 1, 38 Campbell Pde.; ✆ **(02) 9365 1788**) is one of my favourite things to do in summer, especially when sunset coincides with happy hour. See p. 229.

- **Best Gay Night Out.** There's something for everyone seven nights a week no matter what your taste, with DJs, drag performances, male dancers and live entertainment at the **Stonewall Hotel** (175 Oxford St.; ✆ **(02) 9360 1963**). See p. 216.

FREE & DIRT CHEAP CALENDAR OF EVENTS

Sydney loves to party and it does it in style with some of the biggest, busiest, loudest and showiest celebrations in the world. What's more, the best stuff tends to be the free stuff, and we're not just saying that because we're cheap. No matter what time of year you're in town, there's usually something on worth going out of your way for.

JANUARY

Sydney Festival, various Sydney locations `FREE`. The biggest cultural event in the country with more than 80 events involving upwards of 500 artists from Australia and abroad. And the good news is much (but not all) of the line-up is either free or dirt cheap. The last three weeks in January are nonstop theatre, dance, music and visual arts, and free events include two huge outdoor concerts in **The Domain Concert Series** (p. 212). **Festival First Night** sees more than 250,000 people head into the city to check out the action at any one of the 10 outdoor stages, where all of the festival's major talent is on show for free. For information, call ℂ **(02) 8248 6500** or visit www.sydneyfestival.org.au.

Australia Day, various Sydney locations `FREE`. Australia Day marks the anniversary of the First Fleet landing at Sydney Cove. Nowhere puts on a bigger bash on January 26 than Sydney—where it all began. For information, visit www.australiaday.gov.au.

Chinese New Year, various locations around central Sydney `FREE`. Sydney's Chinese New Year Festival is the largest Lunar New Year celebration outside Asia. The festival lasts for three weeks over late January and early February and has more than 50 events, with

Tix for Next to Nix

Sydney Festival has a heap of other great shows, but you don't need to pay full price. The **Tix for Next to Nix** scheme has tickets available for every show playing at the bargain basement price of just $25. There's a Tix for Next to Nix Booth in Martin Place in the city and at Riverside Theatres in Parramatta. It's cash only and you are limited to two tickets per person for that evening's shows.

dragon boat races, acrobats, parades, markets, music, drumming, dance and costumes. Visit www.cityofsydney.nsw.gov.au/cny/ for information.

FEBRUARY

TropFest, The Domain (between Art Gallery and Hospital roads) `FREE`.The largest short film festival in the world is a must-see for any movie buff. Filmmakers vie for fame and glory—and $100,000 in prize money—on the last Sunday in February. The 16 finalists are shown on a huge screen; go early to get a good spot and BYO (bring your own) picnic blanket. For information, visit www.tropfest.com.

Sydney Gay & Lesbian Mardi Gras, Oxford Street, Darlinghurst and various Sydney locations `FREE`. Sydney becomes the centre of the gay universe during the two-week festival that culminates in a parade of costumed dancers and decorated floats. Expect plenty of glitz and glamour for the fabulous parade, held on either the last Saturday night in February or the first in March. For information, visit www.mardigras.org.au.

MARCH

Sydney Harbour Week, various locations around Sydney Harbour `FREE`. Activities range from guided snorkelling tours, harbour rock pool discovery walks, tours of the islands and forts within the harbour, races and regattas, picnic days, lighthouse open days and more during the first week in March. Most events are free. Visit www.sydneyharbourweek.com.au for information.

APRIL

Darling Harbour Hoopla, Darling Harbour `FREE`. The Easter long weekend brings lots of juggling, abseiling, gymnastics, aerial stunts, plate spinning, trampolining, stilt walking and unicycling to the **Acrobatic and Street Theatre Festival**—all for free. Visit www.darlingharbour.com for information.

Surry Hills Festival, Prince Alfred Park, corner Cleveland and Chalmers streets, Surry Hills `FREE`. A great little community festival in mid-April, with free entertainment, a market—and fabulous people-watching opportunities. For information, visit www.shnc.org/festival/.

Acoustica, various venues in Balmain `FREE`. Sydney's own roots, blues and folk festival brings music lovers together in mid-April in and around Balmain. And in the spirit of all that lovin', many of the performances are free. Visit www.acousticafestival.com.au for information.

Anzac Day, various locations in and around Sydney `FREE`. April 25 is Australia's national day of mourning for those who died in wars and conflict. A dawn service is followed by a parade of returned servicemen and women down George and Bathurst streets to the War Memorial in Hyde Park.

May

Kings Cross Festival, Fitzroy Gardens, Potts Point `FREE`. Held on a Sunday in early to mid-May, this festival is all about food, wine, art and live entertainment. This is the Cross, so expect everything from police and navy bands to drag shows. Visit www.kingscrossonline. com.au for information.

Sydney Writers Festival, various Sydney locations `FREE`. Bookworms are in heaven during this mid-May, week-long festival of book readings, author talks, workshops, readings and more. Many (but not all) of the events are free. Visit www.swf.org.au for information.

Vivid Sydney, various Sydney locations `FREE`. A festival of music, light and ideas beginning mid-May, Vivid is all about getting creative and showing off (p. 231). For information, visit www.vivid sydney.com.

Sydney Italian Festival, various Sydney locations. Live *la dolce vita* during this three-week celebration of all things Italian from mid-May. There's some bargain fine Italian dining to be had at countless Italian restaurants and trattorias across town. Visit www.sydney italianfestival.com.au for information.

June

Darling Harbour Jazz & Blues Festival, Darling Harbour `FREE`. See some of the biggest names in jazz and blues from Australia and overseas over the Queen's Birthday long weekend (p. 212). Visit www.darlingharbour.com for information.

Winter Festival, locations vary, but usually around Hyde Park or Cook + Phillip Park. A city park is transformed into a huge outdoor ice rink in mid-June. You have to pay to skate, but entry into the festival site is free. Visit www.winterfestival.com.au for information.

JULY

Biennale of Sydney, Art Gallery of New South Wales and other Sydney locations `FREE`. Held every two years (the next one runs from July to September 2010) the Biennale is a city-wide festival of contemporary international art. For information, visit www.biennale ofsydney.com.au.

Aroma Festival, The Rocks `FREE`. Wake up and smell the coffee at the annual Aroma Festival on a mid-July Sunday. Free entertainment, belly dancing, camel rides, chocolate, coffee-grounds readings and $2 cups of coffee. Visit www.therocks.com for information.

AUGUST

Sydney Design, various Sydney locations `FREE`. An annual festival of design, held in mid-August, with a range of free workshops, events and exhibitions in galleries, museums and public spaces throughout the city, all showcasing the best in local and international design. Visit www.sydneydesign.com.au for information.

SEPTEMBER

Festival of the Winds, Bondi Beach `FREE`. Fly a kite at Australia's largest, most exciting and most colourful festival on a mid-September Sunday. Visit www.waverley.nsw.gov.au for information.

Chamber Music Festival, Verbrugghen Hall, Conservatorium of Music, Macquarie Street, Sydney `FREE`. Student ensembles perform a series of five free concerts at lunchtime in mid-September. For information, visit www.music.usyd.edu.au.

Manly Arts Festival, various venues around Manly `FREE`. Many of the exhibitions, classes and performance are free or—at the very least—dirt cheap. Visit www.manlyartsfestival.com for information.

OCTOBER

Darling Harbour Fiesta, Darling Harbour `FREE`. Dance up a storm at the biggest Latin American and Spanish festival in Australia. There are dance classes, South American–inspired food and arts and crafts stalls and fireworks over the Labour Day long weekend. Visit www.darlingharbour.com for information.

Manly Jazz Festival, various venues around Manly `FREE`. Three days of live jazz on five outdoor stages scattered around the seaside suburb of Manly make this the largest and longest running jazz festival in Australia, held over the Labour Day long weekend. If the sun is shining, there is no better place to be and all the entertainment is free. Visit www.manly.nsw.gov.au/manlyjazz for information.

Art and About, various locations around Sydney `FREE`. Sydney gets all arty-farty during this public art festival, an arts party (usually the first three weeks in October) with exhibitions at numerous art galleries and public spaces around the city as well as street art shows and installations, free art classes and lectures, curator talks, behind-the-scenes tours, performances and events. For information, visit www.artandabout.com.au.

NOVEMBER

Sculpture by the Sea, Bronte to Bondi Coastal Walk `FREE`. Whatever you do, if you are in Sydney in late October or early November don't miss this annual event staged alongside part of the spectacular Bronte to Bondi Coastal Walk. Visit www.sculptureby thesea.com for information. `FINE PRINT` It's very popular, so avoid the weekend, early morning and late afternoon crushes. Go at lunchtime on a weekday instead.

DECEMBER

Carols in the Domain, The Domain (between Art Gallery and Hospital roads) `FREE`. Popular with little kids and wannabe opera stars and held on a Saturday a week or so before Christmas. This huge outdoor concert will bring a smile to even the biggest Grinch and you're expected to sing along. For information, visit www.carolsin thedomain.com.

Sydney-to-Hobart Yacht Race, Sydney Harbour `FREE`. Wave the competitors goodbye as the Sydney-to-Hobart Yacht Race gets underway on Boxing Day (December 26) at around 1pm. It's a pretty amazing sight. The best vantage points: Bradleys Head, Chowder Bay, Georges Heights, Middle Head, Shark Island, Steele Point, Vaucluse Point, South Head, The Gap and North Head.

New Year's Eve, Sydney Harbour `FREE`. The city celebrates with a mega fireworks show on December 31. The first one is at 9pm, so young kids and those who like their sleep don't miss out. You'll need to get there early to secure the best harbourside spots. Visit www.cityofsydney.nsw.gov.au/NYE for information.

Crowne Plaza Coogee Beach (p. 41) offers this panoramic view of the Pacific Ocean for less than you'd expect.

CHEAP SLEEPS

Sleeping around in Sydney is not cheap. Even a standard four- or five-star harbour-view room will set you back around $500 a night on a good day. The great news is that there are some fantastic accommodation bargains to be found—you just need to know where to look for them.

If you want a harbour view, try Darling Harbour rather than Circular Quay, or head to Kings Cross. The best-value city hotels are to be found closer to Central Station than Martin Place, and your dollars will buy you a better beach view if you opt for Coogee rather than Bondi.

Name Your Price

Who says you can't afford that harbour-view suite on the top floor? Thanks to 2009's global financial crisis, haggling is back in vogue, which means there some fantastic hotel bargains to be found—all you have to do ask. If you don't fancy fronting up to the reception desk and negotiating, try **www.Ubid4rooms.com.** It's not an auction site; you just look for a hotel you like and offer the hotel a figure that's less than the already discounted rate you see. You'll hear if your offer is accepted somewhere between 10 minutes and three hours later. It's just like haggling—but far less embarrassing and awkward. You can also make linked bids, where you bid on three hotels at once and see who comes back first—hotels competing for your business often means a lower price. The site doesn't allow silly bids such as $40 for a $400 room, but you'll be surprised to see how low you can go!

Most Sydney hotels are pretty good and they're usually very clean. Even the most basic hotel room will include tea- and coffee-making facilities, a fridge and a colour TV.

We've used a rough guide of $150 or less per double room when choosing hotels to include in this guide. Keep in mind that the published rates in this book are rack rates (what the hotel would *like* to get for its rooms in a perfect world and what they *can* get during busy periods), so always check hotel websites or call the hotel to find out about cheaper rates.

And remember that everything with a harbour view or within cooee of the city will be charging full rates on New Year's Eve and holiday periods, such as at Easter or Valentine's Day. Also, January is the peak holiday time for beachside hotels, but you'll pay less at these times for those in the city centre, which are also generally cheaper on weekends.

1 City Centre & Harbourside

AFFORDABLE

Aarons Hotel   The rooms aren't flash, but they are clean and comfortable and the hotel is right in the heart of things. Rates increase on

CHEAP SLEEPS CITY CENTRE & HARBOURSIDE

790 on George **23**
Aarons Hotel **21**
Base Backpackers **7**
Central Railway Hotel **27**
City Crown Motel **18**
Clarion Suites
  Southern Cross
  Darling Harbour **12**
Cockatoo Island **1**
Great Southern Hotel **19**
Hotel Ibis World Square **11**
Leisure Inn
  Sydney Central **26**
Lord Nelson
  Brewery Hotel **2**
Marque Sydney **24**
Metro Hotel on Pitt **9**
Metro Hotel
  Sydney Central **16**
Old Sydney Holiday Inn **3**
Park Regis City Centre **8**
Pensione Hotel **15**
Quality Hotel
  Cambridge **17**
Railway Square YHA **25**
Rendezvous Stafford
  Hotel Sydney **4**
Sydney Central YHA **20**
Sydney Harbour
  Marriott Hotel **6**
Sydney Harbour YHA **5**
Travelodge Sydney Hotel **13**
Vibe Hotel Sydney **14**
Wake Up **22**
Y Hotel Hyde Park **10**

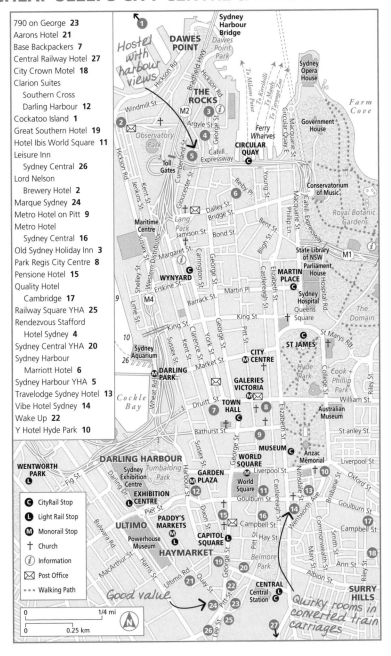

weekends, but still offer a bargain for the centre of Sydney, even if the standard rooms do feel a bit hostel-ish. This is a good budget family option with rooms that can sleep up to six; however, you may like to pay the extra $10 and go for a deluxe room, as standard rooms are small.

37 Ultimo Rd., Sydney. ℂ **(02) 9281 5555.** Fax: (02) 9281 2666. www.aaronshotel. com.au. 93 units. $129–$169 double. Extra person $25. AE, DC, MC, V. Parking station nearby. Train: Central. **Amenities:** Restaurant, bar, Internet kiosk. *In room:* A/C, TV, fridge, hair dryer, Wi-Fi ($4 per hr.; $15 per day).

Central Railway Hotel   This small family-run motel is clean and comfortable, if a little bland, but at a great price. It's around 10 minutes' walk from Central Station, and the area can be a bit dodgy after dark. It's not the place to stay if you're looking for pumping nightlife, but if you are after somewhere nice and quiet, this hotel could be for you. There's no lift, so you'll have to lug your bags up the stairs if you're staying anywhere other than the ground floor.

240 Chalmers St., Strawberry Hills. ℂ **(02) 9319 7800.** Fax: (02) 9319 1004. www. centralrailwayhotel.com. 38 units. $119 double. MC, V. Parking $22. Train: Central or Redfern. **Amenities:** Courtyard. *In room:* A/C, TV, fridge, hair dryer, microwave.

City Crown Motel   It looks like a bit of a dive from the outside, but while the rooms are certainly not swish, their saving grace is that they all have balconies, and you can borrow DVDs from reception for free. It's also in a great spot in the heart of Surry Hills, one of Sydney's most vibrant areas.

289 Crown St., Surry Hills. ℂ **(02) 9331 2433.** Fax: (02) 9360 7760. www.citycrown motel.com.au. 28 units. $115–$162 double. Extra person $20. MC, V. Parking $15. Bus: 378 or 380. **Amenities:** Cafe. *In room:* A/C, TV, DVD player, fridge, free Wi-Fi.

Great Southern Hotel   This classic 1920s pub opposite Central Station has always been a favourite with country folk up for a few days in the big city. It's Heritage Listed, so expect lots of nice Art Deco touches, and it offers small, no-frills rooms. It's undergoing a gradual refurbishment, so ask for one of the newly made-over rooms when you book as all rooms are the same price. You'll get a $5 discount if you don't want your bed made each day, and you'll find good-value steaks on offer in the pub's restaurant.

717 George St., Sydney. ℂ **(02) 9289 4400.** Fax: (02) 9281 5118. www.greatsouthern hotel.com.au. 165 units. $99–$164 double. Extra person $40. AE, DC, MC, V. Parking $30. Train: Central. **Amenities:** Restaurant, bar, fitness room. *In room:* A/C, TV, fridge, hair dryer, Internet (55¢ per min.; $27.50 per day).

Hotel Ibis World Square   The hotel's rooms are small and functional, but unremarkable. It's in a great location in the heart of the Central Business District (CBD), although the area can get a little rough late at night on weekends. Rates tend to be higher on the weekends, but rooms are good value mid-week if you can get a deal online.

382–384 Pitt St., Sydney. ☏ **(02) 8267 3111.** Fax: (02) 8267 3100. www.ibisworld square.com.au. 166 units. $99–$169 double. Extra person $60. AE, DC, MC, V. Parking $25. Train: Central or Town Hall. **Amenities:** Breakfast room, fitness room. *In room:* A/C, TV, fridge, hair dryer, Internet ($8 per hr.; $18 per day).

Leisure Inn Sydney Central   Try to upgrade to a superior room for a little more space; otherwise, rooms are functional, if a little plain. It provides a good budget base close to Central Station and is an easy stroll to universities and Chinatown. Be careful if walking around this area alone at night.

28–30 Regent St., Sydney. ☏ **(02) 8023 3333.** Fax: (02) 9211 4445. www.leisure innhotels.com. 47 units. $99–$189 double. AE, DC, MC, V. No off-street parking. Train: Central or Town Hall. **Amenities:** Laundry. *In room:* A/C, TV, fridge, hair dryer, Wi-Fi ($20 per day).

★ **Lord Nelson Brewery Hotel**   The rooms above this great brewery pub—one of Sydney's oldest: it's been serving cold beers to thirsty locals since 1841—are quite charming and the location, in the heart of the historic Rocks area, is certainly hard to beat. It's a popular pub, so expect some noise on weekends. Rates include breakfast.

19 Kent St., The Rocks. ☏ **(02) 9251 4044.** Fax: (02) 9251 1532. www.lordnelson brewery.com. 9 units (7 w/bathroom). $190 double w/bathroom; $130 w/shared bathroom. AE, DC, MC, V. No off-street parking. Train: Circular Quay. **Amenities:** Restaurant, bar. *In room:* A/C, TV, fridge.

★ **Marque Sydney**   This recently made-over hotel is a great choice if you want to be close to Central Station, Chinatown, or the Entertainment or Convention centres—and even if you don't, you're only minutes away from the sexier end of town near the harbour. Rooms are quite stylish, offer a reasonable amount of space, have lots of the amenities you normally don't get in this price range and the rooftop pool has fantastic views of the city. Splash out an extra $10 to $20 and opt for an executive room—they're much quieter.

Cnr. George and Quay sts., Railway Square. ☏ **(02) 9212 2544.** Fax: (02) 9281 3794. www.marquehotels.com/sydney. 113 units. $135–$220 double. Extra person $65. AE, DC, MC, V. Parking $35. Train: Central. **Amenities:** Restaurant, bar, rooftop pool, sauna. *In room:* A/C, TV, fridge, hair dryer, minibar, MP3 docking station, Internet ($20 per day).

Metro Hotel on Pitt You won't get a view (the hotel is hemmed in by office blocks, which means the rooms are quite dark), but it's a small price to pay for the central location. Rooms are small and the hotel can be popular with large groups, which can mean a long wait if you arrive at the same time they do. That said, for the price, this place is a pretty good option for a night or two. The queen rooms have more space and are the better option if you can afford the upgrade.

300 Pitt St., Sydney. ✆ **(02) 9283 8088.** Fax: (02) 9283 2825. www.metrohotels.com. au. 115 units. $105–$149 double. Extra person $50. MC, V. Parking $25. Train: Town Hall. **Amenities:** Restaurant, bar. *In room:* A/C, TV, fridge, hair dryer, Internet ($10 per hr.; $30 per day).

Metro Hotel Sydney Central Freshened up by a recent refurbishment, the rooms are a bit on the small side. The hotel's in a good location at the southern end of the CBD, which means it's an easy walk to just about anywhere and public transport is right on your doorstep.

431–439 Pitt St., Sydney. ✆ **(02) 9281 6999.** Fax: (02) 9281 6988. www.metrohotels. com.au. 220 units. $99–$145 double. Extra person $40. AE, DC, MC, V. Parking nearby $26. Train: Central. **Amenities:** Restaurant, bar, rooftop pool. *In room:* A/C, TV, fridge, hair dryer, Wi-Fi ($20 per day).

Park Regis City Centre A nice budget hotel in the middle of the business end of the city. Book online and you can often pick up an executive king room with views of Hyde Park for around $150 a night, which is great value. The rooms are contemporary and stylish and the windows actually open, which can be hard to find these days in high-rise hotels. Check out the great views from the sun deck on the 45th floor.

27 Park St. (cnr. Castlereagh St.), Sydney. ✆ **(02) 9267 6511.** Fax: (02) 9264 2252. www.parkregishotel.com.au. 122 units. $125–$260 double. Extra person $40. AE, DC, MC, V. Parking $30. Train: Central. **Amenities:** Rooftop pool and sun deck. *In room:* A/C, TV, fridge, hair dryer, Internet ($7.50 per hr.; $16.50 per day).

Pensione Hotel Cheap and cheerful, this popular little hotel near Chinatown has small, basic rooms; the triple and quad rooms feature bunk beds and can feel a bit like a backpackers' dorm, but if you're sharing with family or friends I guess it doesn't matter. The bathrooms can be poky and the rooms can be noisy on weekends if the bar below is jumping or if you've got a room fronting busy George Street. Ask for a room in the centre of the hotel.

631–635 George St., Sydney. ✆ **(02) 9265 8888.** Fax: (02) 9211 9825. www.pensione. com.au. 68 units. $115–$155 double. Extra person $25. MC, V. Parking station nearby. Train: Central. **Amenities:** Restaurant, bar, breakfast room, kitchenette, Wi-Fi ($7 per hr.; $22 per 5 hr.). *In room:* A/C, TV, fridge, hair dryer.

Quality Hotel Cambridge   This place has good-sized rooms at pretty decent prices, particularly mid-week. Try to snag a room with a balcony for good city views. It's in the south-eastern end of town, which means it's within walking distance of some great Oxford Street and Surry Hills bars and restaurants, and is a short bus ride away from the city centre and Circular Quay.

212 Riley St., East Sydney. ✆ **(02) 9212 1111.** Fax: (02) 9281 1981. www.choicehotels. com.au. 170 units. $99–$150 double. Extra person $25. AE, DC, MC, V. Parking $18– $20. Train: Central. **Amenities:** Restaurant, bar, pool, spa. *In room:* A/C, TV, fridge, hair dryer, Internet (some rooms only; $5 per hr.; $15 per day).

Travelodge Sydney Hotel   Rooms are basic and plain, but they offer great value in the heart of the city; you can walk to just about anywhere in the downtown area from here. Book online and you can often get a room for between $100 and $140.

27 Wentworth Ave., Sydney. ✆ **(02) 8267 1700.** Fax: (02) 8267 1800. www.travelodge. com.au. 406 units. $170 double. Extra person $40. AE, DC, MC, V. Parking $20. Train: Martin Place. **Amenities:** Breakfast room, Internet kiosk. *In room:* A/C, TV, fridge, hair dryer.

★ **Vibe Hotel Sydney**   Vibe hotels always offer great value with a stylish and colourful edge. This one is very handy to both Central Station and the theatre district. Book online and you can save up to $240 per night on the rack rates below.

111 Goulburn St., Sydney. ✆ **(02) 8272 3300.** Fax: (02) 9211 1806. www.vibehotels. com.au. 190 units. $380 double. Extra person $40. AE, DC, MC, V. Parking $22. Train: Central. **Amenities:** Restaurant, bar, rooftop pool. *In room:* A/C, TV, fridge, hair dryer, minibar, Internet ($12.95 per hr.; $24.95 per day).

Y Hotel Hyde Park   Is it a hotel or is it a hostel? Depends on which room you opt for. There are some small basic rooms with bathrooms, and some with shared bathrooms, as well as 'dorm' rooms with four single beds and shared bathroom facilities down the hall. It's run by the YWCA, so it's mostly very clean and it's in a great spot close to the city end of Oxford Street. A light breakfast is included in the room rates. Confirm your booking before you arrive as staff have a deliberate overbooking policy to protect themselves from no-shows.

5–11 Wentworth Ave., Sydney. ✆ **(02) 9264 2451.** Fax: (02) 9285 6288. www.yhotel. com.au. 121 units (68 w/bathroom). $148–$158 double w/bathroom; $110 w/shared bathroom; $37 dorm bed. MC, V. Parking station nearby. Train: Museum. **Amenities:** Cafe, Internet kiosk, communal kitchen. *In room:* (private rooms only) A/C, TV, fridge, hair dryer, Wi-Fi ($5 per hr.; $35 per 12 hr.).

CHEAP SLEEPS

790 on George   Almost all rooms and dorms in this new-ish backpackers' at Central Station have good views over George Street, but the windows don't open so it can get a bit stuffy. The good news is that they are air-conditioned.

790 George St., Sydney. ✆ **(02) 9080 1155.** Fax: (02) 9080 1156. www.790ongeorge. com.au. 280 units (25 private w/shared bathrooms). $76–$82 private w/shared bathroom; $25–$30 dorm bed. MC, V. Train: Central. **Amenities:** Internet kiosk, communal kitchen, laundry, TV lounge. *In room:* A/C, lockers, Wi-Fi ($3 per hr.).

Base Backpackers   Don't expect luxury accommodation here; this is a backpackers' first and foremost—despite what the website says. Women like the separate 'Sanctuary' female-only dorms and there are some private bathroom rooms, but unless you enjoy the backpackers' vibe, you might be better off with a cheap private room elsewhere.

477 Kent St., Sydney. ✆ **(02) 9267 7718.** www.stayatbase.com. 420 units (10 w/bathroom). $120 double w/bathroom; $95 w/shared bathroom; $20–$34 dorm bed. MC, V. Train: Town Hall. **Amenities:** Cafe, Internet kiosk, communal kitchen. *In room:* A/C, lockers.

★ **Cockatoo Island**   As far as camp sites go it's a bit on the pricey side, but as far as harbour views go it's priceless. For $45 a night you can pitch a tent on Cockatoo Island, the largest of the harbour islands, and you're guaranteed an unimpeded view (although be prepared to be woken early by passing boat traffic—you are in the middle of a working harbour, after all). You'll need a sleeping bag, but you can hire camping equipment (a tent, mattress, lantern and camping chairs) on the island and you can buy barbecue packs from the Muster Station Cafe on the island, or bring your own. You can't BYO (bring your own) alcohol, but you can buy beer and wine from the cafe.

Cockatoo Island, Sydney Harbour. ✆ **(02) 8898 9774.** www.cockatooisland.gov.au. 135 unpowered camp sites. $45 per night for 4; camping package (site and equipment rental) $85 per night Sun–Fri; $95 Sat. Ferry: Circular Quay (Wharf 5). **Amenities:** Cafe, electric barbeques, communal kitchen, lockers.

★ **Railway Square YHA**   This quirky youth hostel at Central Station (it's on an old platform) is a new twist to the idea of falling asleep on a train: some of the dorms are in converted train carriages. Private rooms with bathrooms are available, but are usually booked out well in advance.

8–10 Lee St. (cnr. Upper Carriage Lane and Lee St., or entry via the Henry Deane Plaza), Sydney. ✆ **(02) 9281 9666.** Fax: (02) 9281 9688. www.yha.com.au. 280 units, (2 w/ bathroom). $98–$109 double w/bathroom; $30.50–$34 dorm bed. MC, V. Train: Central. **Amenities:** Cafe, Internet kiosk, communal kitchen, outdoor pool, spa, TV room. *In room:* A/C, hairdryer (private rooms only), lockers, Wi-Fi ($3 per hr.; $15 per day).

★ **Sydney Central YHA**   It's a youth hostel with lots of dorm rooms, but you can also get good-sized light and airy double rooms with bathrooms. There's a great swimming pool and it's right across the road from Central Station, so it's close to just about everything.

Cnr. Pitt St & Rawson Pl, Sydney. ✆ **(02) 9218 9000.** Fax: (02) 9218 9099. www.yha. com.au. 500 units (16 private w/bathroom). $102–$118 double w/bathroom; $36–$41.50 dorm bed. MC, V. Parking $20. Train: Central. **Amenities:** Restaurant, bar, Internet kiosk, communal kitchen, games room, laundry, rooftop pool, sauna, TV lounge. *In room:* A/C, hairdryer (private rooms only), lockers, Wi-Fi ($3 per hr.; $15 per day).

★ **Sydney Harbour YHA**   The only backpackers' in The Rocks area, this brand new purpose-built hostel opened in late 2009 and has knock-out harbour and Opera House views from the rooftop sun deck, as well as private double rooms with a view for just over $150, which is dirt cheap in any language.

110 Cumberland St., The Rocks. ✆ **(02) 8272 0900.** Fax: (02) 9261 1969. www.yha. com.au. 106 units (46 w/bathroom). $159 double w/bathroom; $42 dorm bed. MC, V. No parking. Train: Central. **Amenities:** Internet kiosk, communal kitchen, rooftop barbecue, TV lounge. *In room:* A/C, hairdryer (private rooms only), lockers.

Wake Up   If you're looking to party with lots of other backpackers, this could be the place for you. The rooms are clean and it's right near Central Station in the heart of the Sydney backpacker district. It's huge, which can make finding space in the kitchen a little difficult, but the cafe menu has nothing over $10 and there are plenty of cheap eats nearby, so who needs to cook? There usually a DJ or live entertainment in the bar and free city orientation tours on Monday and Friday, plus a guided Coogee to Bondi beach walk on Wednesday.

509 Pitt St., Sydney. ✆ **(02) 9288 7888.** Fax: (02) 9288 7889. www.wakeup.com.au. 540 units (10 w/bathroom). $108 double w/bathroom; $98 private w/shared bathroom; $30–$38 dorm bed. MC, V. Train: Central. **Amenities:** Restaurant, bar, Internet

kiosk, communal kitchen, laundry, TV lounge. *In room:* A/C, TV, hair dryer (private rooms only), lockers, Wi-Fi ($3.50 per hr.).

WORTH A SPLURGE

Clarion Suites Southern Cross Darling Harbour   This is a brand new all-suite hotel on the eastern side of Darling Harbour in the heart of Chinatown and close to the theatre and entertainment districts. Check online for a last-minute booking and you can often pick up a studio, mid-week, for less than $150 a night or a one-bedroom apartment for just a little bit more.

Cnr. Harbour & Goulburn sts., Darling Harbour. © **(02) 9268 5888.** Fax: (02) 9268 5666. www.southerncrosssuites.com.au. 63 units. $350–$370 double. Extra person $40. AE, DC, MC, V. Parking $20. Train: Central or Town Hall. **Amenities:** Restaurant, bar, fitness room, pool, sauna. *In room:* A/C, TV, hair dryer, kitchen, minibar, Wi-Fi ($10 per hr.; $18 per day).

Old Sydney Holiday Inn   If you're going to splurge on a hotel room, it really should be one with a view, and this Holiday Inn at The Rocks has deluxe harbour-view rooms from around $275 a night if you book far enough ahead. Just make sure you specify that you want a room with a harbour view when booking.

55 George St., The Rocks. © **(02) 9252 0524.** Fax: (02) 9251 2093. www.holidayinn. com.au/oldsydney. 175 units. $200–$350 double. Extra person $55. AE, DC, MC, V. Parking $35. Train: Circular Quay. **Amenities:** Restaurant, fitness room, rooftop pool. *In room:* A/C, TV, hair dryer, kitchen, minibar, Internet ($27.50 per day).

Rendezvous Stafford Hotel Sydney   This is less a hotel than a collection of apartments and historic terrace houses in the heart of The Rocks. The studios and apartments are well worth the splurge, particularly in winter when you can often pick up a great rate of around $230 or so a night for a one-bedroom apartment, though you'd be better off going to a cafe or making your own coffee and toast rather than forking out almost $50 for the buffet breakfast. It's in an unbeatable location and many of the rooms offer good views of the harbour, Opera House and bridge.

75 Harrington St., The Rocks. © **(02) 9251 6711.** Fax: (02) 9251 3458. www.rendezvous hotels.com.au. 61 units. $230–$390 double. Extra person $35. AE, DC, MC, V. Parking $45. Train: Circular Quay. **Amenities:** Fitness room, pool, sauna. *In room:* A/C, TV, hair dryer, kitchen, minibar.

★ **Sydney Harbour Marriott Hotel**   Most rooms in this upmarket hotel have good harbour or Opera House views and it's only a few minutes' walk to The Rocks and Circular Quay. It has all the little luxuries you'd expect from a five-star hotel, the beds are super comfortable and you can usually get good packages online.

30 Pitt St., Sydney. ✆ **1800 251 259.** Fax: (02) 9252 2352. www.marriott.com.au. 550 units. $280–$350 double. Extra person $55. AE, DC, MC, V. Parking $45. Train: Circular Quay. **Amenities:** Restaurant, bar, fitness room, pool, sauna. *In room:* A/C, TV, hair dryer, minibar, Internet ($19.95 per day).

2 Kings Cross & Inner East

AFFORDABLE

Arts Hotel   Rooms are a bit uninspiring but it's good value and in a top location on Oxford Street, particularly if you're a keen shopper or sports fan. You can often get a discount on the rack rate. The courtyard (garden) rooms are the quietest. Note that it was formerly known as Sullivans Hotel.

21 Oxford St., Paddington. ✆ **(02) 9361 0211.** Fax: (02) 9360 3735. www.artshotel. com.au. 64 units. $165–$185 double. AE, DC, MC, V. Limited free parking. Bus: 378 or 380. **Amenities:** Breakfast room, fitness room, pool. *In room:* A/C, TV, fridge, hair dryer, free Wi-Fi (garden rooms only).

DeVere Hotel   The fantastic location and good views make up for the slightly tired rooms, which are a reasonable size. Ask for a bayview room on the fourth floor with views over Elizabeth Bay.

44–46 Macleay St., Potts Point. ✆ **(02) 9358 1211.** Fax: (02) 9358 4685. www.devere. com.au. 97 units. $89–$129 double. Extra person $50. MC, V. Parking nearby for $20. Train: Kings Cross. **Amenities:** Breakfast room, Wi-Fi in lobby ($4 per hr.). *In room:* A/C, TV, fridge, hair dryer.

Hotel 59   Hotel 59 is a friendly little B&B on the Rushcutters Bay side of Kings Cross. A (very good) cooked breakfast is included in the tariff. The single rooms are small, but the family rooms are nice and roomy; for the price, it's quite a bargain.

59 Bayswater Rd., Kings Cross. ✆ **(02) 9360 5900.** Fax: (02) 9360 1828. www.hotel59. com.au. 9 units. $110–$121 double. Extra person $25. MC, V. No parking. Train: Kings Cross. **Amenities:** Cafe. *In room:* A/C, TV, fridge, hair dryer, free Wi-Fi (though it doesn't always work).

★ **Hotel Altamont**   Is there really such a thing as a luxury budget hotel? I didn't think so until I checked in to the Hotel Altamont. I'm now a believer and I love this stylish boutique hotel in an old Georgian mansion. It used to be a (rather notorious) nightclub—the Loft suite used to be the club's VIP room, where the Rolling Stones, Madonna and their ilk once partied. Rooms are spacious and some of the bathrooms are huge. I love the courtyard room (room 8); it has its own little garden. It's also pet friendly, but with just 14 rooms you'll need to book well in advance.

207 Darlinghurst Rd., Darlinghurst. ℂ **(02) 9360 6000.** Fax: (02) 9332 2499. www. altamont.com.au. 14 units. $129–$150 double. Extra person $10. AE, DC, MC, V. Limited free parking. Train: Kings Cross. **Amenities:** Bar, rooftop garden. *In room:* A/C, TV, fridge, hair dryer, free Wi-Fi.

Hotel Formule 1 Kings Cross   Hotel Formule 1 is the original no-frills hotel chain, and that's exactly what you get at this one: no frills for not a whole heap of cash. All rooms sleep three and are tiny—just like a private room at a backpackers', but cheaper, and (usually) quieter, although be warned: William Street is where most of the ladies of the night hang out and this hotel is right in the middle of it. Saturday nights are always more expensive than the rest of the week.

191–201 William St., Kings Cross. ℂ **(02) 9326 0300.** Fax: (02) 9326 0155. www. formule1.com.au. 115 units. $79–$129 double/triple. AE, DC, MC, V. Limited parking $20. Train: Kings Cross. **Amenities:** Vending machine in lobby. *In room:* A/C, TV.

The Hughenden   This boutique hotel is set in a historic 1870s mansion in a leafy eastern suburbs shopping and art gallery precinct. The lobby and lounge are much more opulent than the rooms, which are smallish and fairly plain, but it's in a great spot at the top end of Oxford Street near Centennial Park. It's also close to the Sydney Cricket Ground and Football Stadium and is pet friendly. Ask about mid-week deals when you book, which can work out at around $100 a night if you stay for two or three nights.

14 Queen St., Woollahra. ℂ **(02) 9363 4863.** Fax: (02) 9362 0398. www.hughenden hotel.com.au. 35 units. $168–$258 double. AE, DC, MC, V. Bus: 378 or 389. **Amenities:** Restaurant, bar, guest lounge, free Internet. *In room:* A/C, TV, fridge, hair dryer.

Lido Suites   This great little hotel has stylish rooms and is well worth a stay, on the provision that it is early in the week (avoid Thursday, Friday and Saturday if you intend to sleep). It's above a nightclub (and opposite one), so describing it as 'noisy' is an understatement—the music doesn't stop until dawn. That said, you're onto a winner if you stay here on Monday night (mid-week is also around $30 cheaper than weekends). You can't swing a cat in the studios, so opt for the Diva or Barncleuth suites.

CHEAP SLEEPS KINGS CROSS & INNER EAST

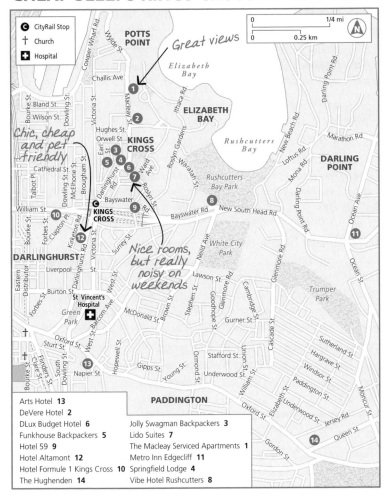

Arts Hotel **13**
DeVere Hotel **2**
DLux Budget Hotel **6**
Funkhouse Backpackers **5**
Hotel 59 **9**
Hotel Altamont **12**
Hotel Formule 1 Kings Cross **10**
The Hughenden **14**

Jolly Swagman Backpackers **3**
Lido Suites **7**
The Macleay Serviced Apartments **1**
Metro Inn Edgecliff **11**
Springfield Lodge **4**
Vibe Hotel Rushcutters **8**

2 Roslyn St., Kings Cross. ℱ **(02) 8354 0956.** Fax: (02) 9360 5670. www.staywell group.com. 36 units. $79–$149 double. Extra person $35. MC, V. No parking. Train: Kings Cross. *In room:* A/C, TV, fridge, hair dryer, microwave, Wi-Fi ($9.50 per hr.; $16.50 per day).

Metro Inn Edgecliff   This hotel is in a good, if slightly noisy location (it's on a very busy road) near Kings Cross. While not really within walking distance, it's right across the road from Edgecliff train station, which will take only minutes to get you into the city, Kings Cross or Bondi Junction (where you can catch the bus to Bondi Beach). Rooms are clean and comfortable: those at the rear are quieter (the higher the better) and have good water views.

230 New South Head Rd., Edgecliff. ℭ **(02) 9328 7977.** Fax: (02) 9360 1216. www. metrohotels.com.au. 34 units. $89–$155 double. Extra person $25. MC, V. Limited free parking. Train: Edgecliff. **Amenities:** Guest lounge. *In room:* A/C, TV, fridge, hair dryer.

Springfield Lodge   This place has nicely renovated rooms in an atmospheric 1930s building at the leafier end of Kings Cross. Rooms are basic but clean, and there's a good cafe downstairs.

9 Springfield Ave., Potts Point. ℭ **(02) 8307 4000.** Fax: (02) 9357 4742. www. springfieldlodge.com.au. 62 units. $120–$140 double. AE, MC, V. Parking station nearby. Train: Kings Cross. **Amenities:** Cafe. *In room:* Ceiling fans, TV, fridge, Internet ($10 per day).

CHEAP SLEEPS

DLux Budget Hotel   Despite the name, DLux is a backpackers', and it's not all that deluxe. All rooms, including the dorms, have fridges and (cubicle-sized) bathrooms, and there are some private rooms, but I'd only stay here if I really had to have my own bathroom as there are better backpackers' nearby. It's in the heart of the red light district and is party central, so if you're looking for somewhere quiet, this is not the place for you. There's a free Saturday barbecue, and free drink vouchers.

30 Darlinghurst St., Kings Cross. ℭ **1800 236 213** (in Australia). www.dluxbudget hotel.com.au. 320 units (20 private). $65 double; $20–$26 dorm bed. MC, V. Train: Kings Cross. **Amenities:** Internet kiosk, communal kitchen, rooftop barbecue area, TV lounge. *In room:* A/C, TV (private rooms only), lockers.

Funkhouse Backpackers   This is another good hostel if you are looking to party, but perhaps not the best choice if you are more interested in sleeping. The dorms are small, but in this case small is good with only three to four beds per dorm. There's a large rooftop barbecue area (the rooftop parties are legendary) and breakfast and Internet access is free.

23 Darlinghurst Rd., Kings Cross. ℭ **(02) 9358 6455.** Fax: (02) 9358 3506. www. funkhouse.com.au. 138 units (15 private rooms, none w/bathroom). $70 double; $25 dorm bed. MC, V. Parking station nearby. Train: Kings Cross. **Amenities:** Internet, communal kitchen, rooftop barbecue area, TV lounge. *In room:* Lockers.

★ **Jolly Swagman Backpackers**   Friendly, clean and quiet with good mattresses, this is one of the few four-star hostels in Sydney and my pick of the bunch in the Cross. It's on a quiet side street and all the communal areas are away from the bedrooms, so you know you'll be able to sleep. Rates include breakfast and a free airport pick-up (if you book a two-night stay).

27 Orwell St., Kings Cross. ✆ **1800 805 870** (in Australia). Fax: (02) 9331 0125. www. jollyswagman.com.au. 135 units (23 private, none w/bathroom). $75 double; $26 dorm bed. MC, V. No parking. Train: Kings Cross. **Amenities:** Communal kitchen, TV lounge, Wi-Fi ($3 per hr.; $10 per day). *In room:* TV and DVD player (private rooms only), fridge, lockers.

WORTH A SPLURGE

★ **The Macleay Serviced Apartments**   A room with view of the Opera House and Harbour Bridge for around $160? That's about as good a deal as you'll ever find in Sydney. If none of those are available the rooms on the east side have a fantastic view over Elizabeth Bay. Rooms on the south side have a view of another building, but they are around $20 cheaper. Don't be misled by the term 'studio apartments': they are more like smallish hotel rooms, but the views make up for it. All in all, the Macleay is a great-value hotel in the more attractive end of Kings Cross.

28 Macleay St., Potts Point. ✆ **(02) 9357 7755.** Fax: (02) 9357 7233. www.themacleay. com. 126 units. $160–$230 double. Extra person $15. AE, DC, MC, V. Parking $15. Train: Kings Cross. **Amenities:** Restaurant, barbecue, free access to local gym, swimming pool. *In room:* A/C, TV, kitchenette, hair dryer, iPod docking station, Wi-Fi ($15 per day).

★ **Vibe Hotel Rushcutters**   A quieter alternative to staying in Kings Cross, this hotel fronts a lovely park on a small harbour bay and is just minutes from Kings Cross, Paddington and Bondi. The rack rates below look expensive, but book online and you can usually get a room for around $130 to $180 a night; look out also for good-value two- and four-night packages.

100 Bayswater Rd., Rushcutters Bay. ✆ **(02) 8353 8988.** Fax: (02) 8353 8999. www. vibehotels.com.au. 245 units. $355–$390 double. Extra person $40. AE, DC, MC, V. Parking $16.50 ($22 valet). Train: Edgecliff. **Amenities:** Restaurant, bar, fitness room, rooftop pool. *In room:* A/C, TV, fridge, hair dryer, minibar, Internet ($24.95 per day).

3 Eastern Suburbs

AFFORDABLE

Bondi Hotel   You'll find the cheapest beach-view private rooms in Bondi here, but they come with a catch: the Hotel Bondi has a 24-hour liquor license, which means it can be noisy until just before

Harbour View Cottages

If you are travelling with a large family, or a few friends, the National Parks and Wildlife Service rents out two historic cottages with sweeping harbour views for weekend and week-long stays. When you divide the rate by the amount of beds on offer (between six and eight), we're talking about a serious bargain. The cottages are all near Watsons Bay, around 20 minutes from the city centre by bus or ferry and all are self contained, have off-street parking and linen and towels are provided, but bring your food and drink.

Constables Cottage has three bedrooms and sleeps eight: $1,400 to $1,700 per week; $700 per weekend. Green Point Cottage is just 30 metres from Camp Cove Beach (the spot where Captain Arthur Phillip first landed in Sydney Harbour in 1788) and sleeps six: $1,050 to $1,700 per week; $600 per weekend. To book, contact the Gap Bluff Centre on ℰ **(02) 9337 2333** or email Gap.Bluff@environment.nsw.gov.au.

dawn, particularly on weekends. Still, if noise doesn't worry you, spend the extra $25 and get a beach-view room with a balcony and watch the sunrise. The bathrooms are the size of a shoe box, but at least you don't have to share.

178 Campbell Pde., Bondi. ℰ **(02) 9130 3271.** Fax: (02) 9130 7974. www.hotelbondi. com.au. 40 units. $110–$165 double. Extra person $20. MC, V. Limited free parking. Bus: 380 or 382. **Amenities:** Bar, restaurant. *In room:* A/C, TV, fridge.

Gemini Hotel   The Gemini Hotel's website infers that it's near the airport. It's not, but they do offer a free shuttle service for the 20 to 30 minute trip (except on public holidays). Randwick's a pleasant place to stay and it's only a 10-minute bus trip away from Coogee Beach. There are lots of good restaurants in the area known as 'The Spot' and public transport will get you to the city centre in no time. It's very close to the University of NSW and several major hospitals. Rooms are a bit on the tired and drab side, but, for the price, this isn't a bad choice.

65 Belmore Rd., Randwick. ℰ **(02) 9399 9011.** Fax: (02) 9398 9708. www.geminihotel. com.au. 97 units. $140 double. Extra person $20. AE, DC, MC, V. Free parking (five-day limit). Bus: 372, 373, 374 or 377. **Amenities:** Breakfast room, Wi-Fi ($10 for entire stay). *In room:* A/C, TV, fridge, hair dryer, minibar.

CHEAP SLEEPS EASTERN SUBURBS & AIRPORT

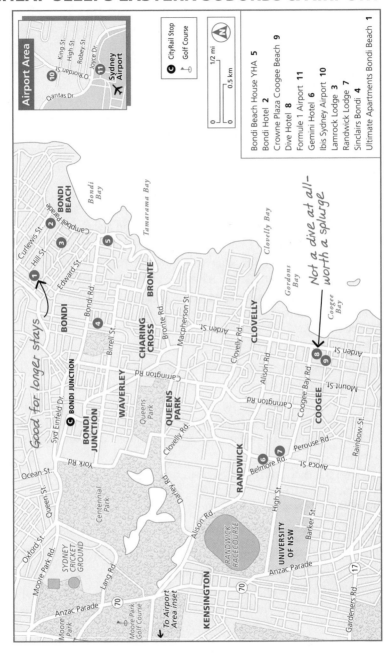

Airport Area

King St. High St. Robey St.
Joyce Dr.
O'Riordan St.
Qantas Dr.
Sydney Airport
10 **11**

CityRail Stop
Golf Course

1/2 mi
0.5 km

Bondi Beach House YHA **5**
Bondi Hotel **2**
Crowne Plaza Coogee Beach **9**
Dive Hotel **8**
Formule 1 Airport **11**
Gemini Hotel **6**
Ibis Sydney Airport **10**
Lamrock Lodge **3**
Randwick Lodge **7**
Sinclairs Bondi **4**
Ultimate Apartments Bondi Beach **1**

Good for longer stays

Not a dive at all—
worth a splurge

Curlewis St. **2**
Hill St. **3**
1
Edward St.
Campbell Parade
BONDI BEACH
5

Bondi Bay

Tamarama Bay

Clovelly Bay

Gordons Bay

Coogee Bay

BONDI
Bondi Rd.
Birrell St.
4
BONDI JUNCTION
Syd Enfield Dr.

CHARING CROSS
BRONTE
Bronte Rd.
Macpherson St.
Arden St.

CLOVELLY
Clovelly Rd.
Alison Rd.

8
9
Arden St.
COOGEE
Mount St.
Coogee Bay Rd.
Rainbow St.

WAVERLEY
Carrington Rd.
Queens Park
QUEENS PARK
Clovelly Rd.
Carrington Rd.

RANDWICK
6 **7**
Belmore Rd.
Perouse Rd.
Avoca St.

Ocean St.
York Rd.
Queen St.
Dalley Rd.
Centennial Park

Oxford St.
Moore Park Rd.
SYDNEY CRICKET GROUND
Lang Rd.
Moore Park
70
Anzac Parade
Moore Park Golf Course

To Airport Area inset

KENSINGTON
Alison Rd.
High St.
RANDWICK RACECOURSE
UNIVERSITY OF NSW
Barker St.
Anzac Parade
70
Gardeners Rd.
17

Randwick Lodge   Of the numerous 'lodges' in old mansions that offer reasonably priced accommodation in Randwick, this one is the pick of the crop. It's in two lovely old terrace houses that were built in 1898 and it's close to the University of NSW and Prince of Wales Hospital. All rooms have bathrooms and are quite charming with lots of heritage touches. Many have balconies.

211 Avoca St., Randwick. ℂ **(02) 9310 0700.** Fax: (02) 9310 0763. www.randwicklodge. com.au. 40 units. $120 double. Extra person $25. MC, V. Parking $10. Bus: 372, 373, 374 or 377. **Amenities:** Courtyard, barbecue, guest kitchen. *In room:* A/C, TV, fridge, Wi-Fi ($10 per day).

Sinclairs Bondi   Don't be misled by the name: Sinclairs is closer to Bondi *Junction* than Bondi *Beach*, but it's an easy 15-minute walk down lively Bondi Road to the beach and you can always catch the bus back up the hill when it's time to go home. It's in a good quiet location, the rooms are a bit on the small side and they're a little cheerless, but comfortable and clean. Rates include a continental breakfast.

11 Bennet St., Bondi. ℂ **0414 342 010.** www.sinclairsbondi.com.au. 23 units (5 w/ bathroom). $99.50 double w/bathroom; $75 w/shared bathroom; $34 dorm bed. Extra person $50. MC, V. Free parking. Bus: 380 or 333. **Amenities:** Breakfast room. *In room:* TV, fridge, microwave, free Wi-Fi.

Ultimate Apartments Bondi Beach   Stay here if you want to live like a Bondi local for a week or so. These studio apartments are a few blocks west of the beach, but they're right in the heart of residential Bondi where the locals hang out. It's not a hotel, so don't expect 24-hour reception, but the rooms are comfortable and they're cleaned weekly.

59 O'Brien St., Bondi. ℂ **(02) 9365 7969.** Fax: (02) 9365 7927. www.apartmentsbondi beach.com. 45 units. $99–$145 double. Extra person $50. MC, V. Free parking. Bus: 389. **Amenities:** Swimming pool, laundry. *In room:* A/C, TV, kitchen, Wi-Fi ($15 per day).

CHEAP SLEEPS

Bondi Beach House YHA   There a number of cheap backpacker lodges in and around Bondi, but this YHA hostel is one of the best, even though it's probably closer to Tamarama Beach than Bondi, a short but gorgeous cliff-top walk away. You'll find great beach views from the rooftop and they offer the use of free snorkelling gear, surf and body boards.

Cnr. Fletcher and Dellview sts., Bondi. ℂ **(02) 9365 2088.** Fax: (02) 9365 2177. www. yha.com.au. 95 units (27 private rooms; 5 w/bathroom). $70–$78 double; $25–$30

Snooze & Fly

If all you want is a place to sleep before an early morning flight, then no-frills **Formule 1 Sydney Airport** is a good bet. It's a 10-minute walk to the domestic terminal (a shuttle bus from the hotel is available for $6) and it's next door to a Krispy Kreme Doughnuts and a McDonald's if you need a fast food fix. 5 Ross Smith Ave., Mascot. ☏ **(02) 8339 1840.** Fax: (02) 8339 1740. www.formule1.com.au. 130 units. $79–$89 double/triple. AE, DC, MC, V. Limited parking $5. Train: Domestic Airport. **Amenities:** Vending machine in lobby. *In room:* A/C, TV.

A step up from Formule 1, **Ibis Sydney Airport** is a comfortable—if bland—airport lodging choice. It also offers a $6 shuttle to the domestic and international terminals, and at least offers you slightly better food choices than the Formule 1. 205 O'Riordan St., Mascot. ☏ **(02) 8339 8500.** Fax: (02) 8339 8585. www.ibishotels.com.au. 200 units. $129–$150 double. AE, DC, MC, V. Limited parking $12. Train: Domestic Airport. **Amenities:** Bar, restaurant. *In room:* A/C, TV, fridge, hair dryer, Internet ($14 per hr.).

dorm bed. MC, V. Limited parking. Bus: 339. **Amenities:** Barbecue, cafe, communal kitchen, TV lounge, Internet kiosk. *In room:* TV (private rooms only), fridge, lockers, Wi-Fi ($15 per day).

Lamrock Lodge   A backpackers' hostel just a couple of blocks back from the beach at the southern end of Bondi. The rooms are basic, even by backpackers' standards, but who cares? You'll probably spend most of your time at the beach.

19 Lamrock Ave., Bondi. ☏ **(02) 9130 5063.** www.lamrocklodge.com. 54 units (31 private; none w/bathroom). $44–$83 double; $23–$36 dorm bed. AE, MC, V. Limited nearby parking. Bus: 380 or 333. **Amenities:** Communal kitchen, Wi-Fi ($4 per hr.; $12 per 4 hr.). *In room:* TV, fridge, microwave.

WORTH A SPLURGE

Crowne Plaza Coogee Beach   You'll get more beach view for your buck if you opt for Coogee rather than Bondi, and if you do want to head to Bondi it's only a few minutes away by bus or taxi. That said, there are plenty of cafes and bars at Coogee to keep you fed and watered. This hotel's opposite the beach, so ask for a room with an ocean view.

242 Arden St., Coogee. ✆ **(02) 9315 7600.** Fax: (02) 9315 9100. www.ichotelsgroup. com. 209 units. $203–$275 double. Extra person $50. AE, DC, MC, V. Parking $20. Bus: 372, 373 or 374. **Amenities:** Restaurant, bar, fitness room, rooftop pool. *In room:* A/C, TV, fridge, hair dryer, minibar, Wi-Fi ($25 per day).

★ **Dive Hotel**   Don't be put off by the name, it's definitely not a dive—but you can *almost* dive into the water from your room. This bright and quirky little boutique hotel is opposite Coogee Beach and three of its rooms have fantastic water views. The bathrooms are tiny, but the beds are comfy and all the rooms have a nice fresh feel. Splurge out on an ocean view room (rooms 1, 2 and 19) for more space. Breakfast is included in the rate.

234 Arden St., Coogee. ✆ **(02) 9665 5538.** Fax: (02) 9665 4347. www.divehotel.com. au. 14 units. $160–$250 double. Extra person $45. MC, V. Parking $20. Bus: 372, 373 or 374. **Amenities:** Breakfast room. *In room:* A/C, TV, kitchenette, Wi-Fi ($10 per day).

4 North Side

AFFORDABLE

Glenferrie Lodge   A pet-friendly hotel on the leafy lower North Shore, just a few minutes' stroll from the harbour's edge and within easy train access to the city; or take a stroll across the Harbour Bridge. Practically next door to Kirribilli House (the Prime Minister's Sydney residence) and Admiralty House (the Governor-General's residence), it's a peaceful alternative to staying in the city. Bathrooms are shared, but a hot breakfast is included in the rate. If you can afford it, opt for the slightly more expensive balcony rooms (rooms 14, 15, 36 and 37); rates are cheaper mid-week.

12A Carabella St., Kirribilli. ✆ **(02) 9955 1685.** Fax: (02) 9929 9439. www.glenferrie lodge.com. 70 units. $129–$149 double; $159–$189 w/balcony. Extra person $30. MC, V. Limited street parking. Train: Milsons Point. **Amenities:** Breakfast room, garden, guest lounge, laundry. *In room:* Ceiling fan, TV, fridge, Wi-Fi ($6 per hr.; $15 per day).

★ **Manly Paradise Motel & Apartments**   It's all about location— this place is right across the road from the beach and just metres from The Corso. The price goes up a bit in summer, but is a good deal during the winter months with reasonable rooms (although they are an

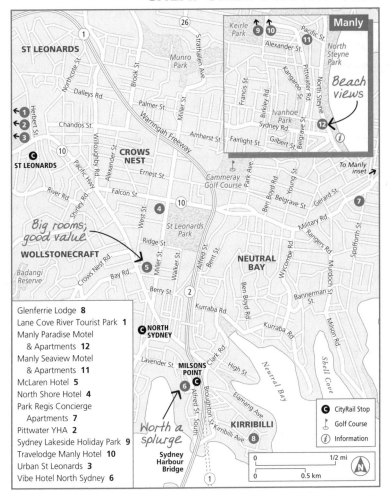

ST LEONARDS

Munro Park

Strathallen Ave.

Keirle Park **9** **10**

Pacific St.

Manly

Alexander St.

North Steyne Park

Beach views

Ivanhoe Park

Sydney Rd.

12

CROWS NEST

ST LEONARDS **10**

Cammeray Golf Course

To Manly inset ↗

7

St Leonards Park

Big rooms; good value

WOLLSTONECRAFT

Badangi Reserve

5

4

10

NEUTRAL BAY

2

Glenferrie Lodge **8**
Lane Cove River Tourist Park **1**
Manly Paradise Motel
  & Apartments **12**
Manly Seaview Motel
  & Apartments **11**
McLaren Hotel **5**
North Shore Hotel **4**
Park Regis Concierge
  Apartments **7**
Pittwater YHA **2**
Sydney Lakeside Holiday Park **9**
Travelodge Manly Hotel **10**
Urban St Leonards **3**
Vibe Hotel North Sydney **6**

NORTH SYDNEY

MILSONS POINT

6

North a splurge

KIRRIBILLI

8

Shell Cove

Neutral Bay

Sydney Harbour Bridge

1

C CityRail Stop
Golf Course
i Information

0   1/2 mi
0   0.5 km

odd shape with a long hallway) that have views of the beach, and there's a great rooftop pool.

54 North Steyne, Manly. ℂ **(02) 9977 5799.** Fax: (02) 9977 6848. www.manly paradise.com.au. 30 units. $160–$220 double. Extra person $15. MC, V. Parking $10. Ferry: Manly. **Amenities:** Rooftop pool. *In room:* A/C, TV, fridge, Internet ($10 per day).

Manly Seaview Motel & Apartments   Despite the name, there are no sea views at this old-style motel a block and a half away from the beach at the north end of Manly. Don't expect anything too flash, but if all you want is a smallish but functional room they are pretty good value for the price, even if it's a little on the daggy side.

19 Pacific St. (cnr. Malvern Ave.), Manly. ✆ **(02) 9977 1774.** Fax: (02) 9977 5298. www.manlyseaviewmotel.com.au. 18 units. $110–$220 double. Extra person $30. MC, V. Free parking. Ferry: Manly. *In room:* A/C, TV, fridge, Wi-Fi ($5 per day).

★ **McLaren Hotel**   The large, pleasant rooms in a 1870s mansion make this another good alternative to CBD accommodation. There is a new wing of accommodation joined to the historic house via an atrium. Ask about any specials before you book.

25 McLaren St., North Sydney. ✆ **(02) 9954 4622.** www.mclarenhotel.com.au. 27 units. $157 double. Extra person $35. MC, V. Free parking. Train: North Sydney. **Amenities:** Breakfast room, garden, guest lounge, free Internet. *In room:* A/C, TV, fridge, hair dryer, minibar, Wi-Fi ($5 per 30 min.; $15 per 5 hr.).

North Shore Hotel   Don't get this place confused with the North *Sydney* Hotel, a pub 50m down the road. The standard rooms are a bit small, but the deluxe and superior rooms offer good value and room to move and are ideal for families as most include a single bed (or two) as well as a double at no extra charge. The hotel is located opposite St Leonards Park and North Sydney Oval and it's only a few minutes by train to the city centre, although it's a bit of an uphill walk from North Sydney Station—hard work if you're dragging luggage. (That said, there is a bus stop right outside the door.)

310 Miller St., North Sydney. ✆ **(02) 9955 1012.** Fax: (02) 9955 4212. www.northshorehotel.com.au. 27 units. $99–$110 double. Extra person $10. MC, V. No parking. Train: North Sydney. Bus: 202, 203, 205, 207 or 208. **Amenities:** Breakfast room, guest lounge. *In room:* A/C, TV, fridge, hair dryer.

Park Regis Concierge Apartments   Some of these apartments have views over Sydney Harbour, although some look down on noisy Military Road, so it pays to double check what you're getting when you book. It's not far to Cremorne Point, where you can catch the ferry to the city, which means you get to *see* the sights on your way *to* the sights. Otherwise, there's a bus stop practically outside the front door.

287 Military Rd., Cremorne. ✆ **(02) 8969 6944.** Fax: (02) 8969 6933. www.parkregishotel.com.au. 56 units. $95–$151 double. Extra person $30. MC, V. Parking $15. Bus: 246, 247 or 249. Ferry: Cremorne. **Amenities:** Restaurant, bar. *In room:* A/C, TV, hair dryer, kitchen, laundry, Internet ($10 per 2 hr.; $27.50 per day).

`FREE` Free Sleeps

There's no place like someone else's home ... especially when it means you can sleep for free. If you're new to Sydney and don't know anyone, you don't have to miss out: here are three great (and above-board) ways to find a stranger's bed to sleep in, for free.

Key Change House Swapping—where you stay in someone's house and they stay in yours for an agreed length of time at no cost to either party—is very easy to arrange, thanks to a swag of house swapping internet sites. Beyond the obvious delights of scoring free accommodation, it's a great way to save money by cooking your own meals and you get peace of mind because someone is taking care of your home. It is also extremely family friendly as you can swap with other families and take advantage of their child's facilities while having plenty of space to play. Swapping is free, but most sites charge a small registration fee, usually around $60 to $70 a year. Try www.aussie houseswap.com.au.

Don't have a house back home you can swap? Try **house sitting:** you stay in someone else's house while they are away for free. There is a catch: you have to maintain the house as if it was your own and you'll have to do some household chores, such as watering the garden, forwarding mail or looking after pets. You can house sit for a week or a year—or longer. There are a raft of websites out there where you can register and most cost hopeful sitters around $50 to $65 a year to register. Check out www.aussiehousesitters.com.au and www.housesit world.com.au.

What's the next best thing to a free bed for the night? A friendly couch to crash on! **Couch Surfing** is a worldwide network of people with couches who offer them up to travellers and visitors for a night or two of free accommodation. There are more than one million registered couch surfers around the world, which means you're sure to find a Sydney sofa to sleep on. Visit www.couchsurfing.org.

Travelodge Manly Hotel You'll usually get a much better deal than the published rate below at this motel near Brookvale Oval. Be warned: it's nowhere near Manly Beach, despite the hotel's name.

4–10 Victor Rd., Brookvale. ℂ **(02) 8978 1200.** Fax: (02) 8978 1300. www.travelodge. com.au. 120 units. $155 double. Extra person $40. AE, MC, V. Free parking. Bus: L90 or 190. **Amenities:** Bar and restaurant at Manly Warringah Rugby League Club, opposite. *In room:* A/C, TV, hair dryer, kitchenette.

Urban St Leonards This colourful little boutique hotel is a good choice if you want to stay on the north side on a weekend. During the week, rates are around the $200 mark when it's popular with business types, but come Friday and Saturday night, you can pick up a room for around $150, and some have balconies.

194 Pacific Hwy. (cnr. Bellevue Ave.), St Leonards. ℂ **(02) 9439 6000.** Fax: (02) 9439 6442. www.hotelurban.com.au. 100 units. $179–$300 double. Extra person $45. AE, MC, V. Limited parking $10. Train: St Leonards. **Amenities:** Licensed cafe. *In room:* A/C, TV, fridge, hair dryer, minibar, Wi-Fi ($8 per 30 min.; $27.50 per day).

CHEAP SLEEPS

★ **Lane Cove River Tourist Park** The Lane Cove River winds through a peaceful bushland valley just beyond the backyard fences of lower North Shore suburbia near Chatswood. It's a national park, and one of the few places you can camp or park your caravan and still be within easy reach of the city centre. The two-bedroom cabins are phenomenal value, especially if you're travelling with kids, who can run wild in the national park.

Plassey Rd., North Ryde/Macquarie Park. ℂ **(02) 9888 9133.** Fax: (02) 9888 9322. www.lanecoverivertouristpark.com.au. 28 cabins; 300 caravan/tent sites. $121–$145 cabin. Extra person $10. $34–$36 caravan/tent site. MC, V. Free parking. Bus: 545 from Chatswood Station. **Amenities:** Barbecue, camp kitchen, games room, Internet kiosk, laundry, swimming pool. *In room (cabins):* A/C, TV, DVD, hair dryer, kitchen.

Pittwater YHA Deep in the bush of Ku-ring-gai Chase National Park, this basic little hostel is a back-to-nature getaway with great kayaking and bushwalking spots and plenty of wildlife to watch. It's hard work to get there, but once you arrive, you may never want to leave.

Towlers Bay Track, Ku-ring-gai Chase National Park. ℂ **(02) 9999 5748.** Fax: (02) 9999 5749. www.yha.com.au. 36 units (2 private; none w/bathroom). $65–$72 double; $25–$28 dorm bed. MC, V. No vehicular access. Bus: E86 from the city or 156 from Manly to Church Point, then a ferry to Halls Wharf, then a 15 min walk. **Amenities:** Barbecue, communal kitchen, canoes, guest lounge. *In room:* Lockers.

Sydney Lakeside Holiday Park There are not many places in Sydney where you can wake up a stone's throw from the beach for less than $40, but in this caravan park behind the beach at Narrabeen you can. It's one of the only seaside caravan parks left in Sydney.

38 Lake Park Rd., North Narrabeen. ✆ **(02) 9913 7845.** Fax: (02) 9970 6385. http://sydney-lakeside-holiday-park.nsw.big4.com.au. 68 cabins, 260 caravan/tent sites. $168–$310 cabin. Extra person $15. $36–$65 caravan/tent site. MC, V. Free parking. Bus: 183 or 185. **Amenities:** Barbecue, camp kitchen, games room, laundry, playground, free Wi-Fi. *In room:* A/C, TV, DVD, hair dryer, kitchen (cabins).

WORTH A SPLURGE

★ **Vibe Hotel North Sydney** Staying on the North Shore makes for a nice change, and it's a lovely stroll over the Harbour Bridge to get to the city. Ask for a Kirribilli or Lavender Bay view and book online for a better price: you'll often find two-night B&B packages for around $150 to $180 a night.

88 Alfred St., Milsons Point. ✆ **(02) 9955 1111.** Fax: (02) 9955 3522. www.vibehotels.com.au. 165 units. $380–$405 double. Extra person $40. Parking $19.50. AE, DC, MC, V. Train: Milsons Point. **Amenities:** Restaurant, bar, outdoor pool. *In room:* A/C, TV, fridge, hair dryer, minibar, Wi-Fi ($12.95 per hr.; $24.95 per day).

5 Inner West

AFFORDABLE

Alishan International Guesthouse The rooms aren't nearly as grand as the outside of this imposing Victorian mansion would lead you to expect. In fact, the doubles are positively poky, so if your budget allows, opt for a family room, which offers more space.

100 Glebe Point Rd., Glebe. ✆ **(02) 9566 4048.** Fax: (02) 9525 4686. www.alishan.com.au. 25 units (all w/bathroom except dorms). $99–$145 double; $27–$35 dorm bed. Extra person $16. AE, MC, V. Limited off-street parking $5. Bus: 431 or 433. **Amenities:** Barbecue area, communal kitchen, guest lounge. *In room:* Ceiling fan, TV, fridge, Wi-Fi ($7 per day).

Aspire Hotel Aspire is in a good location in a residential area, while being close enough to walk into the city across Darling Harbour. The rooms are in need of a refurb, but even so, they good for the price. If you're here in summer ask for a room with a balcony for good city skyline views.

383–389 Bulwara Rd., Ultimo. ℭ **(02) 9211 1499.** Fax: (02) 9281 3764. www.aspire hotel.com. 96 units. $110–$145 double. Extra person $40. AE, MC, V. Parking $25. Light rail/Monorail: Paddy's Markets. **Amenities:** Breakfast room. *In room:* A/C, TV, balcony (some rooms), fridge, hair dryer, Wi-Fi ($5 per hr.; $10 per day).

The Haven Inn The rooms are basic, but almost all have a balcony and kids love the pool in the centre courtyard. Those on the third floor have views of the city skyline. Avoid the corner rooms, which can be noisy as they are above two busy bus routes.

196 Glebe Point Rd., Glebe. ℭ **(02) 9660 6655.** Fax: (02) 9660 6279. www.haveninn sydney.com.au. 59 units. $99–$129 double. Extra person $25. MC, V. Limited parking $15. Bus: 431 or 433. **Amenities:** Pool. *In room:* A/C, TV, DVD (free DVD library), fridge, hair dryer, Wi-Fi ($7.50 per day).

★ **Vulcan Hotel** Vulcan offers stylish, large and newly refurbished rooms in a historic old pub built in 1894. It's worth staying here for the breakfasts alone, although there's not much happening in the area after dark; Darling Harbour and Chinatown are a 10- to 15-minute walk away.

500 Wattle St., Ultimo. ℭ **(02) 9211 3283.** www.vulcanhotel.com.au. 46 units. $139–$169 double. Extra person $30. MC, V. Parking $18. Monorail: Exhibition Centre. **Amenities:** Bar, restaurant. *In room:* A/C, TV, DVD, fridge, Wi-Fi ($10 per day).

Sleeping with the Enemy

Here's a good alternative for those looking for longer and mid-term accommodations, without the constant comings and goings of a back-packers' or cheap hotel or the bother of finding your own apartment. Sleeping with the Enemy (don't let the name scare you away) has several furnished houses sleeping up to nine people in Ultimo and Pyrmont, available for a minimum one-month stay. The crowd is young and international and you can expect to pay rent of around $170 to $200 per week, which includes unlimited computer access (Internet terminals and Wi-Fi) and covers all household bills. For information, call ℭ **1300 309 468** or visit www.sleepingwiththeenemy.com.

CHEAP SLEEPS INNER WEST

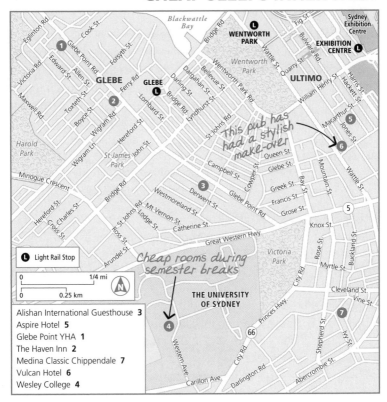

Wesley College   Staying in Edwardian gothic splendour in the middle of Sydney for less than $100 a night—including a hot breakfast—is a pretty good deal, so long as the timing's right. During university semester breaks, Wesley College at the University of Sydney offers casual accommodation in single and twin rooms with a shared bathroom, and the longer you stay the cheaper it gets. Accommodation is available over the summer, from late November to mid-February, excluding the week over Christmas/New Year's Eve. Check out the website for next year's dates.

Western Ave., in the grounds of the University of Sydney. ✆ **(02) 9565 3377.** Fax: (02) 9516 3653. www.wesleycollege-usyd.edu.au. 200 units. $95 double. MC, V. Free parking. Bus: 412, 413, 436, 438, 461, 422 or 424. **Amenities:** Breakfast room, guest lounge, vending machine. *In room:* Phone.

CHEAP SLEEPS

Glebe Point YHA   Popular with those on working holiday or extended stays, this hostel at the water-end of Glebe Point Road is in a residential area with a bus stop directly across the street and Glebe's cheap eats just up the road. It's a quieter alternative to some other more social hostels and backpackers' you'll find in inner eastern suburbs such as Kings Cross and around Central Station.

262 Glebe Point Rd., Glebe. ℂ **(02) 9692 8418.** Fax: (02) 9660 0431. www.yha.com. au. 147 units (24 private; none w/bathroom). $72–$84 double; $26–$35 dorm bed. MC, V. Limited street parking. Bus: 431. **Amenities:** Rooftop barbecue, communal kitchen, TV lounge, *In room:* Lockers, Wi-Fi ($3 per hr.; $15 per day).

WORTH A SPLURGE

Medina Classic Chippendale   About as upmarket as you'll find in the inner west, this apartment hotel is close to the University of Sydney, but the area is a bit rough, so be careful if you're walking around alone late at night. That said, I love the working-class, inner-city, edgy boho vibe of the district, and it's an easy walk to Newtown and Glebe. The spacious apartments have lots of room to move and are a good choice if you need to stay in the area for business or work for a few days, or even weeks.

74–80 Ivy St., Chippendale. ℂ **(02) 9311 8800.** Fax: (02) 9311 8899. www.medina. com.au. 41 units. $150–$255 double. Extra person $50. AE, DC, MC, V. Parking $10. Train: Milsons Point. **Amenities:** Barbecue, cafe, gym, outdoor pool. *In room:* A/C, TV, kitchen, laundry, hair dryer, Internet ($12.95 per hr.; $24.95 per day).

Harry's Cafe de Wheels (p. 66) is arguably a Sydney institution. Make up your own mind as to whether you agree with the masses.

CHEAP EATS

Sydney is a food lover's paradise. Not only do we have some of the freshest and best ingredients at our fingertips, we also enjoy an amazing variety of cuisines and cooking styles; you can eat your way around the world in multicultural Sydney. Yes, we have our fair share of stratospherically expensive restaurants—most of the classy eateries that have a harbour view will set you back $40 to $50 for a main course—but you *don't* have to be rich to eat well in Sydney.

As a general rule of thumb, Asian food is your best bet for a cheap meal, though tapas can also be a good option if you're eating en masse—the more hungry mouths to feed, the cheaper it is. You'll also find great-value no-frills pub grub for little more than $10 (think steaks, schnitzels, pastas, chicken parmigiana—parma for short—and so on). If you need another reason to head to your local, they often also have live music or irreverent bingo—that's dinner and a show for next to nix!

We've stuck to price cap of (roughly) $25 or less for a main dish when compiling this guide, and stayed pretty much in the city centre and inner suburbs, but prices tend to get cheaper the further you go into the suburbs. Chinatown's one of your best bets for truly dirt-cheap dining, but don't discard Surry Hills, Darlinghurst or Newtown as cheap-eat hubs.

Just like Sydney hotels, restaurants with a harbour or ocean view are going to be pricey. Most of the eateries that overlook water tend to be either very high-end or a tourist rip-off; however, surprisingly, some über-expensive gastro temples also offer the best-value eats during daylight hours. Now that's a bargain any way you serve it up.

1 City Centre

The Apprentice *CONTEMPORARY* Many superstar chefs start their careers here in this rooftop training restaurant for the hospitality college at Sydney TAFE. It's amazing value: four courses for $27. The only catch is that it's a set menu.

Level 7, Building E, Ultimo College, cnr. Harris and Thomas sts., Haymarket. ℂ **(02) 9217 5527.** www.sit.nsw.edu.au/theapprentice. MC, V. Lunch and dinner Mon–Fri (during term). Train: Central.

Asagao *JAPANESE* This is one of a chain of Japanese takeaway stores that stud the city. Some are much better than others, and this one near Pitt Street Mall is pretty good. There's a sushi train, but the ready-to-eat bento boxes and teriyaki sets are better value in my opinion. Beware of long office-crowd lines during lunchtime.

239 Pitt St., Sydney. ℂ **(02) 9283 6522.** Sushi $3–$5, mains $12–$15. No credit cards. Lunch and dinner Mon–Sat. Train: Town Hall.

Athenian *GREEK* Tuck into a huge Greek lamb casserole, mezes or seafood specialities, such as barbecued octopus and fried whitebait, in this imposing, elegant old bank. A couple of the seafood mains are

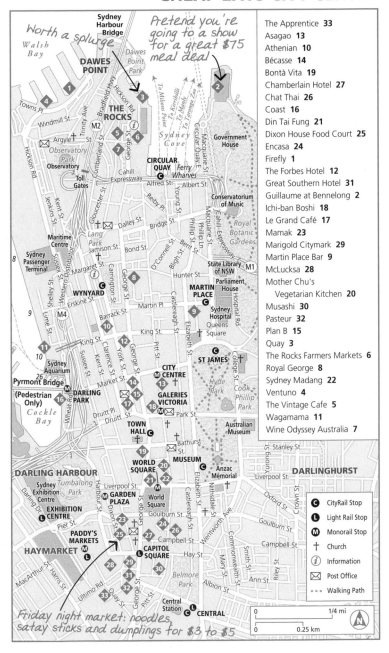

Worth a splurge

Pretend you're going to a show for a great $75 meal deal

Friday night market: noodles, satay sticks and dumplings for $3 to $5

The Apprentice **33**
Asagao **13**
Athenian **10**
Bécasse **14**
Bontà Vita **19**
Chamberlain Hotel **27**
Chat Thai **26**
Coast **16**
Din Tai Fung **21**
Dixon House Food Court **25**
Encasa **24**
Firefly **1**
The Forbes Hotel **12**
Great Southern Hotel **31**
Guillaume at Bennelong **2**
Ichi-ban Boshi **18**
Le Grand Café **17**
Mamak **23**
Marigold Citymark **29**
Martin Place Bar **9**
McLucksa **28**
Mother Chu's
    Vegetarian Kitchen **20**
Musashi **30**
Pasteur **32**
Plan B **15**
Quay **3**
The Rocks Farmers Markets **6**
Royal George **8**
Sydney Madang **22**
Ventuno **4**
The Vintage Cafe **5**
Wagamama **11**
Wine Odyssey Australia **7**

C CityRail Stop
L Light Rail Stop
M Monorail Stop
† Church
ⓘ Information
✉ Post Office
••• Walking Path

0   1/4 mi
0   0.25 km

a bit above our $25 limit, but the rest of the menu of classic Greek dishes hovers around the $20 mark.

11 Barrack St., Sydney. ℂ **(02) 9262 2624.** Mains $16–$30. AE, DC, MC, V. Lunch and dinner Mon–Sat. Train: Wynyard.

Bontà Vita *ITALIAN/MALAYSIAN*   Italian and Malaysian are an unlikely cuisine mix, but the signature dish of this place— the Rizza— works. It's kind of like a roti, stuffed with various fillings, and then topped with a pizza-like sauce.

Regent Place, 501 George St., Town Hall (enter via Bathurst St., opp. St Andrews Cathedral). ℂ **(02) 9267 2212.** www.bontavita.com.au. Mains $12–$26. AE, DC, MC, V. Lunch and dinner daily. Train: Town Hall.

Chamberlain Hotel *PUB GRUB*   Ten bucks buys a plate piled high with your choice of fish and chips, steak and mash, schnitzel and chips or pasta every night (except Sunday), 5.30pm to 8.30pm. It's not flash, but it's filling. Wednesday night sees a (chicken) parma and pale ale deal for the same price. There's a good bistro menu and Thai food after 10pm.

428 Pitt St., Haymarket. ℂ **(02) 9288 0888.** www.chamberlainhotel.com.au. Mains $9–$17. MC, V. Lunch and dinner daily. Train: Central.

Chat Thai *THAI*   There is always a queue outside, but it's worth the wait for treats such as crying tiger (grilled marinated beef served with a fiery chilli, tomato and tamarind relish) or spicy green papaya salad. There's always a good selection of just-made sweet coconut-infused dumplings and rice cakes for dessert.

20 Campbell St., Haymarket. ℂ **(02) 9211 1808.** www.chatthai.com.au. Mains $11–$26. MC, V. Lunch and dinner daily. Train: Central.

★ **Din Tai Fung** *CHINESE*   I have just one word for this place, but I'll say it thrice: dumplings, dumplings, dumplings. I'd argue that these are among the best dumplings in Sydney. It's the only Aussie outpost of the legendary Taipei-based global chain and there's usually a long queue, but if your idea of culinary heaven is a steaming hot soup dumpling you'll be happy to wait.

Level 1, World Square Shopping Centre, 644 George St., Sydney. ℂ **(02) 9264 6010.** Mains $11–$18. AE, MC, V. Lunch and dinner daily. Train: Town Hall.

Encasa *SPANISH*   Think fast Spanish tapas and paella served in a rambunctious dining room. This is not the place to go for a quiet

Cheap Eat Streets

Some streets are made for walking, but in Sydney you'll find some are made for eating. The competition for your dinner dollar is fierce, and places that don't deliver the goods go out of business fast, so remember the golden rule: if there's a crowd inside, the food is good.

- **Cleveland Street, Surry Hills:** The stretch of Cleveland Street that spears through Surry Hills is packed with cheap-as-chips Turkish, Lebanese and Indian restaurants.

- **Crown Street, Surry Hills:** Crown Street, running north–south from Oxford to Cleveland streets, is eating central. Some of it is positively pricey, but much of it is super cheap.

- **Dixon Street, Haymarket:** If you can't find a dirt cheap Chinese (or Thai or Vietnamese) meal in and around Chinatown, you're just not looking.

- **Glebe Point Road, Glebe:** The top end of Glebe Point Road is chock-full of cafes and inexpensive restaurants; it's a mixed bag of international cuisines.

- **King Street, Newtown:** Cheap and cheerful is the name of the game in Newtown, with a veritable feast of Thai, Vietnamese, a few Indian and Turkish and more than a couple of Italian eateries all vying for your dinner dollars.

- **Norton Street, Leichhardt:** Leichhardt is the heart of Italian Sydney; this is the place to go for dishes just like your nonna used to make.

- **Park and John streets, Cabramatta:** These streets are home to some of the tastiest pho (noodle soup) this side of Saigon. Most places charge less than $10 a bowl.

- **The Spot, Randwick:** The corner of St Pauls and Perouse roads is known as 'The Spot'. It's home to a cluster of great affordable restaurants, with Thai, Indian, Spanish, Italian and a couple of excellent fish cafes.

romantic dinner for two, but the tapas is good value and the pizzas are interesting. It gets a bit hot and steamy in the middle of summer.

423 Pitt St., Sydney. ✆ **(02) 9211 4257.** Mains $12–$26. AE, MC, V. Lunch Tues–Fri, dinner Mon–Sat. Train: Central.

Firefly *TAPAS*   Right next door to the Sydney Theatre Company, this breezy tapas wine bar has great views of the Harbour Bridge. It's a great place for a pre- or post-show nibble, and you might run into some of the stars of the show—it's a favourite hangout. I love the roast beetroot salad and the prosciutto-wrapped haloumi, but there's no shortage of choice.

Pier Seven, 17 Hickson Rd., Walsh Bay. ✆ **(02) 9241 2031.** www.fireflybar.com.au. Mains $7–$19. AE, MC, V. Lunch Mon–Sat; dinner daily. Train: Circular Quay.

The Forbes Hotel *CONTEMPORARY*   Good-value, no-nonsense meals have made this gorgeous historic pub a long-time favourite with the office crowd, who come here for pasta at lunch and steak or seafood after work.

30 York St., Sydney. ✆ **(02) 9299 3703.** www.theforbeshotel.com.au. Mains $16–$24. AE, DC, MC, V. Lunch and dinner Mon–Sat. Train: Wynyard or Martin Place.

Great Southern Hotel *PUB GRUB*   A little bit of cash buys a big plate of food at this pub bar near Central. A 250g grain-fed rump steak is just $9, while the most expensive thing on the blackboard menu is a steak smothered in king prawns and creamy garlic sauce at $16.

717 George St., Sydney. ✆ **(02) 9289 4400.** Mains $8–$16. AE, DC, MC, V. Lunch and dinner daily. Train: Central.

Ichi-ban Boshi *JAPANESE*   Sydney's best ramen and udon are to be found in this very popular Japanese noodle shop, hidden away inside Galeries Victoria. I can't get enough of the silky noodles (which are made on-site), the practically perfect gyoza and the sukiyaki *don* (thinly sliced marinated beef in sukiyaki sauce on a bed of rice). Be prepared to queue at lunchtime, or get there early to beat the crowd.

Level 2, Galeries Victoria, 500 George St., Sydney. ✆ **(02) 9262 7677.** www.ichiban boshi.com.au. Mains $16–$22. No credit cards. Lunch and dinner daily. Train: Town Hall.

Le Grand Café *FRENCH*   One of Sydney's best French chefs, Justin North of Bécasse fame (p. 62), turns out classic French fare at bargain prices at this lovely little cafe at the French language and cultural centre, Alliance Française. A perfect spot for a light lunch.

257 Clarence St., Sydney. ℂ **(02) 9264 7164.** www.afsydney.com.au. Mains $8–$12. No credit cards. Lunch Mon–Sat; early dinner (5–6pm) Mon–Thurs. Train: Town Hall.

Mamak *MALAYSIAN*   This place gets five out of five for the $5 rotis alone; for a couple of dollars more they come filled with spicy chicken or lamb. But save plenty of room for the satay—and dessert, of course: lusciously sweet rotis served with ice-cream and coconut paste. Yum!

15 Goulburn St., Haymarket. ℂ **(02) 9211 1668.** Mains $8–$16. AE, MC, V. Lunch and dinner daily. Train: Central.

★ **Marigold Citymark** *CHINESE*   In the heart of Chinatown, the Marigold is one of Sydney's best spots for weekend yum cha, boasting more than 100 different varieties of dim sum. The 800 seats fill fast, but the service is faster. It's good value at the best of times, but get a group of six together and you can feast on eight courses for $38. Another good reason to go there is the dim sum degustation for two, where $25 gets you 11 courses, but only at dinner from Sunday through Thursday.

Levels 4 and 5, 683 George St., Haymarket. ℂ **(02) 9281 3388.** Mains $18–$33. AE, MC, V. Lunch and dinner daily. Train: Central.

Martin Place Bar *PUB GRUB*   There are few dishes on the all-day bar menu that cost more than $20, making this a good place for a good-value meal in the centre of the city. If you order from the lunch menu, expect to pay a couple of dollars more.

51 Martin Place, Sydney. ℂ **(02) 9231 5575.** www.martinplacebar.com.au. Mains $9–$25. MC, V. Lunch and dinner Mon–Fri. Train: Martin Place.

King of the (Food) Court

If you're looking for a wide choice of good and cheap Asian food, you can't do much better than **Dixon House Food Court.** It's home to 14 or 15 food outlets, offering everything from *nasi lemak* and *roti chanai* to beef pho, freshly squeezed sugar-cane juice and steamed pork buns. The cuisines stretch all the way from China and Nepal to Japan, Korea, Vietnam, Malaysia and Indonesia. Almost all of it will leave you with change from a $10 note. You'll find the food court on the corner of Dixon and Little Hay streets, Haymarket and it's open daily from 10.30am until 8.30pm.

BYO

Many of the smaller restaurants and neighbourhood eateries in Sydney are BYO, which stands for 'bring your own', meaning you can bring a bottle of wine or a few beers, even if the restaurant is licensed. Some may charge a corkage fee of a few dollars, but it's still much less than buying a bottle in-house. It's a great way to save money, so ask when booking and keep an eye out for those three magic letters.

McLucksa *SINGAPOREAN*   A food-court standout; at this place, you can forget about swish service—or anything else, for that matter—and concentrate on the food. And with a name like this, you've gotta try the laksa.

Level 3, Market City, 9–13 Hay St., Haymarket. © **(02) 9211 1922.** Mains $8–$9. No credit cards. Lunch and dinner daily. Train: Central.

Mother Chu's Vegetarian Kitchen *TAIWANESE*   I can't believe it's not meat! Steeped in the Buddhist tradition of making vegetables look (and almost taste) just like meat, this is a vegetarian restaurant that even appeals to carnivores. My favourite is the crispy noodle nest, full of cashews and peas and other goodies on a bed of fried noodles, and do try the vegetarian Peking duck ($40 for two; must be ordered a day ahead). There's no alcohol and it's decidedly ambience-free.

367 Pitt St., Sydney. © **(02) 9283 2828.** Mains $9–$17. AE, MC, V. Lunch and dinner Mon–Sat. Train: Town Hall.

Musashi *JAPANESE*   Wagyu for way less than $30? Bring it on! This great-value Japanese restaurant serves up all the favourite dishes in *izakaya* fashion (a Japanese version of tapas), which is designed to share. Beyond the melt-in-the-mouth beef sirloin, there are plenty of brilliant sushi, sashimi and fish dishes, such as the delectable baby snapper simmered in soy and mirin.

477 Pitt St., Haymarket. © **(02) 9280 0377.** www.masuya.com.au. Mains $15–$28. AE, MC, V. Lunch Mon–Fri; dinner daily (no bookings after 12.15pm for lunch or 6pm for dinner). Train: Central.

Pasteur *VIETNAMESE*   Pasteur is authentic Vietnamese, right down to the plastic furniture and jar of chopsticks on the table. It's all about the food here, rather than the decor or the service. Order the pho—a rich and satisfying beef noodle soup that is a staple of any Vietnamese eatery.

709 George St., Haymarket. ⓒ **(02) 9212 5622.** Mains $8–$12. No credit cards. Lunch and dinner daily. Train: Central.

★ **Plan B** *CAFE*   Ten dollars might seem like a lot to pay for a burger, but you'll think again once you've sunk your teeth into the 600-day-old grain-fed Wagyu beef burger at this hole-in-the-wall cafe next door to (and run by) one of Sydney's best French restaurants, Bécasse (p. 62). Just as brilliant are the homemade sausage rolls and a-cut-above-the-average sandwiches with fillings such as crisp pork belly, hoisin sauce and spring onion.

204 Clarence St., Sydney. ⓒ **(02) 9283 3450.** www.becasse.com.au. Mains $7–$10. AE, DC, MC, V. Breakfast and lunch Mon–Fri. Train: Town Hall.

Royal George *PUB GRUB*   Modelled on a traditional English pub, this is where the beautiful people go when they feel like toning it down. The meals are hearty, high quality and good value, with favourites such as shepherd's pie alongside more adventurous plates such as pork, apple and chorizo terrine with celery salad featuring on a menu that doesn't break the $20 barrier.

320–330 George St., Sydney. ⓒ **(02) 9240 3000.** www.merivale.com/ivy/royal george. Mains $14–$18. AE, DC, MC, V. Lunch and dinner Mon–Sat. Train: Martin Place.

Sydney Madang *KOREAN*   Perennially packed despite being hidden down a laneway off Pitt Street, this tiny little Korean canteen offers great food and fast service. Five kinds of *kimchi*, table-top barbecues and sizzling steamboats for two ($35 to $40) make this a great spot for a late-night feed—it's open until 2am on weekdays and 3am on Friday and Saturday nights.

371A Pitt St (enter via an alley just north of Liverpool St), Sydney. ⓒ **(02) 9264 7010.** Mains $13–$18. MC, V. Lunch and dinner daily. Train: Town Hall

Ventuno *ITALIAN*   The full name of this buzzy but glam restaurant at Walsh Bay—Ventuno Pizzeria Enoteca Birreria—is a mouthful, but it does describe the restaurant's specialities: antipasti, pizza, pasta, Italian wines and boutique Italian beers. Go on Sunday night and have your choice of pizza and a glass of house wine or Italian boutique beer for $20.

21 Hickson Rd., Walsh Bay. ℂ **(02) 9247 4444.** www.ventuno.com.au. Mains $14–$26. AE, MC, V. Lunch and dinner daily. Train: Circular Quay.

The Vintage Cafe *MEDITERRANEAN*   Come here for tasty *petisco* plates (also known as tapas) dished up with live bossa nova and jazz at dinner and weekend lunch. The breakfast omelette, filled with capsicum, tomato, Spanish onion, mushrooms, oregano and feta cheese, is a good reason to visit.

R2 Nurse Walk, The Rocks. ℂ **(02) 9252 2055.** Mains $9–$17. MC, V. Breakfast and lunch daily; dinner Thurs–Sat. Train: Circular Quay.

Wagamama *ASIAN*   To be honest, the food served up at this British chain of eateries is not the most authentic Asian food in town, but it's user-friendly if you're not used to this type of cuisine and nothing's too hot or too spicy. This makes it a great place to take kids, especially considering they can eat for free on weekends, public holidays and during school holidays.

49 Lime St., Kings Street Wharf (other venues at Galeries Victoria and city). ℂ **(02) 9299 6924.** www.wagamama.com.au. Mains $17–$23. AE, MC, V. Lunch and dinner daily. Train: Wynyard.

WORTH A SPLURGE

★ **Bécasse** *FRENCH*   One of Sydney's most highly awarded fine diners, this is a good choice if you're eager to impress clients, as long as you have a corporate credit card. If you don't, try the Producers Lunch, a fixed seasonal menu that focuses on Australian produce, instead. For $50 you'll get two courses and a glass of wine.

204 Clarence St., Sydney. ℂ **(02) 9283 3440.** www.becasse.com.au. Mains $45. 10-course degustation $130. AE, DC, MC, V. Lunch Mon–Fri; dinner Mon–Sat. Train: Town Hall.

★ **Coast** *ITALIAN*   Popular with those who have expense accounts, this highly awarded swish restaurant overlooks Darling Harbour and has a fantastic chef's market menu that is well worth the splurge. The shared four-course menu changes daily and features whatever is fresh and best for just $59. There's a slightly cheaper version for lunch: two courses for $39 or three for $50, plus a glass of wine. There are two catches: you don't get to choose your dishes and the whole table must join in at dinner.

The Roof Terrace, Cockle Bay Wharf, Darling Park. ℂ **(02) 9267 6700.** www.coast restaurant.com.au. Mains $23–$44. AE, MC, V. Lunch Mon–Fri; dinner Mon–Sat. Train: Town Hall.

★ **Guillaume at Bennelong** *CONTEMPORARY/FRENCH* You would expect a restaurant in the Opera House to be a touristy rip-off, but Guillaume at Bennelong is anything but. With mains starting at $40 and reaching into three figures, it normally wouldn't qualify as dirt cheap, but go early (opens at 5.30pm; must be out by 8pm) and take advantage of three courses for $75.

Sydney Opera House, Bennelong Point. ℂ **(02) 9241 1999.** www.guillaumeat bennelong.com.au. Mains $40–$120. AE, DC, MC, V. Lunch Thurs–Fri; dinner Mon–Sat. Train: Circular Quay.

`FREE` Free Booze

Fancy a free tipple or two? You'll have to sit through the sales pitch, but these places are happy to give you a free taste or two—just try not to look desperately thirsty.

- **Amato's Liquor Mart:** Free wine-tasting sessions every Thursday (5 to 8pm), Friday (4 to 8pm) and Saturday (noon to 8pm). It's at 267–277 Norton Street, Leichhardt (ℂ **(02) 9560 7628;** www. amatos.com.au), so expect lots of luscious Italian varietals.

- **Five Ways Cellars:** This tiny wine shop at 4 Heeley Street, Paddington (ℂ **(02) 9360 4242**) serves hand-picked boutique wines at the Saturday (noon to 6pm) wine-tasting session.

- **Moncur Cellars:** The focus is on French and Italian wines at 60 Moncur Street, Woollahra (ℂ **(02) 9327 9715**). Every Friday night (5 to 7pm) and Saturday afternoon (1 to 4pm) you can taste some for free. Check out the website for details of what wines and when: www.woollahrahotel.com.au. There are also regular free wine education evenings.

- **Ultimo Wine Centre:** These guys know just about everything there is to know about wine and are keen to share it with you. Free wine tastings every Saturday from 12.30pm (until whenever the bottles run out) at shop C21/99 Jones Street, Ultimo (ℂ **(02) 9211 2380;** www.ultimowinecentre.com.au).

★ **Quay** *CONTEMPORARY*   If you're searching for some wow factor, head to Quay. It was named 2009 Restaurant of the Year by two of the country's most respected food guides and it has an unbeatable view of the Opera House and Harbour Bridge. Night-time's pricey, but the view's as good, if not better, during daylight hours, when you can get two courses for $75.

Overseas Passenger Terminal, The Rocks. ✆ **(02) 9251 5600.** www.quay.com.au. 4 courses $145. AE, DC, MC, V. Lunch Tues–Fri; dinner daily. Train: Circular Quay.

Wine Odyssey Australia *CONTEMPORARY*   This is the place to go to taste the best of Australian wine (including Penfolds' legendary Grange), with a whopping 44 of them available by the taste in the DIY tasting room, half and full glass—and another 200 by the bottle. But what makes this place much more are the sensational food and wine flights: each 'flight' includes three glasses of wine and three perfectly matched small dishes for less than $35.

39–43 Argyle St., The Rocks. ✆ **(02) 8114 0256.** www.wineodyssey.com.au. Mains $25–$29. AE, MC, V. Lunch and dinner Tues–Sun. Train: Circular Quay.

2 Kings Cross

★ **Aperitif** *FRENCH/MEDITERRANEAN*   Tucked away in a tiny terrace on a back street, this great late-night restaurant specialises in tasting plates to share. The cuisine is hard to pin down—think French, Spanish, Italian and a touch of Moroccan. The sophisticated room, fantastic selection of wine by the glass and a great cocktail list make this an easy place to linger over several hours.

7 Kellett St., Kings Cross. ✆ **(02) 9357 4729.** Mains $18–$25. AE, MC, V. Dinner Wed–Mon. Train: Kings Cross.

Bay Bua *VIETNAMESE*   With 105 dishes on the menu, it might take you a while to decide on your order, but I can pretty much guarantee that you won't be disappointed. It's all delicious—especially the calamari stuffed with pork. And the bonus: the room is more opulent than you would expect, given the bargain-basement prices.

2 Springfield Ave., Potts Point. ✆ **(02) 9358 3234.** www.baybua.com.au. Mains $9–$18. MC, V. Dinner daily. Train: Kings Cross.

Bei Amici *ITALIAN*   It can be hard find somewhere to eat in Sydney on Monday nights, as it's often chef's night off, which makes the amazing Monday-night $33 deal at this intimate and elegant little

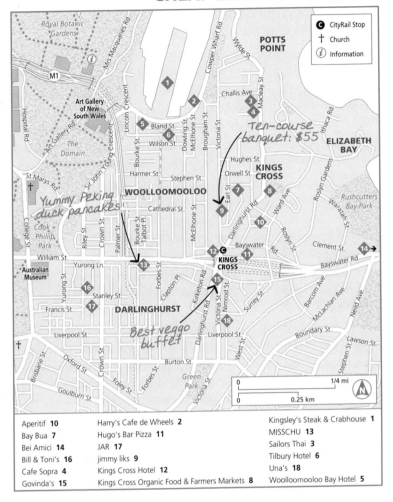

Royal Botanic Gardens

Mrs Macquaries Rd.

Cowper Wharf Rd.

Wylde St.

POTTS POINT

C CityRail Stop
† Church
ⓘ Information

M1

Challis Ave.

Macleay St.

Art Gallery of New South Wales

Lincoln Crescent

1

2

3
4

Bland St.
5

Dowling St.
McElhone St.

Brougham St.

Victoria St.

Wilson St.

Ten-course banquet: $55

ELIZABETH BAY

Ithaca Rd.

The Domain

Art Gallery Rd.

Sir John Young Crescent

Bourke St.

Harmer St.

Stephen St.

Hughes St.

Orwell St.
KINGS CROSS

Roslyn Gardens

St Marys Rd.

†

WOOLLOOMOOLOO

Cathedral St.

Earl St.
7

8

Yummy Peking duck pancakes

Cook + Phillip Park

College St.

Riley St.

Crown St.

Palmer St.

Bourke St.
Talbot St.

McElhone St.

Darlinghurst Rd.

9

10

Ward Ave.

Roslyn St.

Rushcutters Bay Park

Waratah St.

Clement St.
14 →

William St.

Australian Museum

Yurong Ln.

Forbes St.

Clapton Pl.

Bayswater
11

C

12
KINGS CROSS

Bayswater Rd.

Barcom Ave.

McLachlan Ave.

Neild Ave.

Yurong St.

16

Stanley St.

17

Francis St.

DARLINGHURST

Kirketon Rd.

15

Victoria St.

Nimrod St.

Surrey St.

18

Best veggo buffet

Liverpool St.

Darlinghurst Rd.

West St.

Liverpool St.

Boundary St.

Lawson St.

Stephen St.

†

Brisbane St.

Oxford St.

Crown St.

Forbes St.

Foley St.

Burton St.

Green Park

Victoria St.

| 0 | | 1/4 mi |
| 0 | 0.25 km | |

Goulburn St.

N

Aperitif **10**	Harry's Cafe de Wheels **2**	Kingsley's Steak & Crabhouse **1**
Bay Bua **7**	Hugo's Bar Pizza **11**	MISSCHU **13**
Bei Amici **14**	JAR **17**	Sailors Thai **3**
Bill & Toni's **16**	jimmy liks **9**	Tilbury Hotel **6**
Cafe Sopra **4**	Kings Cross Hotel **12**	Una's **18**
Govinda's **15**	Kings Cross Organic Food & Farmers Markets **8**	Woolloomooloo Bay Hotel **5**

eatery all the harder to resist. The price gets you three courses of the chef's choosing. To top it off, everything you eat will be organic, biodynamic or handmade.

2B Mona Rd., Darling Point. ℂ **(02) 9328 0305.** Mains $21–$33. AE, MC, V. Lunch Fri; dinner Mon–Sat. Train: Edgecliff.

Bill & Toni's *ITALIAN* You'll get simple, honest and hearty Italian food in this unpretentious Sydney institution that also serves great coffee and is kid friendly. If you're hungry don't go past the spag bol or veal schnitzel.

74 Stanley St., East Sydney. ℭ **(02) 9360 4702.** Mains $9–$15. No credit cards. Lunch and dinner daily. Bus: 372, 373, 378 or 380.

★ **Govinda's** *INDIAN/VEGETARIAN*   It's vegie paradise and a great place for a first date that's cheap as chips without seeming stingy. Dine out on the gourmet vegetarian buffet, then retire upstairs and lay back on the cushions at the comfiest movie house in town (p. 222). Just be careful you don't fall asleep—and try not to canoodle too much.

112 Darlinghurst Rd., Darlinghurst. ℭ **(02) 9380 5155.** www.govindas.com.au. Buffet $19.80, meal and movie deal $28.60. AE, MC, V. Dinner daily. Train: Kings Cross.

OVERRATED **Harry's Cafe de Wheels** *PIES*   This late-night pie cart is in almost every Sydney guidebook, but I just don't see what's great about the pie-and-mushy-pea combos. I think it's a tourist trap, but many of my friends argue that it's a quintessential Sydney experience that's not to be missed. Make up your own mind.

Cnr. Cowper Wharf Roadway and Brougham Rd., Woolloomooloo. ℭ **(02) 9357 3074.** Mains around $5. No credit cards. Breakfast, lunch and dinner (until very late) daily. Bus: 311.

Hugo's Bar Pizza *ITALIAN*   There is nothing finer than a pork-belly pizza and a couple of cocktails at Hugo's. If you go before 10pm, the pizzas are $5. It's hard to believe the designer-clad people who frequent Hugo's would eat pizza, but it does make for good people-watching—and most of them seem keen to be seen.

33 Bayswater Rd., Kings Cross. ℭ **(02) 9332 1227.** www.hugos.com.au. Mains $18–$28. AE, MC, V. Dinner Tues–Sun. Train: Kings Cross.

JAR *CONTEMPORARY*   JAR stands for 'Just Another Restaurant', but it's clearly not. This is a great little place has consistently good food and service. Go early (in before 6pm; out by 8pm) and you get three courses and a glass of wine or beer for $29.50. The chicken liver parfait with pear chutney is to die for.

Cnr. Crown and Stanley sts., East Sydney. ℭ **(02) 9331 5375.** www.justanother.com.au. Mains $22–$28. AE, MC, V. Lunch Mon–Fri; dinner Mon–Sat. Bus: 372, 373, 378 or 380.

★ **jimmy liks** *ASIAN*   It's very hip and groovy, so join the shared table and enjoy the fantastic food. Try jimmy's selection, a great-value 10-course banquet that showcases the best of the menu.

186 Victoria St., Potts Point. ℭ **(02) 8354 1400.** www.jimmyliks.com. Mains $22–$33. 10-course selection $55. AE, MC, V. Dinner daily. Train: Kings Cross.

Kings Cross Hotel *PUB GRUB*   Wash a $4 burger down with a $4 beer after 6pm on Tuesday. What's not to love? Or head to the main bar of this iconic corner pub in the middle of the Cross on Thursday night, for a pizza and five games of Tranny Bingo (not a game for the uptight or morally righteous) for $10. Head upstairs to the slightly more salubrious Balcony Bistro for the amazing two-for-one meal deal on Wednesday evening.

248 William St., Kings Cross. ℭ **(02) 9331 9900.** www.kingscrosshotel.com.au. Mains $7–$26. AE, MC, V. Breakfast, lunch and dinner daily. Train: Kings Cross.

Kingsley's Steak & Crabhouse *STEAK/SEAFOOD*   Okay, neither the crab nor the steak make it under our $25 budget, but the $18 Sunday roast does. It's on for lunch and dinner and it's just as good as (if not better than) Mum used to make.

9 Cowper Wharf Rd., Woolloomooloo. ℭ **1300 546 475.** www.kingsleys.com.au. Mains $25–$56. AE, MC, V. Lunch and dinner daily. Bus: 311.

★ **MISSCHU** *VIETNAMESE*   The Queen of Rice Paper Rolls normally only does catering, but has a hole-in-the-wall where you can buy her amazingly delicious finger food and dumplings to take away. Try not to dither once you get to the counter—just do as I do: get the tofu dumplings, the melt-in-your-mouth Peking duck pancakes and the banana leaf boat.

Cnr. Bourke and William sts., Darlinghurst. ℭ **(02) 8356 9988.** Rolls $2–$9. No credit cards. Lunch Mon–Fri. Bus: 324.

Sailors Thai *THAI*   The prices at this low-key Thai restaurant might look expensive, but it is one of the best places for Thai eats in Sydney and $60 will easily feed two. Set up by the only Thai-food chef to have earned a Michelin star, David Thompson, this place dishes out authentic food. Try the betel leaf with smoked trout and caramelised peanuts.

71A Macleay St., Potts Point. ℭ **(02) 9361 4498.** Mains $16–$28. AE, DC, MC, V. Lunch Fri; dinner Mon–Sun. Train: Kings Cross.

Tilbury Hotel *CONTEMPORARY*   Even though the a la carte menu *just* breaks our $25 barrier, you can get one of Sydney's great food bargains for $20 on Thursday nights from 6 to 8pm at this stylish pub. Dish on the Deck is a dozen freshly shucked Sydney rock oysters, with two glasses of Yarra Burn sparkling rosé or Stella Artois beers.

12–18 Nicholson St., Woolloomooloo. ℭ **(02) 9368 1955.** www.tilburyhotel.com.au. Mains $25–$28. MC, V. Lunch and dinner Tues–Sun. Bus: 311.

Una's *AUSTRIAN*   You'll get schnitzel, sauerkraut, spätzle and steins of beer at this friendly Darlo institution. It's always packed; after all, nothing fills you up as fast as pork knuckle and rosti on a cold winter night. There aren't many choices for vegetarians beyond the potato pancakes and pickled cabbage, and the service is best described as no-frills, but the serves are huge.

340 Victoria St., Darlinghurst. ℂ **(02) 9360 6885.** Mains $14–$22. No credit cards. Lunch and dinner daily. Train: Kings Cross.

Woolloomooloo Bay Hotel *PUB GRUB*   This lively pub has some great weekday meal-and-beer deals, mostly for $11. It's a chicken parma and a beer on Monday; steak and a beer on Wednesday; seafood and a beer on Thursday—and the beer is premium bottled stuff. On Tuesday you can choose anything you like for $15 and still get a free beer, or splash out on Friday with a $15 scotch fillet—don't forget the free beer!

2 Bourke St., Woolloomooloo. ℂ **(02) 9357 1177.** Mains $11–$27. MC, V. Lunch and dinner daily. Bus: 311.

3 Surry Hills & Waterloo

Agave *MEXICAN*   Really good Mexican restaurants are hard to find in Sydney, but this newbie is shaping up pretty well. You'll find all the classic Mexican favourites, including dishes you don't get in most Tex-Mex joints, such as *pollo en mole poblano* (chicken in a rich chocolate chili sauce). Head there for the Sunday night special: two courses and a glass of wine or beer for $39.

2/406 Crown St., Surry Hills. ℂ **(02) 9326 9072.** Mains $19–$28. MC, V. Breakfast (until 3pm) Sat and Sun, dinner daily. Bus: 372, 373, 378 or 380.

★ **The Beresford** *ITALIAN*   Another made-over pub that was once all working-class and is now all style, this is a great place to go for Sunday lunch, when you can get four courses for $45. It's very good eating the rest of the week, too, but expect to pay more—although the pasta dishes will keep you under budget.

354 Bourke St., Surry Hills. ℂ **(02) 9357 1111.** www.theberesford.com.au. Mains $15–$34. MC, V. Lunch Wed–Sun, dinner daily. Bus: 372, 373, 378 or 380.

Betty's Soup Kitchen *CAFE/SOUP*   This is comfort food of the highest order, perfect if you are craving your nanna's cooking. There is, of

CHEAP EATS SURRY HILLS & WATERLOO

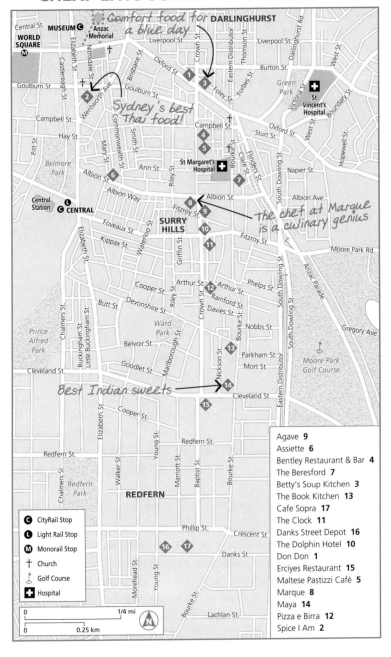

Comfort food for a blue day

Sydney's best Thai food!

The chef at Marque is a culinary genius

Best Indian sweets

CityRail Stop

Light Rail Stop

Monorail Stop

Church

Golf Course

Hospital

0   1/4 mi
0   0.25 km

Agave **9**
Assiette **6**
Bentley Restaurant & Bar **4**
The Beresford **7**
Betty's Soup Kitchen **3**
The Book Kitchen **13**
Cafe Sopra **17**
The Clock **11**
Danks Street Depot **16**
The Dolphin Hotel **10**
Don Don **1**
Erciyes Restaurant **15**
Maltese Pastizzi Café **5**
Marque **8**
Maya **14**
Pizza e Birra **12**
Spice I Am **2**

course, a good selection of homemade soup, but also lots of hearty favourites such as goulash and even fish fingers. There's usually a $10 soup-and-salad lunch deal, and you can get your choice of soup, pasta or a pie and salad for $10 on Monday and Tuesday.

84 Oxford St., Darlinghurst. ℭ **(02) 9360 9698.** Mains $8–$13. No credit cards. Lunch and dinner daily. Bus: 372, 373, 378 or 380.

The Book Kitchen *CONTEMPORARY*   The Book Kitchen has new and used books for food lovers and very good organic food, sourced fresh from the markets, so the menu changes on an almost daily basis. It's a great spot for lunch, although breakfast is pretty hard to resist if you are close by. Be prepared to wait for a table on weekends.

255 Devonshire St., Surry Hills. ℭ **(02) 9310 1003.** www.thebookkitchen.com.au. Mains $16–$26. AE, MC, V. Breakfast and lunch daily, dinner Fri and Sat. Bus: 372, 373, 378 or 380.

Cafe Sopra *ITALIAN*   Fresh, simple, seasonal and very, very flavoursome Italian food is what you'll get, where the ingredients are sourced from the provedore next door. They don't take bookings, so you'll usually have to wait for a table, but it's worth it for some of the best pasta in town.

7 Danks St., Waterloo (another venue at Potts Point; map p. 65). ℭ **(02) 9699 3174.** www.fratellifresh.com.au. Mains $18–$25. MC, V. Lunch daily. Bus: 301.

The Clock *CONTEMPORARY*   This pub pulls a mixed crowd: 20-something hipsters upstairs, fashionable 30s downstairs while locals, artists and musicians mix over the pool tables. The one thing you can sure of is that the bistro appeals to all of them. You'll get great beer-battered fish and chips, seafood spaghettini, burgers, steaks and tasting plates to share.

470 Crown St., Surry Hills. ℭ **(02) 9331 5333.** Mains $14–$25. MC, V. Lunch and dinner daily. Bus: 310 or 302.

Danks Street Depot *CONTEMPORARY*   Another great little neighbourhood eatery that uses seasonal produce with a changing daily menu. Dinner's a bit pricey, but lunch is good value. I love the corned Waygu beef toasted sandwich, although the zucchini fritters with tomato and cucumber salsa and the pappardelle with braised rabbit are pretty good as well. Early birds can get three courses and glass of wine for $35 if they're seated by 6pm (Friday and Saturday only).

2 Danks St (Cnr. Young St), Waterloo. ℂ **(02) 9698 2201.** www.danksstreetdepot. com.au. Mains $17–$34. AE, MC, V. Breakfast and lunch daily, dinner Thurs–Sat. Bus: 301.

The Dolphin Hotel *CONTEMPORARY*   This is a favourite with locals who meet here for drinks, pool or a good-value meal in the bistro with lots of classics. It manages to be both casually stylish and comfortable at the same time.

412 Crown St., Surry Hills. ℂ **(02) 9331 4800.** Mains $18–$25. MC, V. Lunch and dinner daily. Bus: 372, 373, 378 or 380.

Don Don *JAPANESE*   There are not many places in Sydney where you can feed two for $10, but this hole-in-the-wall Japanese restaurant does just that. There are no entrees or mains, just large bowls full of noodles and other Japanese delights. They're almost all less than $10 and they're almost all large enough to feed two.

80 Oxford St., Darlinghurst. ℂ **(02) 9331 3544.** Mains $9–$14. No credit cards. Lunch and dinner Mon–Sat. Bus: 372, 373, 378 or 380.

Erciyes Restaurant *TURKISH*   Great meze plates, delectable dips and tasty pides (Turkish pizzas) make this a great cheap eatery during the week. The live belly dancing on Friday and Saturday turns it into a fun and economical night out.

409 Cleveland St., Surry Hills. ℂ **(02) 9319 1309.** www.erciyesrestaurant.com.au. Mains $14–$22. MC, V. Lunch and dinner daily. Bus: 372 from Railway Square.

★ **Maltese Pastizzi Café** *MALTEZE*   I don't use the word 'icon' lightly, but this tiny cafe is one, having turned out the freshest, lightest, flakiest, yummiest *pastizzi* since the 1950s. There are 10 varieties to choose from, including apple, curried beef, mushy peas and ricotta. At $1.50 each, I defy you to have just one.

310 Crown St., Surry Hills. ℂ **(02) 9361 6942.** Pastizzi: $1.50 each, $9 a dozen. No credit cards. Sun and Mon 9am–6pm, Tues–Sat 9am–8pm. Bus: 372, 373, 378 or 380.

Maya *INDIAN*   Downstairs is one of the best Indian sweet shops in Sydney, where you'll find a dazzling array of coconut- and cardamom-rich dainties that come in all shapes and colours. They're almost all less than $2 a piece, so eat your fill and get some to take home, or head upstairs to the Tandoori restaurant for choice South Indian delights.

472 Cleveland St., Surry Hills. ℂ **(02) 9699 8663.** www.maya.net.au. Mains $13–$18. AE, MC, V. Lunch and dinner daily. Bus: 372 from Railway Square.

Pizza e Birra *ITALIAN*   Sure, it's not the cheapest pizza in town, but it's up there with the best in terms of taste. Cooked in the wood-fired oven and with properly sparse toppings, these pizzas are about as close to the real things as you'll find. I love the tomato sauce–free *pizza bianchi*.

500 Crown St., Surry Hills. ℰ **(02) 9332 2510.** Mains $19–$29. AE, MC, V. Lunch Thurs–Sun, dinner daily. Bus: 372 or 374.

★ **Spice I Am** *THAI*   Spice I Am is cheap as chips and has great food to boot. Expect to queue, but, once inside, the fiery home-cooked fare is dished out at a fast and furious rate. It's strictly BYO.

90 Wentworth St., Surry Hills. ℰ **(02) 9280 0928.** www.spiceiam.com. Mains $14–$26. No credit cards. Lunch and dinner Tues–Sun. Train: Central.

WORTH A SPLURGE

Assiette *FRENCH*   This charming little French restaurant is one of Sydney's hidden gems, where one of the city's most talented young chefs turns out some very fine French food. The braised lamb shoulder, spinach, pine nuts and rosemary cannelloni is always superb, as is the fig pizza when they are both in season. It's worth the splurge any night of the week, but you can't beat the Friday three-course $30 lunch deal. Be sure to book.

48 Albion St., Surry Hills. ℰ **(02) 9212 7979.** www.restaurantassiette.com.au. Mains $35. AE, DC, MC, V. Lunch Fri, dinner Tues–Sat. Train: Central.

★ **Bentley Restaurant & Bar** *CONTEMPORARY*   The decor, food and clientele are sleek and sophisticated at this swish inner-city pub. Some of the dishes look more like works of art and, thankfully, they taste as good as they look. If you're into your food and like trying old flavours in astonishing new ways, you'll love this place at lunch, when you can get 10 (small) courses for $50.

320 Crown St., Surry Hills. ℰ **(02) 9332 2344.** www.thebentley.com.au. Tapas $5–$16, mains $29–$40. AE, DC, MC, V. Lunch and dinner Tues–Sat. Bus: 373, 372, 378 or 380.

★ **Marque** *FRENCH*   Another one of Sydney's best restaurants, Marque has a simple dining room that belies the complexity of the food. The focus is on molecular gastronomy; opt for the degustation to enjoy the full experience. If you can't afford it, have a three-course lunch for just $45 on Friday. The chef is a culinary wizard.

355 Crown St., Surry Hills. ℰ **(02) 9332 2225.** www.marquerestaurant.com.au. Mains $48, 8-course degustation $145. AE, MC, V. Dinner Mon–Sat. Bus: 372, 373, 378 or 380.

4 Eastern Beaches

Aquarium Bistro & Bar *PUB GRUB*   The bistro downstairs is open for lunch and dinner and its specials include an $8 chicken schnitzel on Monday, a $2 steak (when purchased with a $4 drink) on Wednesday and $10 pizza on Thursday.

169 Dolphin St., Coogee. ✆ **(02) 9964 2900.** www.beachpalacehotel.com.au. Mains $15–$18, share platters $22–$25. MC, V. Lunch Sat and Sun, dinner Fri–Sun. Bus: 372, 373 or 374.

Banana Palm *VIETNAMESE*   My best friend Anna swears this place has the best salt-and-pepper chili squid in Sydney, and I think she might just be right. The Indo–French decor has lots of wood panelling and black-and-white photos of a vanished Vietnam—you could be in an elegant hotel in Hanoi. The only downside to eating here: there's no pho.

260 Arden St., Coogee. ✆ **(02) 9665 1212.** Mains $19–$23. AE, DC, MC, V. Dinner Mon–Sat. Bus: 372, 373 or 374.

Blue Groper Bistro *STEAK/SEAFOOD*   On a warm summer's day a table on the deck at the Clovelly Hotel's bistro is hard to beat (although the view's not great). There's mixed grill Monday, Italian Wednesday and seafood Friday, although you can find good steak and seafood fare here any night (or day) of the week.

381 Clovelly Rd., Clovelly. ✆ **(02) 9665 1214.** www.clovellyhotel.com.au. Mains $17–$26. MC, V. Lunch and dinner daily. Bus: 339.

Blue Wave Bistro *PUB GRUB*   You get the same (if not better) gob-smacking view as the much more fashionable North Bondi Italian Food downstairs (p. 78), but even though the food's not quite as classy (nor are the diners), with deals such as $7 steaks on Wednesday, who's complaining? There is a catch: it's a Returned Services League (RSL) club, so you'll have to join if you live within 5km ($20 annually). Those who live beyond the eastern suburbs can sign in as guests rather than paying the fee. Summer evenings, especially on weekends, can get loud and crowded around sundown.

North Bondi RSL, 120 Ramsgate Ave., North Bondi. ✆ **(02) 9130 3152.** Mains $12–$25. MC, V. Lunch and dinner daily. Bus: 380 or 389.

★ **Bondi Social** *CONTEMPORARY*   Tapas-sized tasting plates designed to share make this a great place to get together with friends on the balcony overlooking Bondi Beach. It's even better if you go during happy hour (p. 229).

Level 1, 38 Campbell Pde, Bondi. ℰ **(02) 9365 1788.** www.bondisocial.com. Mains $11–$17. AE, MC, V. Lunch Sat and Sun, dinner Tues–Sun. Bus: 380.

Bondi Tucker *CONTEMPORARY*   This colourful cafe caters mainly for locals, which means its good value and, despite its ocker-ish name, quite stylish. It's famous for its desserts (they're yummy *and* gluten free), it's kid friendly and it's a great spot for brunch, but best value is the $25 set menu: two courses and a glass of wine or a beer.

80 Hall St., Bondi. ℰ **(02) 9130 8080.** Mains $14–$32. AE, MC, V. Breakfast Sat and Sun, lunch and dinner daily. Bus: 380.

★ **Doyles on the Wharf** *SEAFOOD*   Treat yourself to some of the best fish and chips in town from Doyles on the Wharf. The legendary Doyle family have been dishing up fabulous seafood since 1885. Eat on the beach or in shady Robertson Park, but avoid weekends if you can as queues can be painfully long. Don't confuse it with Doyles on the Beach, where you'll get similar food, but pay double for it.

Fishermans Wharf, Watsons Bay. ℰ **(02) 9337 6214.** www.doyles.com.au. Mains $11–$18. MC, V. Lunch daily. Bus: 324, 325 or 380. Ferry: Watsons Bay.

★ **Fishmongers** *SEAFOOD*   The chips: hand cut from Sebago potatoes—and frequently voted the best in Sydney. The fish: five-spice barramundi or garlic and sesame salmon. Eat on one of the wooden tables on the footpath or take it two blocks east to the beach for a perfect fish-and-chip experience.

42 Hall St., Bondi. ℰ **(02) 9365 2205.** www.mongers.com.au. Mains $11–$19. No credit cards. Lunch and dinner daily. Bus: 380.

Flying Squirrel *TAPAS*   Tapas in size rather than flavour, the food here is a mix of French, Italian and South East Asian. It also does great cocktails, but it's very popular with locals and you can't book, so snaring a seat in this tiny little bar can be tricky unless you're prepared to go early or you're just plain lucky.

249 Bondi Rd., Bondi. ℰ **(02) 9130 1033.** www.flyingsquirreltapasparlour.com.au. Mains $8–$15. MC, V. Dinner Tues–Sun. Bus: 380.

Gertrude & Alice *CAFE*   From the outside it looks just like a poky second-hand bookshop, but there are a couple of tables and chairs squeezed in among the shelves. If there's a space, grab it, grab a

CHEAP EATS EASTERN BEACHES

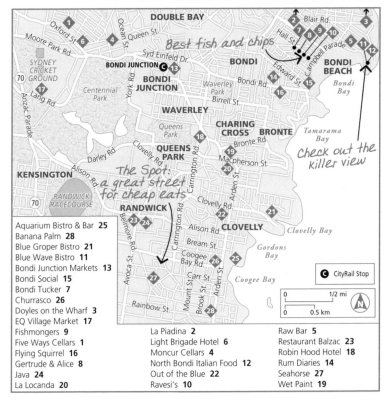

Map annotations: Best fish and chips · Check out the killer view · The Spot: a great street for cheap eats

Restaurant index (map numbers):

Aquarium Bistro & Bar **25**
Banana Palm **28**
Blue Groper Bistro **21**
Blue Wave Bistro **11**
Bondi Junction Markets **13**
Bondi Social **15**
Bondi Tucker **7**
Churrasco **26**
Doyles on the Wharf **3**
EQ Village Market **17**
Fishmongers **9**
Five Ways Cellars **1**
Flying Squirrel **16**
Gertrude & Alice **8**
Java **24**
La Locanda **20**

La Piadina **2**
Light Brigade Hotel **6**
Moncur Cellars **4**
North Bondi Italian Food **12**
Out of the Blue **22**
Ravesi's **10**

Raw Bar **5**
Restaurant Balzac **23**
Robin Hood Hotel **18**
Rum Diaries **14**
Seahorse **27**
Wet Paint **19**

C CityRail Stop

book, order a coffee and some cake or a bowl of lentil stew, and settle back for an hour or so.

46 Hall St., Bondi. **© (02) 9130 5155.** Mains $8–$13. MC, V. Lunch and dinner daily. Bus: 380.

Java *INDONESIAN* There's nothing flash about this busy, noisy neighbourhood eatery, but the food is good and very well priced. Go here for cheap and cheerful chicken satay, gado gado, beef rendang and other Indonesian staples. The $52 *rijsttafel* for two (two entrees and two main courses) is great value.

151 Avoca St., Randwick. **© (02) 9398 6990.** Mains $9–$16. No credit cards. Lunch and dinner Wed–Mon. Bus: 372, 373, 376 or 377.

La Locanda *ITALIAN* There's only ever a choice of three homemade pastas, four classic northern Italian dishes and four desserts on offer at

Fresh from the Farm

Farmers' and growers' markets are a great place to pick up the fixings for a tasty meal. Most stalls will offer you a free taste, but beware: this makes you more determined to buy! Here are some of the city's best; for more, visit www.organicfoodmarkets.com.au.

- **Bondi Junction Markets:** The Oxford Street Mall, Bondi Junction becomes a one-stop shop for lots of edible goodies on Thursday and Friday from 9am to 5pm.

- **EQ Village Markets:** The Entertainment Quarter (EQ) Village Market on Lang Road, Moore Park is one for the gourmets every Wednesday from 10am to 3.30pm and Saturday from 10am to 3.30pm.

- **Everleigh Farmers Market:** Redfern doesn't usually spring to mind when you think of sourcing produce straight from the farm, but think again. The weekly farmers' market next door to CarriageWorks at Eveleigh Railyards, 243 Wilson Street, Darlington sells organic and bio-dynamic foods from across New South Wales each Saturday from 8am to 1pm.

- **Kings Cross Organic Food & Farmers Markets:** Try some of the sweet treats on offer at Burgitta's Bites stall. It's Happy Crepe Hour from 8.30 to 10.30am (I know that's *two* hours, but the Cross has always been about excess). It's at the Fitzroy Gardens, Macleay Street, Kings Cross every Saturday from 9am to 2pm.

- **North Side Produce Market:** You'll find fresh fruit, veg and gourmet produce at Civic Park on Miller Street, North Sydney on the third Saturday of every month from 8am to noon.

- **The Rocks Farmers' Markets:** Growers display not only their produce, but also their food miles at Jack Mundey Place on the corner of Argyle and George streets in The Rocks each Friday from 9am until 3pm.

this tiny neighbourhood bistro, but they are all good. It's worth going for the pappardelle with duck and pea ragu alone.

65B Macpherson St., Bronte. ☏ **(02) 9389 3666.** www.lalocanda.com.au. Mains $22–$28. MC, V. Dinner Tues–Sun. Bus: 378.

La Piadina *CAFE/ITALIAN*   La Piadina has the best Italian flatbread in town. The actual cafe is nearly all kitchen, but it's not about the place, it's about the *piadina*. A *piadina* is a round flatbread, stuffed with, well, *stuff*: mozzarella, lamb sausage, prosciutto, ricotta, wild mushrooms, Nutella . . . Once you have one, you'll be addicted.

106 Glenayr Ave., Bondi. ☏ **(02) 9300 0160.** Mains $8–$18. No credit cards. Lunch and dinner Tues–Sun. Bus: 380.

Light Brigade Hotel *CONTEMPORARY*   This gorgeous Art Deco pub has a very nice (and expensive) bistro upstairs, but the hearty meals available in the main bar are great value. Think steak and chips, bangers and mash and shepherd's pie.

2A Oxford St. (cnr. Jersey Rd.), Woollahra. ☏ **(02) 9357 0888.** Mains $13–$23. AE, MC, V. Dinner daily. Bus: 378 or 389.

Out of the Blue *BURGERS*   It might look like your everyday take-away food joint, but believe me, the burgers here are so much better than average. The chicken burger with mouth-watering garlic mayo is what most of the locals line up to get, but the fish and chips are pretty good, too.

272 Clovelly Rd., Clovelly. ☏ **(02) 9315 8380.** Mains $6–$9. No credit cards. Lunch and dinner Wed–Sun. Bus: 339.

Raw Bar *JAPANESE*   There is nothing finer than eating super-fresh fish *from* the sea, *by* the sea, which is exactly what you'll get at this tiny sushi bar at the northern end of Bondi Beach. The $40 dinner bento box is almost big enough to share between two; the others are under the $25 mark. Service can be a bit hit and miss, but the view is amazing.

Cnr. Warners and Wairoa aves., Bondi. ☏ **(02) 9365 7200.** Mains $15–$25. AE, MC, V. Lunch and dinner daily. Bus: 380 or 389.

Robin Hood Hotel *PUB GRUB*   It's your basic neighbourhood pub, with loud music, a pool table, comfy couches and lots of happy chatter. It's also where you can chow down on a great-value $8 steak or schnitzel.

203 Bronte Rd., Charing Cross. ℂ **(02) 9389 3477.** Mains $8–$14. MC, V. Lunch and dinner daily. Bus: 378.

Rum Diaries *TAPAS*   It would be very easy to walk past this little place and not notice it at all, but step inside and you're transported into an opulent rum and cocktail bar that dishes up some very fine tapas. Don't be put off by the prices; I regularly eat here with friends and have rarely spent more than $35 a head after several hours of determined grazing.

288 Bondi Rd., Bondi. ℂ **(02) 9300 0440.** www.rumdiaries.com.au. Mains $8–$26. MC, V. Dinner daily. Bus: 380.

Seahorse *ITALIAN/SEAFOOD*   Unpretentious, tasty Italian seafood can be found at this neighbourhood eatery. Service can be patchy at times, but it's kid friendly and the portions are large.

26 St Pauls St (The Spot), Randwick. ℂ **(02) 9398 4444.** Mains $22–$26. MC, V. Lunch Thurs and Fri, dinner Mon–Sat. Bus: 372, 373 or 374.

WORTH A SPLURGE

Churrasco *BRAZILIAN*   Like your meat? $35 buys you as much meat (and rice, beans and potatoes) as you can eat at this Brazilian-style barbecue restaurant. The slow-roasted meat keeps coming until you say enough is enough. Take a big appetite with you, but leave your vegetarian friends at home.

240 Coogee Bay Rd., Coogee (also at Woolloomooloo). ℂ **(02) 9665 6535.** www.churrasco.com.au. Mains $35. AE, MC, V. Dinner daily, lunch Sun. Bus: 372, 373 or 374.

North Bondi Italian Food *ITALIAN*   This is where the young, beautiful and very cool head to eat in Bondi, and who can blame them: the food is as good as they look. Be prepared to wait; it doesn't take bookings.

118 Ramsgate Ave., Bondi. ℂ **(02) 9300 4400.** www.idrb.com. Mains $18–$29. AE, DC, MC, V. Lunch Fri–Sun, dinner daily. Bus: 380.

Ravesi's *CONTEMPORARY*   This place gets a mention not just for its stunning Bondi Beach views, but also for dirt-cheap Fiesta Friday, where you can get a $10 tapas plate (normally $25); and Casual Sunday, where you get gourmet pizzas, waygu burgers and so on for $10—and nothing is more than $20. Try the three-course set menu for $35 Monday through Thursday.

Cnr. Campbell Pde and Hall St., Bondi. ℂ **(02) 9365 4422.** www.ravesis.com.au.
Mains $25–$35. MC, V. Dinner Mon–Sat. Bus: 380 or 389.

★ **Restaurant Balzac** *CONTEMPORARY*   Balzac boasts excellent
French and English food with service to match. Go on Friday for a
fixed-price lunch (four courses for $50) or on the last Sunday of each
month for a special nine-course degustation dinner for $100. You'll
need to book ahead.

141 Belmore Rd., Randwick. ℂ **(02) 9399 9660.** www.restaurantbalzac.com.au.
Mains $29–$40. AE, DC, MC, V. Lunch Fri, dinner Tues–Sat and last Sun of each month.
Bus: 372, 373 or 374.

★ **Wet Paint** *CONTEMPORARY*   The locals would like to keep this
place a secret, but I guess word has to get out sometime. This fabulous restaurant has a menu that is vaguely inspired by Cajun/Creole
traditions. The prices are over the $25 mark, but it's worth it for food
this good. Besides, who can resist a restaurant that dishes up $12 chili
chocolate margaritas for dessert?

56–60 Macpherson St., Bronte. ℂ **(02) 9369 4634.** www.wetpaint.com.au. Mains
$25–$28. MC, V. Dinner Tues–Sat. Bus: 378.

5 North Side & Northern Beaches

Ainoya *JAPANESE*   A good little neighbourhood eatery offering quite
reasonable sashimi and other Japanese standards.

34 Burton St., Kirribilli. ℂ **(02) 9922 1512.** Mains $17–$27. AE, MC, V. Dinner Tues–
Sun. Train: Milsons Point.

A La Facon de Shimizu *JAPANESE/FRENCH*   A rather bizarre fusion
of Japanese and French bistro-style cuisine that somehow works—just
try the rack of lamb with miso sauce. Servings are generous and the
food is good, although service can be a tad slow.

57 Willoughby Rd., Willoughby. ℂ **(02) 9958 8785.** Mains $24–$27. AE, MC, V. Dinner
Wed–Sun. Bus: 273 from Wynyard.

Billy Blue Brasserie *CONTEMPORARY*   Treat yourself to some fine
dining at dirt-cheap prices and head along to the show-case restaurant for William Blue College of Hospitality and Tourism for a spectacular three-course meal for just $29, cooked by the super-chefs of
tomorrow.

Level 9, Northpoint Building, 171 Pacific Hwy, North Sydney. ℭ **(02) 9492 3290.** www.williamblue.edu.au. Mains $15. No credit cards. Lunch Mon–Fri and dinner Mon, Wed–Fri during school term. Train: North Sydney.

Fishmongers *SEAFOOD*   The northern outpost of the fabulous Bondi fish shop is just one block back from the beach. Don't get your fish and chips from anywhere else.

11 Wentworth St., Manly. ℭ **(02) 9977 1777.** www.mongers.com.au. Mains $11–$19. No credit cards. Lunch and dinner daily. Ferry: Manly.

The Greedy Goat *CAFE*   This fantastic little beachside cafe is one of the few in the area that won't cost you an arm and a leg. It's a great spot for lunch or a long brunch. Check the website for details about summertime dinner opening hours.

1031 Barrenjoey Rd., Palm Beach. ℭ **(02) 9974 2555.** www.thegreedygoat.com.au. Mains $16–$20. No credit cards. Breakfast and lunch Wed–Mon. Bus: L90.

Kyushu *JAPANESE*   I have a friend who reckons this is the best Japanese on the North Shore, and going by the crowd that's always inside, it's probably a good call. It's very popular at lunchtime with office workers.

9–11 Grosvenor St., Neutral Bay. ℭ **(02) 9953 8272.** Mains $13–$15. AE, MC, V. Lunch Wed–Sat, dinner Tues–Sat. Bus: 243, 247 or 249.

Malabar *INDIAN*   The Goan fish curry and the chicken biryani are worth making the trek over the bridge, but the real speciality of this place is the dosa, a delicious South Indian rice and lentil pancake stuffed with minced lamb, spiced potatoes or smeared with coconut chutney and served with *sambar*, a lentil broth.

334 Pacific Hwy, Crows Nest. ℭ **(02) 9906 7343.** www.malabarcuisine.com.au. AE, MC, V. Mains $13–$22. Lunch and dinner daily. Bus: 273 from Wynyard.

★ **Manly Wharf Hotel** *SEAFOOD/PUB GRUB*   Soak up the views at this great seaside pub at the end of Manly Wharf over a shared plate of herb-crusted calamari, chili prawns, hot pepperoni pizza or oh-so-'90s nachos.

Manly Wharf, East Esplanade, Manly. ℭ **(02) 9977 1266.** www.manlywharfhotel.com.au. Mains $17–$30. MC, V. Lunch and dinner daily. Ferry: Manly.

North Sydney Noodle Market *ASIAN*   Every summer Friday night, Civic Centre Park is home to a noodle market. Grab a glass of wine and a bowl of noodles, take a picnic blanket and sit back and soak in the free entertainment and feel-good vibe.

Cnr. Miller and McLaren sts., North Sydney. ☎ **(02) 9936 8272.** Mains around $10. No credit cards. Dinner Fri Oct–Apr. Train: North Sydney.

The Oaks *STEAK/SEAFOOD/PIZZA*   The beer garden, with its massive oak tree, is the place to be on a balmy evening. Go here for great-value steaks that you barbecue yourself and pots of mussels with just about any sauce you can think of, as well as gourmet pizzas. It gets very busy (and loud) on Friday and Saturday nights and summer Sunday afternoons.

118 Military Rd., Neutral Bay. ☎ **(02) 9953 5515.** Mains $18–$26. MC, V. Lunch and dinner daily. Bus: 243, 244 or 247.

Phuong *VIETNAMESE*   A classic neighbourhood Vietnamese restaurant offering all the traditional staples, such as pho, hotpots, pork and vermicelli, at reasonable prices.

87 Willoughby Rd., Crows Nest. ☎ **(02) 9439 2621.** Mains $11–$17. AE, MC, V. Lunch Mon–Fri, dinner daily. Bus: 273 from Wynyard.

Prasit's Northside Thai *THAI*   Prasit's used to be one of the best cheap Thai restaurants in Sydney. It's still one of the best Thai eateries, but, sadly, it's not as cheap as it once was. Try the grilled squid stuffed with spicy rice, the chicken and dried shrimp and the banana flower salad.

77 Mount St., North Sydney. ☎ **(02) 9957 2271.** www.prasits.com.au. Mains $24–$29. AE, MC, V. Lunch and dinner Mon–Fri. Train: North Sydney.

★ **Ripples** *CONTEMPORARY*   Ripples is a fantastic little BYO restaurant right under the Harbour Bridge. It's 100% alfresco with great harbour views and it's half the price of an equivalent on the south side of the bridge. I love the apple hotcakes with rhubarb compote and cinnamon crème fraiche for breakfast after a few laps at the North Sydney Olympic Pool next door.

Olympic Dr, Milsons Point. ☎ **(02) 9929 7722.** Mains $24–$29. AE, MC, V. Breakfast, lunch and dinner daily. Train: Milsons Point.

The Sandbar Café *CAFE*   A great place to eat after a morning spent in the surf. You don't have to worry about being a bit sandy and salty at this super-casual beachfront takeaway outlet run by the much more expensive Le Kiosk next door.

1 Marine Pde, Shelly Beach. ☎ **(02) 9977 4122.** Mains $8–$15. No credit cards. Lunch daily. Ferry: Manly.

CHEAP EATS NORTH SIDE

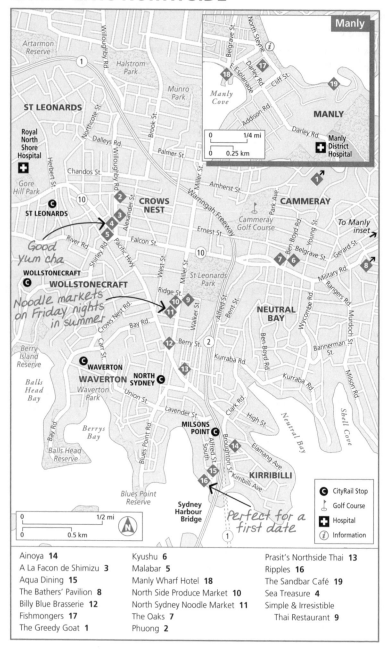

Manly

Ainoya **14**
A La Facon de Shimizu **3**
Aqua Dining **15**
The Bathers' Pavilion **8**
Billy Blue Brasserie **12**
Fishmongers **17**
The Greedy Goat **1**

Kyushu **6**
Malabar **5**
Manly Wharf Hotel **18**
North Side Produce Market **10**
North Sydney Noodle Market **11**
The Oaks **7**
Phuong **2**

Prasit's Northside Thai **13**
Ripples **16**
The Sandbar Café **19**
Sea Treasure **4**
Simple & Irresistible
    Thai Restaurant **9**

A Taste of Sweden, Ikea Style

With a menu that has nothing over $7, you can't get much more dirt cheap than the restaurant (think canteen) at the Ikea in Rhodes Shopping Centre, 1 Oulton Avenue (off Homebush Bay Drive), Rhodes (© **(02) 8002 0400;** no credit cards). It may be that the only reason it has a bargain-priced eatery is that it takes so long to navigate yourself through the store that you're starving once you get there, but with meals ranging from $2.50 to $6.95—a cooked breakfast of sausage, bacon, egg, hash brown and tomato will set you back just $2.50— who cares?

Sea Treasure *CHINESE*   If you're on the north side and can't make it to Chinatown for yum cha, Sea Treasure is the next best thing. It's loud and busy and the service is patchy, but the seafood is fresh and the dumplings and mango pancakes are good.

46 Willoughby Rd., Crows Nest. © **(02) 9906 6388.** Mains $14–$33. AE, MC, V. Lunch and dinner daily. Bus: 273 from Wynyard.

Simple & Irresistible Thai Restaurant *THAI*   The name is an accurate description of this great little Thai restaurant. Order the papaya salad with king prawns or the pineapple fried rice—the servings are large enough for two, so a little cash goes a long way, particularly if you've got a group of friends and can share.

283 Miller St., North Sydney. © **(02) 9929 6696.** Mains $14–$18. MC, V. Lunch Mon– Sat, dinner Mon–Sun. Train: North Sydney.

WORTH A SPLURGE

Aqua Dining *CONTEMPORARY*   Great views of the Harbour Bridge and Opera House make this fine-dining restaurant above North Sydney Swimming Pool and beside Luna Park a good alternative to those city-side eateries. It's pretty expensive, but go for lunch or Sunday dinner and you can get three courses for $69.

Cnr. Paul and Northcliff sts., Milsons Point. © **(02) 9964 9998.** Mains $25–$39. AE, MC, V. Lunch and dinner daily. Train: Milsons Point.

★ **The Bathers' Pavilion** *CONTEMPORARY*   This place is definitely not cheap, but it *is* worth a budget blow-out. The perfect place for a long, long lunch, this airy restaurant on beautiful Balmoral Beach serves up great seasonal produce with French flair. There's simply no better place to be.

4 The Esplanade, Balmoral Beach. ℂ **(02) 9969 5050.** www.batherspavilion.com.au. 3 courses $115. AE, DC, MC, V. Breakfast Sun, lunch and dinner daily. Bus: 247 from Wynyard.

6 Inner West

AIR (All India Restaurant) *INDIAN*   The authentic Indian tucker served up here is a cut above what you find at your average neighbourhood curry house—as is the decor—yet there's nothing on the menu over $20.

1/2A Rowntree St., Balmain. ℂ **(02) 9555 8844.** www.all-india.com.au. Mains $15–$20. AE, MC, V. Dinner daily. Bus: 433 or 434.

Annandale Hotel *PUB GRUB/ASIAN*   Most of time I head to this pub for the live bands or the free flicks (p. 208), but every now and then I find myself unable to resist Pub Cha, a fusion of all sorts of Southeast Asian snacks under $10, followed by a Paddle Pop ice-cream for dessert. Perfect! You'll need to book a table.

17–19 Parramatta Rd., Annandale. ℂ **(02) 9550 1078.** www.annandalehotel.com. Yum cha $3–$7 per serve. MC, V. Lunch Sat, Sun and public holidays. Bus: 412, 413, 436, 437, 438 or 440.

★ **Arabella** *LEBANESE*   It's happy bellies all round here, with good food and great belly dancing. Order a banquet (minimum two people), sit back and enjoy the show on Friday and Saturday night. The stuffed vine leaves and kofta skewers (lamb minced with onion and parsley) are the best in Newtown.

489 King St., Newtown. ℂ **(02) 9550 1119.** www.arabella.com.au. Mains $20–$26. MC, V. Lunch Sun, dinner daily. Train: Newtown.

Badde Manors *VEGETARIAN/CAFE*   I don't know why I love this place so much—the service is always off-hand—but it's a Glebe institution and the food's pretty good (vegetarian lunches, heavenly cakes, great gelato). Check out the angels of the cappuccino machine on the external awning.

1/37 Glebe Point Rd., Glebe. ✆ **(02) 9660 3797.** Mains $9–$15. MC, V. Breakfast, lunch and dinner daily. Bus: 431 or 433.

Baja Cantina *MEXICAN*   Better than average Tex-Mex dishes—although staff insist it's 'Californian Mexican'. Servings are huge and it's popular on weekends, so book ahead.

43–45 Glebe Point Rd., Glebe. ✆ **(02) 9571 1199.** Mains $15–$25. AE, MC, V. Lunch Thurs–Sat, dinner daily. Bus: 431 or 433.

★ **Bank Hotel** *THAI*   Inner-city Newtown has always attracted a mixed crowd of pleasure seekers. Same goes for the Bank Hotel, whether it's locals having an after-work beer in the public bar or happy diners tucking into duck curry at the Sumalee Thai courtyard restaurant. Try the $10 curry-and-a-schooner deal in the public bar Monday through Thursday from 6pm.

324 King St., Newtown. ✆ **(02) 8568 1988.** www.bankhotel.com.au. Mains $12–$38. MC, V. Lunch and dinner daily. Train: Newtown.

Banks Thai *THAI*   It's the real deal as far as decor and ambience goes, the service is warm and friendly and the prices are almost as cheap as Thailand too. The food? Fresh and generous, but the spice and chili meters have been wound back several notches for Western tastebuds.

91 Enmore Rd., Enmore. ✆ **(02) 9550 6840.** Mains $10–$19. MC, V. Lunch and dinner daily. Train: Newtown.

Belli Bar *ITALIAN*   Leichhardt is the centre of the Italian community in Sydney, so it's a safe bet that almost any Italian restaurant in this neighbourhood is going to be worth eating at. Belli Bar doesn't disappoint. Apart from the pastas and good breakfast dishes, it's home to the best *tramezzini* south of Sicily—thick white bread sandwiches filled with all sorts of good stuff.

80 Norton St., Leichhardt. ✆ **(02) 9564 6232.** Mains $15. No credit cards. Breakfast and lunch Mon–Sat. Bus: 438 or 440.

Carpaccio *ITALIAN*   With this name, you know that the delicious thinly sliced raw meat is going to be a speciality. But the real specials of this oh-so-Italian eatery are the set menus: $20 a head gets you all the pizza you can eat, plus a glass of beer or wine on Tuesday, Wednesday or Thursday.

Shop 8, 39–45 Norton St., Leichhardt. ✆ **(02) 9550 9365.** www.carpaccio.com.au. Mains $18–$32. AE, MC, V. Lunch and dinner daily. Bus: 440 or 438.

CHEAP EATS INNER WEST

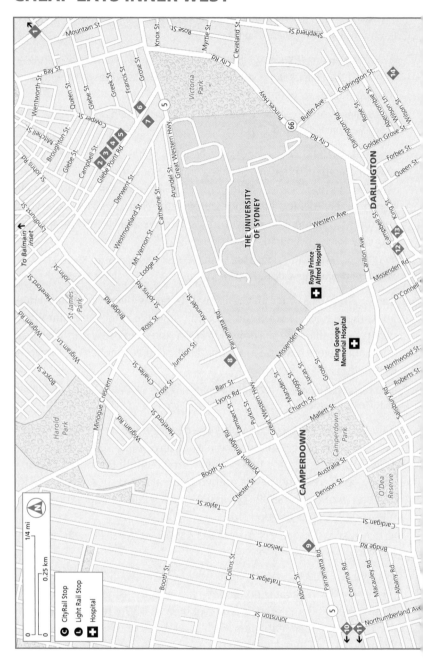

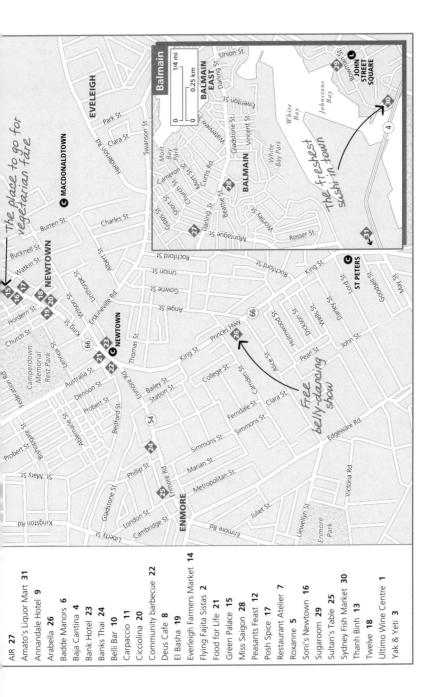

The place to go for vegetarian fare

EVELEIGH

MACDONALDTOWN

Balmain

BALMAIN EAST

BALMAIN

The freshest sushi in town

NEWTOWN

EVELEIGH

Camperdown Memorial Rest Park

NEWTOWN

Free belly-dancing show

ENMORE

ST PETERS

AIR **27**
Amato's Liquor Mart **31**
Annandale Hotel **9**
Arabella **26**
Badde Manors **6**
Baja Cantina **4**
Bank Hotel **23**
Banks Thai **24**
Belli Bar **10**
Carpaccio **11**
Cicciolina **20**
Community barbecue **22**
Deus Cafe **8**
El Basha **19**
Everleigh Farmers Market **14**
Flying Fajita Sistas **2**
Food for Life **21**
Green Palace **15**
Miss Saigon **28**
Peasants Feast **12**
Posh Spice **17**
Restaurant Atelier **7**
Roxanne **5**
Soni's Newtown **16**
Sugaroom **29**
Sultan's Table **25**
Sydney Fish Market **30**
Thanh Binh **13**
Twelve **18**
Ultimo Wine Centre **1**
Yak & Yeti **3**

Cicciolina *ITALIAN*   This stylish but affordable Italian trattoria has great service and a workable wine list, and is fabulous for people-watching. If you want to keep within the $25-or-less budget you'll need to stick mainly to pastas, pizzas and risottos, but there's a wide choice and the servings are large.

224 King St., Newtown. ℂ **(02) 9516 1166.** Mains $18–$29. MC, V. Dinner daily. Train: Newtown.

Deus Cafe *ITALIAN*   Some of Sydney's best gnocchi can be found in among the motorcycles. Be warned, the food might be affordable, but the custom bikes are not, so if you are tempted to live out your *Easy Rider* fantasies, you might want to lock up your wallet.

98 Parramatta Rd (enter via Lyons Rd), Camperdown. ℂ **(02) 9557 6866.** www.deus. com.au. Mains $20–$25. MC, V. Breakfast and lunch daily, dinner Wed–Sat. Bus: 438, 440 or 480.

El Basha *LEBANESE*   Home to the best grilled haloumi cheese in town, El Basha has been a favourite with hungry students and Newtown locals for more than 30 years. Go there and you'll soon see why.

233 King Street, Newtown. ℂ **(02) 9557 3886.** Mains $14–$23. No credit cards. Lunch and dinner daily. Train: Newtown.

Flying Fajita Sistas *MEXICAN*   You'll need to book ahead to score a table on Taco Tuesday, where you can gorge yourself on $3 tacos and $3 tequila shots. The rest of the week's pretty good value too, with plenty of filling choices for less than $20 and great platters for two for $45. Approach the selection of hot sauces on the 'Wall of Pain' at your own risk.

65 Glebe Point Rd., Glebe. ℂ **(02) 9552 6522.** Mains $19–$26. MC, V. Dinner Tues–Sun. Bus: 431 or 433.

Green Palace *THAI/VEGAN*   Good vegan food can be hard to find, which explains why this place is perennially popular despite the no-frills fit-out. You know it's good when there's a monk at the table beside yours!

182 King St., Newtown. ℂ **(02) 9550 5234.** Mains $12–$17. MC, V. Lunch and dinner daily. Train: Newtown.

Miss Saigon *VIETNAMESE*   Cheap eats can be hard to find in Balmain, but this little terrace-house restaurant does unassuming but very fresh and tasty Vietnamese food, especially the roll-your-own rice paper rolls.

248 Darling St., Balmain. ℂ **(02) 9818 3250.** Mains $6–$17. MC, V. Lunch and dinner daily. Bus: 433 or 434.

Here, Fishy, Fishy . . .

Sydney Fish Market is the world's second-largest seafood market, in terms of variety, outside of Japan and it auctions more than 100 species daily at Bank Street, Pyrmont (© **(02) 9004 1143**; www.sydney fishmarket.com.au). Take a 90-minute behind-the-scenes tour and catch the auction action, then breakfast (or lunch) on the freshest sushi and fish and chips in town at half the price you'll pay in restaurants and cafes—you are, after all, cutting out the middle man. The market is open daily from 7am and tours start at 6.50am sharp on Monday and Thursday. They cost $20 for adults and $10 for kids 6 to 13 years old. All tour-takers must wear enclosed shoes.

Posh Spice *INDIAN*   Experience Bollywood glam in the heart of Newtown with live dancing on Friday and Saturday nights. If you can't make it on the weekend, don't panic, there are flat-screen TVs blaring all over the place. Great fun and good food (and scrummy cocktails); it's definitely *not* the place to go for a quiet night out.

Level 1, 196 King St., Newtown. © **(02) 9557 6399.** www.poshspice.com.au. Mains $17–$25. AE, MC, V. Dinner Tues, Thurs–Sun. Train: Newtown.

Roxanne *CONTEMPORAY*   The sexy plush dining room full of thick red velvet and candles with a jazz soundtrack makes this a good choice for a romantic night for two that won't break the bank. The menu's eclectic, with everything from Cajun hotpots to Japanese scallops.

39 Glebe Point Rd., Glebe. © **(02) 9552 6087.** Mains $17–$28. MC, V. Breakfast and lunch Sat and Sun, dinner Tues–Sun. Bus: 431 or 433.

Soni's Newtown MEDITERRANEAN   If you can get your head around the concept of Greek/Italian tapas, you'll love this place. The food is great and four dishes are more than enough for two, so it works out to be dirt cheap. Head upstairs before or after for some of the best cocktails around at Madame Fling Flong (p. 223).

169 King St., Newtown. © **(02) 9565 2471.** www.sonisnewtown.com.au. Mains $10–$19. No credit cards. Dinner daily. Train: Newtown.

★ **Sultan's Table** *TURKISH*   It might look like a takeaway joint (it is), but you can linger over some authentic Turkish food in the courtyard out the back. Try *guvec*, a tender lamb stew with vegetables served in a claypot or the delicious Sultan's Kebab: succulent skewered meatballs with tomatoes and eggplant. You'll be back for more.

179 Enmore Rd., Enmore. ✆ **(02) 9557 0229.** Mains $7–$16. No credit cards. Lunch and dinner daily. Train: Newtown.

Thanh Binh *VIETNAMESE* The tastiest Vietnamese rice paper roll ingredients are delivered to your table and you roll your own. The weekend noodles-only lunch is particularly popular with hungry locals, with nothing over $14.

111 King St., Newtown. ✆ **(02) 9557 1175.** www.thanhbinh.com.au. Mains $19–$21. MC, V. Lunch Sat and Sun, dinner Tues–Sun. Train: Newtown.

Twelve *ITALIAN* Twelve has serious Italian food at not-so-serious prices. In fact, most of the mains come in well under the $20 mark and you can get a set dinner menu of three courses for $45. The rigatoni with beef ragu is amazingly good. It's a great spot for people watching and it's kid friendly.

222 King St., Newtown. ✆ **(02) 9519 9412.** www.twelvenewtown.com.au Mains $12–$24. AE, MC, V. Lunch Thurs–Sun, dinner Tues–Sun. Train: Newtown.

Yak & Yeti *NEPALESE* The Yak & Yeti has been dishing up great Nepalese classics for what seems like forever. If you haven't sampled Nepalese fare, it's a cross between North Indian and Pakistani. The goat curry is a favourite, although the thali platters, which a have a bit of everything, are also good value.

41 Glebe Point Rd., Glebe. ✆ **(02) 9552 1220.** Mains $9–$18. MC, V. Dinner daily. Bus: 431 or 433.

WORTH A SPLURGE

Peasants Feast *ORGANIC* We all know that you have to pay a bit extra for organic food, but we also know that organic food is very good for you, which makes this restaurant, one of the few 100% organic restaurants in Sydney, the place to go to feel good about what you eat.

121A King St., Newtown. ✆ **(02) 9516 5998.** www.peasantsfeast.com.au. Mains $27–$30. MC, V. Dinner daily. Train: Newtown.

Restaurant Atelier *FRENCH* This stylish classical French bistro in a historic cottage would normally be a little out of our price range, except for the mid-week dinner special where you get three courses for $59 on Tuesday, Wednesday and Thursday. Roasted pheasant or rolled rabbit anyone?

22 Glebe Point Rd., Glebe. ℂ **(02) 9566 2112.** www.restaurantatelier.com. Mains $32–$38. AE, MC, V. Dinner Tues–Sat. Bus: 431 or 433.

Sugaroom *CONTEMPORARY*   Take a seat by the window and watch the tugboats and container ships cruise by. Great prices given the location, but if you go for lunch, $40 will get you two courses and a glass of wine.

1 Harris St., Pyrmont. ℂ **(02) 9571 5055.** www.sugaroom.com.au. Mains $28–$32. AE, DC, MC, V. Lunch Tues–Sun, dinner Tues–Sat. Bus: 443 or 449.

Cooking with Karma

Who says there's no such thing as a free lunch? OK, they might be a little bit more soup kitchen than fine diner, and you might have to pretend to be interested in finding some religion, but the food is free and there's generally no questions asked, plus you'll feel good giving a donation to a good cause!

- FREE The Hare Krishna **Food for Life** mobile van pulls up outside the Newtown Neighbourhood Centre (opposite the train station on the corner of Australia and King streets, Newtown; ℂ **0404 187 390**) every evening at 6pm. It's 100% vegetarian and a bit bland: no onions, garlic or chilli are used, but it's free, though a donation will keep your karma on track.

- FREE Once a month the Newtown Neighbourhood Centre holds a **barbecue** at the Newtown Town Hall (1 Bedford Street), usually on a Thursday between noon and 1.30pm. They are held in order to support worthy causes, such as Hepatitis Awareness, so donations are appreciated. Visit www.newtowncentre.org for dates.

Luna Park (p. 108) has been a Sydney icon since 1935—and has free entry.

EXPLORING SYDNEY

I n a city as gorgeous as Sydney it's all about getting out in the great outdoors and soaking it up, which is almost always free—or certainly dirt cheap. A day at the beach is a superb way to spend no money at all; Sydney has some of the best in the world, so it's the perfect place to keep from cracking open your wallet. On the rare occasions that the sun's not shining, there are plenty of free activities to keep you entertained indoors: most of the city's best museums, galleries and historic houses are free to enter. Commercial art galleries can also be great places to see quality art for free—just don't give into temptation or you'll well and truly blow the budget! What are you waiting for? Get out there and explore!

1 Exploring the Harbour for Free (or Dirt Cheap)

Cockatoo Island `FREE`   The largest of the harbour islands, Cockatoo has seen service as an imperial prison, an industrial school, a reformatory and a gaol before being reborn as one of Australia's biggest shipyards. Take a self-guided tour of the former shipbuilding site or pitch a tent (p. 30) for a camp site with a million-dollar, if somewhat noisy, view. The island is also home to regular exhibitions and art installations.

Cockatoo Island. ✆ **(02) 8969 2131.** www.cockatooisland.gov.au. Admission free (ferry costs extra). Information centre open daily 10am–4pm. Ferry: Circular Quay (Wharf 5). Map p. 95.

Ferries and RiverCats   No trip to Sydney is complete without a harbour cruise, but the average leisure boats aren't cheap. The good news is that the average price of an adult ferry ticket is around $6, which makes a ride across Sydney Harbour one of the world's great bargains. My favourite trip is the half-hour run through The Heads on the Manly Ferry, but other great trips include Watsons Bay in the eastern suburbs, Mosman Bay on the lower North Shore and Balmain in the inner west. For a longer cruise climb aboard the RiverCat for a one-hour trip up the Parramatta River to Sydney's second-oldest settlement. Take a return trip on one of the more frequent all-stops services to Rydalmere (one stop before Parramatta) and you've got a fantastic two-hour dirt-cheap cruise that shows you more of the harbour than you would get to see on most of the commercial cruises.

Circular Quay. ✆ **131 500.** www.sydneyferries.info. Admission $5.20–$7.70 adults, $2.60–$3.80 kids. MC, V. Daily 6am–midnight. Train: Circular Quay. Map p. 96.

Headland Park & Chowder Bay `FREE`   This former military site on Middle Head has great views, as well as walking tacks, a sculpture trail, spectacular lookouts (many of which were off limits to the public until a couple of years ago) and some interesting historic fortifications. The beach at Chowder Bay is lovely and has a netted swimming enclosure for safe swimming.

Via Middle Head Rd., Mosman. ✆ **(02) 8969 2100.** www.harbourtrust.gov.au. Daily during daylight hours. Bus: 244 from Wynyard. Map p. 98.

★ **Mrs Macquarie's Chair** `FREE`   Wrapped around Farm Cove, the Royal Botanic Gardens and surrounding Domain were set aside as

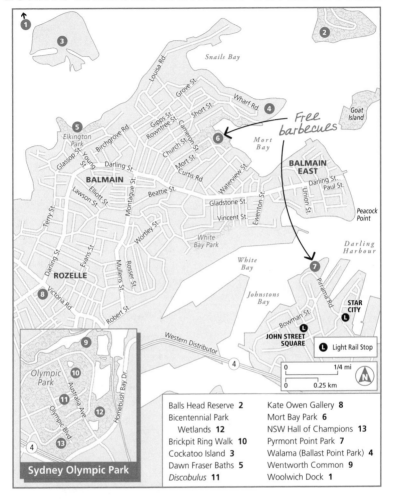

Snails Bay

Wharf Rd.

Goat Island

Free barbecues

Louisa Rd.

Grove St.

Short St.

Gipps St.

Rowntree St.

Cameron St.

Church St.

Mort St.

Curtis Rd.

Waterview St.

Mort Bay

BALMAIN EAST

Elkington Park

Birchgrove Rd

Glassop St.

Young St.

Darling St.

BALMAIN

Elliott St.

Lawson St.

Beattie St.

Montague St.

Gladstone St.

Vincent St.

Ewenton St.

Darling St.

Paul St.

Union St.

Peacock Point

Terry St.

Evans St.

Wortley St.

Rosser St.

Mullens St.

Darling St.

ROZELLE

Victoria Rd.

Robert St.

White Bay Park

White Bay

Johnstons Bay

Darling Harbour

STAR CITY

Piramá Rd.

Bowman St.

Western Distributor

JOHN STREET SQUARE

L Light Rail Stop

0 ___ 1/4 mi
0 ___ 0.25 km

Olympic Park

Australia Ave

Olympic Blvd

Homebush Bay Dr.

Sydney Olympic Park

Balls Head Reserve **2**	Kate Owen Gallery **8**
Bicentennial Park Wetlands **12**	Mort Bay Park **6**
	NSW Hall of Champions **13**
Brickpit Ring Walk **10**	Pyrmont Point Park **7**
Cockatoo Island **3**	Walama (Ballast Point Park) **4**
Dawn Fraser Baths **5**	Wentworth Common **9**
Discobulus **11**	Woolwich Dock **1**

Governor Phillip's private reserve in 1788, just weeks after the first fleeters set up camp in Sydney Cove. In 1810, Governor Macquarie ordered convicts to carve a ledge in the sandstone on the eastern point of the cove so his wife could admire the view, which today looks across to the Opera House, Harbour Bridge and Fort Denison. It is still one of the best views in town. FINE PRINT Go early in the day to avoid the stream of brides who flock here to have their photo taken.

Mrs Macquaries Rd., Mrs Macquaries Point, The Domain. Daily 24 hr. Train: Circular Quay. Map p. 96.

EXPLORING CITY CENTRE

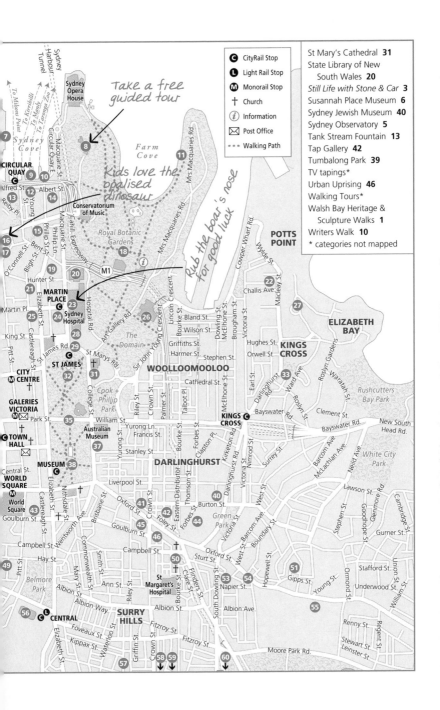

Legend

- **C** CityRail Stop
- **L** Light Rail Stop
- **M** Monorail Stop
- † Church
- (i) Information
- ✉ Post Office
- - - - Walking Path

St Mary's Cathedral **31**
State Library of New
    South Wales **20**
Still Life with Stone & Car **3**
Susannah Place Museum **6**
Sydney Jewish Museum **40**
Sydney Observatory **5**
Tank Stream Fountain **13**
Tap Gallery **42**
Tumbalong Park **39**
TV tapings*
Urban Uprising **46**
Walking Tours*
Walsh Bay Heritage &
    Sculpture Walks **1**
Writers Walk **10**
* categories not mapped

Take a free guided tour

Kids love the opalised dinosaur

Rub the boar's nose for good luck

EXPLORING EASTERN SUBURBS & LOWER NORTH SHORE

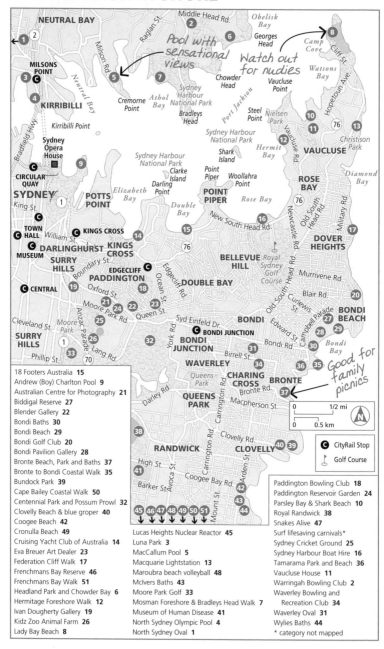

EXPLORING MANLY & MACQUARIE UNIVERSITY

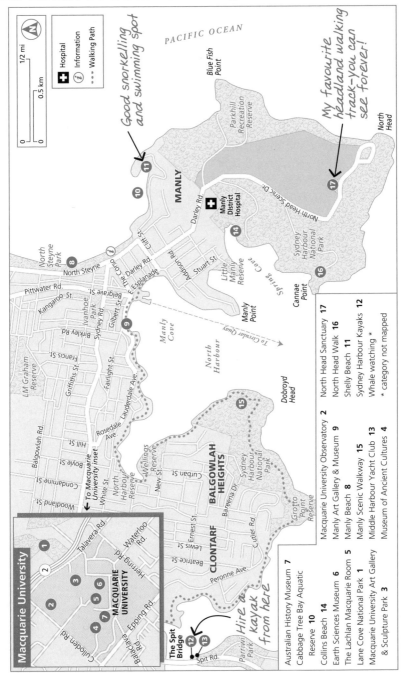

PACIFIC OCEAN

Good snorkelling and swimming spot

My favourite headland walking track—you can see forever!

Blue Fish Point

Parkhill Recreation Reserve

North Head

MANLY

Darley Rd.

Manly District Hospital

North Head Scenic Dr.

Sydney Harbour National Park

North Steyne Park

North Steyne

Pittwater Rd.

Kangaroo St.

The Corso

Belgrave St.

E. Esplanade

Ivanhoe Park

Sydney Rd.

Gilbert St.

Addison Rd.

Stuart St.

Little Manly Reserve

Spring Cove

Cannae Point

Manly Point

Manly Cove

North Harbour

To Circular Quay

Birkley Rd

Francis St.

Griffiths St.

Fairlight St.

Lauderdale Ave.

Rosedale Ave.

LM Graham Reserve

Balgowlah Rd.

Hill St.

Boyle St.

Condamine St.

Woodland St.

To Macquarie University inset

White St.

North Harbour Reserve

Wellings Reserve

New St.

Curban St.

Baeena Dr.

BALGOWLAH HEIGHTS

Dobroyd Head

Sydney Harbour National Park

Grotto Point Reserve

CLONTARF

Lewis St.

Ernest St.

Cutler Rd.

Beatrice St.

Peronne Ave.

Parriwi Park

Spit Rd.

The Spit Bridge

Hire a kayak from here

Macquarie University

Talavera Rd.

Herring Rd.

Waterloo Rd.

MACQUARIE UNIVERSITY

Culloden Rd.

Balaclava Rd.

Epping Rd.

Australian History Museum **7**

Cabbage Tree Bay Aquatic Reserve **10**

Collins Beach **14**

Earth Sciences Museum **6**

The Lachlan Macquarie Room **5**

Lane Cove National Park **1**

Macquarie University Art Gallery & Sculpture Park **3**

Macquarie University Observatory **2**

Manly Art Gallery & Museum **9**

Manly Beach **8**

Manly Scenic Walkway **15**

Middle Harbour Yacht Club **13**

Museum of Ancient Cultures **4**

North Head Sanctuary **17**

North Head Walk **16**

Shelly Beach **11**

Sydney Harbour Kayaks **12**

Whale watching *

* category not mapped

Legend

- ✚ Hospital
- ⓘ Information
- ··· Walking Path

1/2 mi

0.5 km

EXPLORING INNER WEST

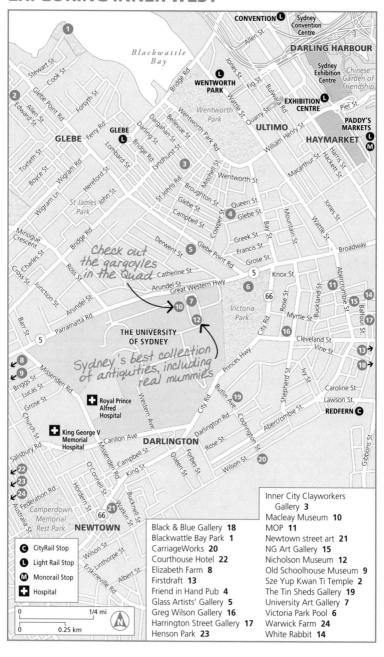

Blackwattle Bay

CONVENTION **L** Sydney Convention Centre

DARLING HARBOUR

Sydney Exhibition Centre

Chinese Garden of Friendship

WENTWORTH PARK **L**

Wentworth Park

EXHIBITION CENTRE **L**

ULTIMO

William Henry St.

Pier St.

PADDY'S MARKETS

HAYMARKET **L M**

GLEBE GLEBE **L**

St James John St Park

Check out the gargoyles in the Quad

Knox St.

Victoria Park

THE UNIVERSITY OF SYDNEY

Sydney's best collection of antiquities, including real mummies

Royal Prince Alfred Hospital

King George V Memorial Hospital

DARLINGTON

REDFERN **C**

Camperdown Memorial Rest Park

66

NEWTOWN

C CityRail Stop
L Light Rail Stop
M Monorail Stop
✚ Hospital

0		1/4 mi
0	0.25 km	

Black & Blue Gallery **18**
Blackwattle Bay Park **1**
CarriageWorks **20**
Courthouse Hotel **22**
Elizabeth Farm **8**
Firstdraft **13**
Friend in Hand Pub **4**
Glass Artists' Gallery **5**
Greg Wilson Gallery **16**
Harrington Street Gallery **17**
Henson Park **23**

Inner City Clayworkers Gallery **3**
Macleay Museum **10**
MOP **11**
Newtown street art **21**
NG Art Gallery **15**
Nicholson Museum **12**
Old Schoolhouse Museum **9**
Sze Yup Kwan Ti Temple **2**
The Tin Sheds Gallery **19**
University Art Gallery **7**
Victoria Park Pool **6**
Warwick Farm **24**
White Rabbit **14**

EXPLORING UPPER NORTH SIDE

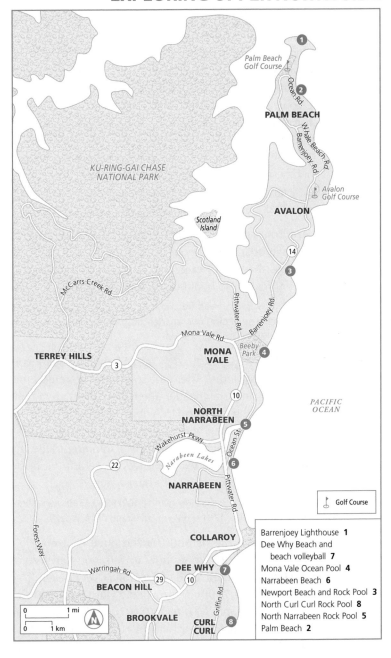

Palm Beach
Golf Course

PALM BEACH

Ocean Rd.

Whale Beach Rd.

Barrenjoey Rd.

KU-RING-GAI CHASE
NATIONAL PARK

Avalon
Golf Course

AVALON

Scotland
Island

14

McCarrs Creek Rd.

Pittwater Rd.

Barrenjoey Rd.

Mona Vale Rd.

Beeby
Park

TERREY HILLS

3

**MONA
VALE**

10

PACIFIC
OCEAN

**NORTH
NARRABEEN**

5

Wakehurst Pkwy

Ocean St.

Narrabeen Lakes

22

6

NARRABEEN

Pittwater Rd.

Golf Course

COLLAROY

Forest Way

Barrenjoey Lighthouse **1**
Dee Why Beach and
   beach volleyball **7**
Mona Vale Ocean Pool **4**
Narrabeen Beach **6**
Newport Beach and Rock Pool **3**
North Curl Curl Rock Pool **8**
North Narrabeen Rock Pool **5**
Palm Beach **2**

DEE WHY

7

Warringah Rd.

29

10

BEACON HILL

0   1 mi
0   1 km

BROOKVALE

**CURL
CURL**

Griffin Rd.

8

North Head Sanctuary FREE   The army gunners that lived on North Head when it was the School of Artillery would have enjoyed one of the most breathtaking views in Sydney. Now that guarding the entrance to the harbour with guns is not seen as so important it's open to anyone who is keen on a bushwalk or is looking for a picnic site with panoramic views. You can also take a tour of the North Fort, now known as the **Australian Army Artillery Museum,** on Wednesday, Saturday and Sunday (admission $11 adults, $5 kids; no credit cards). And there are also guided tours of the parade grounds and World War II tunnels on the second Sunday of every month (adults $12, kids $8).

Scenic Dr., Manly. ✆ **(02) 8969 2100.** www.harbourtrust.gov.au. Daily 10am–4pm. Ferry: Manly, then bus 135 (from Manly Wharf). Map p. 99.

Sydney Harbour Boat Hire   You don't have to be rich to cruise the harbour in your own boat. A four-hour charter of a 20-foot half-cabin cruiser can cost less than $12 per person per hour, as long as there are eight of you on board. No boat license is required.

Rose Bay Marina, 594 New South Head Rd., Rose Bay. ✆ **(02) 9328 4748.** www. sydneyharbourescapes.com.au. Four-hour charter from $360 (up to 8 guests). AE, MC, V. Bus: 323, 324, 325. Map p. 98.

★ Sydney Harbour Kayaks   Explore Sydney Harbour at sea level—just you, a kayak and a paddle. There are a number of guided tours you can do, but hiring one is a cheaper alternative if you are a confident paddler. Over on the north side, Sydney Harbour Kayaks will hire you a sea kayak for $20 an hour. It's a good base from which to explore Middle Harbour, which has much less shipping traffic than the main harbor. Kayaking is an excellent way to get off the beaten tourist track and investigate the harbour's backwaters.

Under the eastern side of The Spit Bridge, Mosman. ✆ **(02) 9960 4389.** www.sydney harbourkayaks.com.au. MC, V. Bus: 178 from Wynyard (Stand C). Map p. 99.

Yacht Racing FREE   Sail the harbour for the price of a couple of post-race beers. If you already know how to sail, you can try your luck at either the **Cruising Yacht Club of Australia** (New Beach Road, Darling Point; ✆ **(02) 8292 7800**) or the **Middle Harbour Yacht Club** (Lower Parriwi Road, The Spit, Mosman; ✆ **(02) 9969 1244**) as they are sometimes short of crew for their twilight races (most evenings in summer) or winter race series on Sunday. Register online or simply turn up on the day; see the websites for more details (www.mhyc. com.au and www.cyca.com.au). If you're a landlubber like me and don't know your port from your starboard or your gunwale from your galley, $15 will get you a spot on board the spectator ferry during the **18 Footers Australia** championship races, where you're guaranteed to be in the heart of the action. The ferry leaves Double Bay Wharf at 2.15pm each race day throughout the season and tickets can be purchased at the office.

18 Footers Australia: Double Bay Wharf (alongside the clubhouse and rigging area), Double Bay. ℂ **(02) 9363 2995.** www.18footers.com.au. Admission $15 adults, free kids under 14. MC, V. Train: Edgecliff. Bus: 232 or 326. Map p. 98.

2 Museums & Attractions

Anzac Memorial `FREE`   This beautiful Art Deco building in Hyde Park is the main New South Wales war memorial, dedicated to all the Australians who have served in a war, but built in 1934 to commemorate those who died in WWI from New South Wales. It is the main focus of the Anzac Day (April 25) activities in Sydney and the end point of the annual parade. Inside is the Hall of Memory, an eternal flame and a moving bronze statue of a dead Anzac borne aloft on a shield by his mother, sister, wife and child, called *Sacrifice*. The ground floor is an exhibition space with displays reflecting the various anniversaries of conflict.

Hyde Park South, Sydney. ℂ **(02) 9267 7668.** www.anzacmemorial.nsw.gov.au. Daily 9am–5pm. Train: Museum. Map p. 96.

Army Museum of New South Wales   One for military buffs, this museum inside the original District Military Prison has a display of weapons, medals, uniforms and other militaria dating from the first days of the penal colony to the present. You can also take a tour of the gorgeous sandstone barracks that were built in the 1840s and, according to the tour guide, 'the largest stone building still in use in the Southern Hemisphere' at 10am on Thursday. Admission includes a rousing performance by the resident band.

Victoria Barracks, Oxford St., Paddington. ℂ **(02) 9339 3330.** Admission $2 adults, $1 kids. No credit cards. Thurs 10am–12.30pm, Sun 10am–4pm. Bus: 378 or 380. Map p. 96.

Australian History Museum `FREE`   This museum is home to 3500 items that reflect Australia's history from pre-colonisation to today. There's lots of everyday stuff on show and I love the Greek cafe display with cafe objects and food products that make me nostalgic for the corner cafe in the tiny outback town where I grew up—there really was a Greek cafe in every country town!

Building W6A, Macquarie University, Balaclava Rd., North Ryde. ℂ **(02) 9850 8870.** www.austhistmuseum.mq.edu.au. Mon, Tues, Thurs and Fri 9.30am–4.30pm, Wed 9am–noon (subject to change; call first). Train: Macquarie University. Map p. 99.

Australian Museum   Everything you'd expect to find in this grand natural history and science museum is here. Most kids head straight for the dinosaurs, mummy or skeletons, depending on their age and penchant for ghoul. They also like the Notorious Australian Insects and Spiders display on level two—Australian upside-down fly or hairy cicada, anyone? For grown-up visitors (and locals) the Surviving Australia exhibition is a good chance to get a close up look at some of the country's most deadly creatures. *Free alert:* You'll still have to pay the $12 entry fee, but once you're inside you can take a free guided tour at 11am and 2pm (no need to book; just turn up). The museum throws open its doors for free entry once or twice a year during open days, when you can go behind the scenes and see collections that are normally off limits to the public. Details are published on the website.

6 College St. (opp. Hyde Park), Sydney. ℂ **(02) 9320 6000.** www.austmus.gov.au. Admission $12 adults, $6 kids. AE, MC, V. Daily 9.30am–5pm. Train: Museum. Map p. 96.

★ **Australian National Maritime Museum** FREE   All those big boats you can see moored on the western side of Darling Harbour—the massive destroyer HMAS *Vampire,* the largest big-gun destroyer built in Australia; the submarine HMAS *Onslow;* the attack-class patrol boat and the colourful replica of the *Endeavour,* the tiny sailing ship that Cook discovered Australia in—belong to the Australian National Maritime Museum. Inside you'll find all sorts of displays relating to Australia's maritime heritage, from commerce to navigation to the history of the bathing suit (or 'cossie', as it's known) and travelling exhibitions.

2 Murray St., Darling Harbour. ℂ **(02) 9298 3777.** www.anmm.gov.au. Admission to museum is free, boats cost extra. Big ticket: $32 adults, $17 kids, $70 family (includes entry to *HMB Endeavour* replica, destroyer *HMAS Vampire*, submarine *HMAS Onslow* and the 1874 tall ship *James Craig*). AE, MC, V. Daily 9.30am–5pm (6pm in Jan). Map p. 96.

Barrenjoey Lighthouse FREE   There have been three lighthouses on this point overlooking Pittwater on the northern end of Palm Beach; the current sandstone incarnation dates from 1881. It's a bit of a rough and steep walking track to get there, but the views are worth the trek. You can take a guided tour on Sunday afternoons, otherwise access is free.

Barrenjoey Rd., Palm Beach. ✆ **(02) 9457 9322.** Access daily; tours $3, Sun 11am–3pm. Bus: 190 (from Wynyard). Map p. 101.

Brickpit Ring Walk `FREE`   One hundred years ago the brickpit at Homebush Bay produced almost three billion bricks. Today, it's a flooded pond on the Sydney Olympics site and is home to the very rare and endangered green and golden bell frog. A circular walkway that is 550m in circumference and 18m above the ground has been built, so you can peer down into the water without harming the fragile environment.

Enter via Marjorie Jackson Pkwy. or Australia Ave., Sydney Olympic Park. ✆ **(02) 9714 7888.** www.sydneyolympicpark.com.au. Daily during daylight hours. Train: Sydney Olympic Park. Map p. 95.

Customs House `FREE`   Built in 1845 and the headquarters of the Australian Customs Service until 1990, Customs House includes the City of Sydney Library (p. 154) on the first floor. Customs House is home to Cafe Sydney (p. 206), a very fine restaurant that does a great free jazz session on Sunday afternoons. But the main reason to pop inside, other than the lure of free books, newspapers and magazines, is to check out the fantastic model of the city central business district (CBD) under your feet (p. 238). You'll often find some very good photographic and art exhibitions on display here and they are always free.

31 Alfred St., Circular Quay. ✆ **(02) 9242 8595.** Library open Mon–Fri 10am–7pm, Sat–Sun 11am–4pm, closed public holidays. Train: Circular Quay. Map p. 96.

Earth Sciences Museum `FREE`   This museum is a good spot for rock hounds. Part of Macquarie University, it has lots of rocks, minerals, gems and fossils on display, plus everything you need to know about earthquakes, weather and soil. There's also an earth sciences garden, featuring plants and fossils from the days of Gondwana.

Building E5A, Macquarie University, Balaclava Rd., North Ryde. ✆ **(02) 9850 8183.** www.museums.mq.edu.au. Mon–Fri 9am–5pm (appointments recommended). Train: Macquarie University. Map p. 99.

Kidz Zoo Animal Farm   Introduce your kids to the farmyard and let them cuddle the child-friendly guinea pigs, rabbits, chicks, kid goats, sheep and lambs in the Entertainment Quarter (EQ) Showring.

Lang Road (next to the SCG), Moore Park. www.entertainmentquarter.com.au. Admission $5. AE, MC, V. Wed and Sat 8.30am–1.30pm, Sun 10am–1.30pm (weather permitting). Bus: 339, 355, 372, 373, 374, 376, 377, 391, 392, 394, 395, 396, 397 or 399. Map p. 98.

A Ticket to Time Travel

The Historic Houses Trust (HHT) has a collection of 12 excellent museums scattered across Sydney. Entry into most is between $8 and $10 each and a $30 **Ticket Through Time** (available for purchase at all HHT museums except Government House; MC, V) gives unlimited entry to all properties over a three-month period—a saving of more than $50 if you visit them all. Visit www.hht.net.au for information.

● When it was built in the 1830s **Elizabeth Bay House** (7 Onslow Avenue, Elizabeth Bay; ℂ **(02) 9356 3022**) was 'the grandest house in the Colony'—despite the fact it was never finished. Go there just to see the elegant domed saloon and geometric staircase. Admission is $8 for adults and $4 for kids and it's open Friday to Sunday, 9.30am to 4pm. Map p. 96.

● Built in 1793, **Elizabeth Bay Farm** (70 Alice Street, Rosehill; ℂ **(02) 9635 9488**) is the oldest surviving cottage in Australia. Macarthur is credited as the father of the Australian wool industry, and was also one of the main political protagonists behind the 'rum rebellion' that overthrew Governor Bligh on January 26, 1808 (the only successful armed coup in Australian history). Admission is $8 for adults and $4 for kids. It's open Friday to Sunday, 9.30am to 4pm. Map p. 100.

● ★ FREE **Government House** is Sydney's version of Buckingham Palace. Well, not really, but it *was* designed by the same architect (Edward Blore) and it was home to 27 successive Governors. Check out the stunning collection of glass art and modern furniture mixed in with the antiques at Macquarie Street, Sydney (ℂ **(02) 9931 5222**). Free guided tours start every 30 minutes Friday to Sunday 10.30am to 3pm. Call ahead as the house closes if a vice-regal function is being held there. Map p. 96.

● ★ **Hyde Park Barracks,** the elegant 1817 sandstone building in Queens Square (Macquarie Street, Sydney; ℂ **(02) 8239 2311**) was designed by convict architect Francis Greenway and it's the best place to learn more about convict New South Wales. Admission is

$10 for adults and $5 for kids. It's open daily from 9.30am to 5pm. Map p. 96.

- ★ What makes the **Justice & Police Museum** so wonderfully chilling is the array of weapons and forensic photographs, most of which was collated in 1910 to instruct new constables in the wicked ways of criminals. Head to the corner of Albert and Phillip streets in Circular Quay (✆ **(02) 9252 1144**) on Saturday or Sunday from 10am to 5pm. Admission is $8 for adults and $4 for kids. Map p. 96.

- FREE The **Mint,** a gorgeous old sandstone building at 10 Macquarie Street, Sydney (✆ **(02) 8239 2288**), dates back to 1811. It's mainly used for offices and functions these days, so there's not that much to see. It's open from Monday to Friday 9am to 5pm. If you are interested in the making of money, go instead to the **Museum of Australian Currency Notes** (p. 109). Map p. 96.

- Built on the ruins of the first governor-general's house, the **Museum of Sydney** explores colonial and contemporary Sydney through found objects, video and changing exhibitions. It's on the corner of Phillip and Bridge streets, Sydney (✆ **(02) 9251 5988**). Admission is $10 for adults and $5 for kids and it's open daily from 9.30am to 5pm. Map p. 96.

- ★ **Susannah Place Museum,** the row of four tiny terrace houses and shop at 58–64 Gloucester Street, The Rocks (✆ **(02) 9241 1893**) was home to more than 100 families over 150 years. Admission (including the one-hour guided tour) costs $8 for adults and $4 for kids. It's open Saturday and Sunday from 10am to 5pm. Map p. 96.

- Built by statesman and explorer William Charles Wentworth, early-19th-century **Vaucluse House** (Wentworth Rd., Vaucluse; ✆ **(02) 9388 7922.**) is worth visiting to learn about the scandals he survived. Admission is $8 for adults and $4 for kids from Friday to Sunday, 9.30am to 4pm. Map p. 98.

The Lachlan Macquarie Room FREE   Melbourne may well have the childhood Yorkshire home of Captain Cook, but Sydney has Lachlan Macquarie's front parlour. Macquarie was the fifth governor of New South Wales (1810–1821) and is the man behind many of the grand buildings in Macquarie Street. The original ground-floor parlour room of his house on the Isle of Mull in Scotland has been painstakingly reconstructed inside the library at the university that bears his name and a collection of artefacts and memorabilia.

Building C7A, Macquarie University, Balaclava Rd., North Ryde. ℂ **(02) 9850 7554.** www.lib.mq.edu.au/lmr/. Mon–Fri 9am–5pm (by arrangement). Train: Macquarie University. Map p. 99.

Lucas Heights Nuclear Reactor FREE   On the first Saturday of every month you can join a free tour of Australia's only nuclear reactor. Being a little nervous of glowing in the dark ever after, I confess that this particular tour is still on my to-do list, but the Commonwealth Scientific and Industrial Research Organisation (CSIRO) boffins who run the show say you'll learn all about neutron scattering and neutron beams, and get to see the accelerators, the mass spectrometer and neutron guide hall. Homer Simpson, eat your heart out! It's a sensitive site, so you must book (and provide ID details) at least three days in advance (deadline is the Wednesday before).

New Illawarra Rd., Lucas Heights. ℂ **(02) 9717 3111.** www.ainse.edu.au. Tours Sat 10am and 2pm. Train: Sutherland or Engadine and then take a taxi from there. Map p. 98.

Luna Park FREE   The various incarnations of the big smiling face at the gate of Luna Park has been a Sydney icon since 1935. Little kids like the carousel and Coney Island, bigger kids prefer the high-octane rides like the Wild Mouse roller-coaster and the Flying Saucer. I like hanging upside down in mid-air as the Rotor's floor drops away.

1 Olympic Dr., Milsons Point. ℂ **(02) 9033 7676.** www.lunaparksydney.com. Entry free, some rides cost extra. Mon 11am–6pm, Fri 11am–11pm, Sat 10am–11pm, Sun 10am–6pm (closed Tues–Thurs). Train: Milsons Point. Ferry: Milsons Point. Map p. 98.

Macquarie Lightstation FREE   The current lighthouse (ca. 1883) near the Gap at Watsons Bay is an exact copy of an earlier one that was designed by convict architect Francis Greenway.

Old South Head Rd., Vaucluse. ℂ **(02) 8969 2131.** www.harbourtrust.gov.au. Entry to the grounds is free; tours of the lighthouse every two months, $5 adults, $3 kids. Check the website for next tour dates; bookings are essential. Bus: 324 or 380. Map p. 98.

Macquarie University Observatory It's not free, but the $10 star-gazing sessions are $5 cheaper than those at Sydney Observatory (p. 114). The observatory is open to the public every Friday night from March through to November, except when it's raining, and staff and students will take you on a guided tour of the night sky. Bookings are essential; call ahead if the weather looks doubtful.

Macquarie University, Balaclava Rd., North Ryde. ✆ **(02) 9850 8914.** www.astronomy. mq.edu.au/observatory/. Fri 7.30pm–9pm (8.30pm–10pm during daylight saving). Admission $10 adults, $5 kids, $25 families. No credit cards. Train: Macquarie University. Map p. 99.

Museum of Ancient Cultures FREE This is a great museum if you love really, really old stuff. It is home to more than 7000 artefacts, including the largest papyrus collection in the Southern Hemisphere and one of the country's best collections of ancient coins.

Level 3, Building X5B, Macquarie University, Balaclava Rd., North Ryde. ✆ **(02) 9850 9263.** www.mac.mq.edu.au. Mon–Fri 9am–4.30pm (museum can sometimes close at short notice; call first). Train: Macquarie University. Map p. 99.

★ **The Museum of Australian Currency Notes** FREE Ever wondered what happens to old (polymer) banknotes? They are shredded, melted and turned into garbage bins! It's just one of the interesting little monetary snippets you'll learn at this shiny new museum underneath the Reserve Bank of Australia. The museum is much more interesting than it sounds—but then, anything to do with money usually is. There's plenty of it on show here (money, that is) with displays that trace the history of the Aussie coinage and bank notes from the early days to some brilliant modern-day forgeries that are almost impossible to detect.

66 Martin Pl., Sydney. ✆ **(02) 9551 9743.** www.rba.gov.au/Museum. Mon–Fri 10am–4pm (except public and bank holidays). Train: Martin Place. Map p. 96.

Museum of Freemasonry FREE OVERRATED I suspect you actually have to be a freemason to really enjoy this museum. Don't come here in the hope of learning the secret handshake and other mysterious business like I did, because you'll leave none the wiser. And you won't necessarily learn much about the meanings and reasons behind the elaborately embroidered and bejewelled aprons, quasi-military medals and very silly hats. . . In fact, you might well leave more confused than ever, but you will glean plenty of entertaining trivia. For example, who knew that some of Australia's most iconic culinary masterpieces (Vegemite, Freddo Frogs, Aeroplane Jelly, Cherry Ripes and Milo) were all created by masons?

Level 3, 279 Castlereagh St., Sydney. ℂ **(02) 9284 2872.** www.mof.org.au. Mon–Fri 8.30am–4.30pm. Train: Central. Map p. 96.

Museum of Human Disease It's not free—in fact, it's a bit on the pricey side—but it deserves a mention just because it's so darn weird and icky. All sorts of real body bits floating in jars—gullets to guts, tumours, growths and insanely long intestinal worms—are on show. This museum was originally designed as a teaching resource for medical students, but it seems they just can't keep the curious crowds away. *Free alert:* Entry includes a free audio tour. It's a hit with easily bored and hard-to-impress teenage boys, but it's not for the squeamish. FINE PRINT The museum is not considered suitable for children under 15.

Ground floor, Samuels Building, University of NSW, cnr. High and Botany sts., Kensington. ℂ **(02) 9385 1522.** www.diseasemuseum.unsw.edu.au. Mon–Fri 3–5pm. Admission $10 adults, $5 kids under 15. No credit cards. Bus: 391, 392, 393, 394, 395, 396, 397, 398 or 400. Map p. 98.

National Opal Collection FREE Yes, it's in a jewellery shop, but this little opal museum done up to resemble a cave is great place to take kids who are obsessed with dinosaurs. Associated with the Australian Museum it purports to be 'the world's only permanent exhibition of opalised fossils' and the star of the show is Nessie, a rare 2m-long opalised pliosaur skeleton, thought to be between 115 and 110 million years old and unearthed in the South Australian outback in 1968. Australia is the only country, apparently, where opalised fossils are found and there are lots of dinosaur teeth and bones on display as well as boulder opals, opalised tree ferns and other pretty prehistoric stuff. Staff don't even seem to mind if all you do is visit the museum; there's no hard sell. The tricky bit is resisting the temptation to buy!

60 Pitt St., Sydney. ℂ **(02) 9247 6344.** www.nationalopal.com. Mon–Fri 9am–6pm, Sat–Sun 10am–4pm. Train: Circular Quay. Map p. 96.

NSW Hall of Champions FREE Relive all your favourite moments in sport and be inspired by the 300 or so champions honoured in this sporting museum. As it's on the site of the 2000 Olympics, expect plenty of Olympics memorabilia as well.

Sydney Olympic Park Sports Centre, Olympic Boulevard, Sydney Olympic Park. ℂ **(02) 9763 0111.** www.sydneyolympicpark.com.au. Daily 9am–5pm. Train: Sydney Olympic Park. Map p. 95.

FREE Old & Pretty Stuff at the University of Sydney

The University of Sydney has some pretty impressive collections that you can see for free. All surround the Quadrangle at the Camperdown campus and are open Monday to Friday, 10am to 4.40pm and Sunday noon to 4pm.

- If you like looking at dead and dried insects in glass cases, you'll love the **Macleay Museum.** There are more than half a million specimens here, all collected in the late 18th century by Alexander Macleay, who was the Colonial Secretary for New South Wales in the early days of the colony. There are also some great photographs of various exploratory and anthropological expeditions from the 1850s through to the middle of the 20th century and a good collection of Aboriginal and Torres Strait Islander artefacts. Map p. 100.

- ★ It might be tiny, but the three-roomed **Nicholson Museum** (℃ **(02) 9351 2812**) is home to the largest collection of antiquities in Australia. Most of it was collected by one of the university founders, Sir Charles Nicholson, though it has been added to over the past 150 years through various university-funded archaeological excavations. My favourite exhibits are the Egyptian mummies and the is a treasure trove of ancient pottery, sculpture, glass and tools from Greece, Italy, Cyprus, Egypt and the Middle East. Map p. 100.

- The university has some 3500 works of art, most donated or left as a bequest. It includes lots of Australian art, as well as a collection of Japanese prints and 19th century European works. The **University Art Gallery** (℃ **(02) 9351 6883**), a small exhibition space near the Quadrangle, has a program of changing exhibitions from the collection. Map p. 100.

Old Schoolhouse Museum FREE   If your kids are complaining about how hard school is, take them to this little museum that reflects a typical schoolroom of 100 years ago to show them how lucky they really are. Teachers, too, will probably find the collection of old school memorabilia interesting.

Cnr. Macquarie and Smith sts. (inside the grounds of Arthur Phillip High School), Parramatta. ✆ **(02) 9635 8936.** Second Sun of every month 11am–3pm. Train: Parramatta. RiverCat: Parramatta. Map p. 100.

★ **Powerhouse Museum**   There's something for everyone in this huge museum. Home to more than 385,000 objects (so they tell me; I haven't counted) that relate to history, science, technology, design, industry, decorative arts, music, transport and space exploration. There's always an engaging exhibition or two and the focus is always hands-on and interactive, so it's a winner with kids who are easily bored. Free alert: Join one of the free 45-minute highlight tours, led by volunteers who know a vast amount about everything in the museum. There's no need to book; just ask when the next tour is scheduled to depart when you buy your entry ticket.

500 Harris St., Ultimo. ✆ **(02) 9217 0111.** www.powerhousemuseum.com. Admission $10 adults, $5 kids. AE, MC, V. Daily 10am–5pm. Monorail: Paddy's Markets. Map p. 96.

Pyrmont Bridge FREE   Built in 1902, Pyrmont Bridge is the oldest surviving electrical swing bridge in the world. It's powered by electricity, can swing open and shut in 45 seconds and is still operating. You can see it in action on Saturday, Sunday and most public holidays at 10.30am, noon, 1pm, 2pm and 3pm (weather permitting). It is also opened as required for shipping and it's closed to vehicular traffic. Walking across it is a great way to get from the city centre to Darling Harbour. If you're keen to know more, call to arrange a free tour.

End of Market St., Darling Park. ✆ **(02) 9299 7541.** Monorail: Darling Park. Map p. 96.

Rail Heritage Central FREE   One for train spotters, rail enthusiasts and lovers of nostalgia, this surprisingly interesting display of railway memorabilia inside the old booking office on the country platform at Central Station has a great collection of old tickets.

Main Concourse, Central Station. ✆ **(02) 9379 1110.** www.nswrtm.org. Mon–Fri 9am–4pm, Sat and Sun 9am–5pm. Train: Central. Map p. 96.

★ **The Rocks Discovery Museum** `FREE` This modern museum is housed in a restored 1850s sandstone warehouse and focuses on The Rocks, with displays relating to the traditional owners (the Cadigal), the establishment of the colony and various other aspects of life in The Rocks over the next 220 years, from the outbreak of the bubonic plague in 1900 and widespread demolition to make way for the Sydney Harbour Bridge in the 1930s to the Green Bans of the 1970s. There's a great collection of artefacts found in archaeological digs and some terrific archival film footage.

Kendall Lane (off Argyle St.), The Rocks. ℂ **(02) 9240 8680.** www.rocksdiscovery museum.com. Daily 10am–5pm. Train: Circular Quay. Map p. 96.

St Mary's Cathedral `FREE` Unlike Paris, Rome or Prague, Sydney's not a city that's particularly famous for its beautiful churches, but the catholic St Mary's Cathedral is an exception. It's built in the 'Gothic Revival' style; squint hard enough and you could be forgiven for thinking you are in Europe. Most of it was built in 1868, although the spires were only completed in 2000. A small museum and historical exhibition shows lots of catholic convict artefacts down in the crypt. It's open most days, but does close for special events (such as weddings) so call ahead to check opening times.

St Mary's Rd., Sydney. ℂ **(02) 9220 0400.** www.stmaryscathedral.org.au. Mon–Fri 9am–5pm. Train: St James. Map p. 96.

★ **State Library of New South Wales** `FREE` It's not only one of the country's leading libraries, but it is also one of the city's best museums—something that not even most locals realise. There are always a couple of interesting displays (it was Australian cookbooks from colonial times to the current celebrity chef craze last time I was there) and excellent exhibitions, ranging from photography to historical collections, as well as talks and weekly movies (p. 223). You can also take a 75-minute heritage and history tour (bookings required). And it's all free!

Macquarie St., Sydney. ℂ **(02) 9273 1414.** www.sl.nsw.gov.au. Mon–Thurs 9am–8pm, Fri 9am–5pm, Sat and Sun 10am–5pm. Train: Martin Place. Map p. 96.

Sydney Jewish Museum `FREE` Entry to this museum dedicated to the Holocaust and Australian Jewish History is free on many non-Jewish public holidays, such as New Year's Day, Australia Day (January 26), Easter and the Monday of long weekends. On other days, you'll have to pay the $10 entry fee, but once you have you can join

Sunday with Kids

Sunday is a great day to go exploring with the kids and several museums offer special activities and programs that are designed specifically for the young 'uns.

- Especially for under-eights, **Cog's Workshop** weekend craft classes at the Powerhouse Museum (500 Harris Street, Ultimo; ✆ **(02) 9217 0111**; www.powerhousemuseum.com; p. 112) are free with museum entry. Every Saturday and Sunday 10.30am to noon and daily from 11am to 3pm during school holidays. Map p. 96.

- `FREE` Sunday afternoon is all about kids at the Art Gallery of New South Wales (Art Gallery Road, The Domain; ✆ **(02) 9225 1700**; www.gallerykids.com.au; p. 115) with free performances and storytelling at 2.30pm. The **Gallery Kids** program includes daily character performances during school holidays, as well as kids' art classes and special art tours for tots. Map p. 96.

- The Sunday **Kids on Deck** program at the Australian National Maritime Museum (2 Murray Street, Darling Harbour; ✆ **(02) 9298 3777**; www.anmm.gov.au; p. 104) has everything from arts and crafts, games and puzzles to stories and dress-ups and is usually a hit with wannabe pirates. It's held Sunday from 11am to 3pm and daily 10am to 4pm during the school holidays. Map p. 96.

one of the free 45-minute tours, led by volunteers at noon on Monday, Wednesday, Friday and Sunday.

148 Darlinghurst Rd. (cnr. Burton St.), Darlinghurst. ✆ **(02) 9360 7999.** www.sydney jewishmuseum.com.au. Admission $10 adult, $6 kids. AE, DC, MC, V. Sun–Thurs 10am–4pm, Fri 10am–2pm, closed Sat, Jewish holidays and Christmas Day. Bus: 311 or 389. Map p. 96.

Sydney Observatory `FREE`   Australia's oldest observatory was built in 1858. It was also a working one until the increasing light pollution made observations too difficult in the 1970s, and it is now a museum.

Watson Rd., Observatory Hill, The Rocks. ✆ **(02) 9921 3485.** www.sydneyobservatory. com.au. Daily 10am–5pm, nightly star-gazing tours (bookings essential). Admission free during the day, star-gazing tours $15 adult, $10 kids. Train: Circular Quay. Map p. 96.

Sze Yup Kwan Ti Temple `FREE` This Chinese temple hidden away in the leafy back streets of residential Glebe Point is dedicated to Kwan Ti, a warrior god. It's not only Sydney's oldest Chinese temple, but a very pleasant spot to take some time out and savour the tranquillity.

2 Edward St., Glebe. Daily 9am–5pm. Bus: 431 or 433. Map p. 100.

Woolwich Dock `FREE` Those who are interested in all things maritime and industrial will enjoy this historic dry dock, where the Parramatta and Lane Cove rivers meet. You can still see boats being lifted in and out of the 300m cut sandstone dock. There's a cantilevered lookout platform with great views of the Harbour Bridge and dock below it, and there are some good walking trails.

Woolwich Rd., Woolwich. ✆ **(02) 8969 2100.** www.harbourtrust.gov.au. Daily during daylight hours. Ferry: Woolwich, then 20-min. walk. Map p. 95.

3 Art Galleries

2 Danks Street `FREE` Nine galleries are housed in a former warehouse that is this arts hub, showing everything from Aboriginal art from the central deserts to fine art reproductions and everything in between. Seven spaces are home to permanent galleries and two are available to rent by artists, so there's always something new on show.

2 Danks St., Waterloo. www.2danksstreet.com.au. Tues–Sat 11am–6pm, Sun 11am–4pm. Bus: 301, 302, 303, 304, 339 or 343. Map p. 96.

★ **Art Gallery of New South Wales** `FREE` If you have time to visit only one major art gallery in Sydney make it this one as it will give you a crash course in Australian art. There's always an international exhibition or two and it's a great way to spend a rainy afternoon. There are heaps of free guided tours, but the best is the collection highlights tour daily at 11am (except Monday), 1pm and 2pm. Wednesday night is Art After Hours (p. 225).

Art Gallery Rd., The Domain. ✆ **(02) 9225 1700.** www.artgallery.nsw.gov.au and www.artafterhours.com.au. Daily 10am–5pm; Art After Hours Wed 5–9pm. Train: Martin Place, then 10-min. walk. Map p. 96.

Asia–Australia Arts Centre `FREE` Also known as Gallery 4A, this is where you can catch some of the best exhibitions of modern Asian art outside of the main state galleries. They often host free lectures, Asian movies and panel discussions as well.

181–187 Hay St., Haymarket. ✆ **(02) 9212 0380.** www.4a.com.au. Tues–Sat 11am–6pm. Train: Central. Map p. 96.

★ **Australian Centre for Photography** FREE Both a photographic gallery *par excellence* and a college with exhibitions from both senior students and leading Australian and international photographers that are always interesting (p. 245).

257 Oxford St., Paddington. ✆ **(02) 9332 1455.** www.acp.org.au. Tues–Fri noon–7pm, Sat and Sun 10am–6pm. Bus: 333, 378 or 380. Map p. 98.

Black & Blue Gallery FREE There's performance art and other out-there stuff on show at this artist-run gallery in Redfern. Exhibitions change monthly.

302/267–271 Cleveland St. (cnr. Elizabeth St.), Redfern. ✆ **(02) 9699 6038.** www.blackandbluegallery.com.au. Thurs–Sat 11am–6pm. Bus: 372. Map p. 100.

Blender Gallery FREE There's a new exhibition to see every three or four weeks at this gallery dedicated to (in its own words) 'new wave art forms guaranteed to strike a chord on individual levels'. The photographic exhibitions are usually excellent.

16 Elizabeth St., Paddington. ✆ **(02) 9380 7080.** www.blender.com.au. Tues–Sun 10am–6pm. Bus: 378 or 380. Map p. 98.

FREE TV Tapings

If you want to witness the magic of television first-hand, all you have to do is ask. Lots of TV shows—especially game shows, chat shows and reality TV shows—need real live people in the audience to clap and cheer at the right moments and add atmosphere. Most of the tapings are free, but there are a few catches. Generally, unless it's a kids' show, under 16s are not allowed and tickets are allocated on a first-come, first-served basis. Due to high demand for some shows, tickets are allocated on a ballot system once you've registered or completed a booking form online. To apply for tickets check the website for the show you want to attend.

Bondi Pavilion Gallery `FREE`   There's a new exhibition on here every two weeks, although sometimes the view outside is better than what's on show inside. But just when you think it's all crap, there'll be a show that knocks your socks off, so it's worth having a quick peek inside when you're at the beach.

Bondi Pavilion, Queen Elizabeth Dr., Bondi. © **(02) 8362 3400.** www.waverley.nsw. gov.au. Daily 10am–5pm. Bus: 380 or 389. Map p. 98.

★ **Brett Whiteley Studio** `FREE`   Tucked away down a back alley, the studio of late artist Brett Whiteley can be hard to find (look for the tell-tale matches out the front), but it's worth the effort. It's full of memorabilia, photographs, objects, postcards, furniture, musical items and sketchbooks, but the main reason to visit is the changing exhibitions of the artist's works. On Saturday the studio is often host to a life-drawing workshop, so if nudity offends go on Sunday.

2 Raper St. (near Devonshire and Crown sts.), Surry Hills. © **1800 679 278** (in Australia). www.brettwhiteley.org. Sat and Sun 10am–4pm. Bus: 301, 302 or 303 from Castlereagh St (near King St). Map p. 96.

CarriageWorks `FREE`   The old Eveleigh railway sheds have been transformed into a contemporary arts centre with theatre spaces, galleries and an exhibition space. There's usually some weird and wonderful installation art to see and a range of exhibitions with everything from art by homeless people to urban industrial design, photography and sculpture. Check the website for details of what's on.

245 Wilson St., Redfern. © **(02) 8571 9099.** www.carriageworks.com.au. Mon–Fri 10am–5pm, Sat 9am–1pm. Train: Redfern. Map p. 100.

Chalk Horse `FREE`   Chalk Horse is a commercial art gallery that promotes the work of emerging artists. There are often some really good photographic essays on show here.

94 Cooper St., Surry Hills. © **(02) 9211 8999.** www.chalkhorse.com.au. Wed–Sat noon–6pm. Bus: 301 or 302. Map p. 96.

China Heights `FREE`   Shows change weekly in this third-storey warehouse gallery and studio space and include works by local artists, photographers and designers.

Level 3, 257 Crown St., Darlinghurst. www.chinaheights.com. Sat–Wed noon–5pm. Bus: 378 or 380. Map p. 96.

FREE Art for Free

The University of NSW's College of Fine Arts (COFA; www.cofa.unsw. edu.au) likes to show off the art of its students. And why not? They're among the best in the city.

- Check out the work of some of the country's best artists before they get famous at **COFAspace,** on the ground level of E Block, corner of Oxford Street and Greens Road in Paddington (© **(02) 9385 0684**) from Monday to Friday 10am to 4pm. Showcasing the work of students, the gallery has a little bit of everything at any given time, from mixed media and photography to traditional ink and paper works. Map p. 96.

- The **Ivan Dougherty Gallery** at the corner of Selwyn Street and Albion Avenue, Paddington (© **(02) 9385 0726**) holds 10 exhibitions each year, all with a focus on Australian and international 20th century and contemporary art. It's open Monday to Saturday from 10am to 5pm. Map p. 98.

- The **Kudos Gallery** at St Sophia Hall, 6 Napier Street, Paddington (© **(02) 9326 0034**) shows the work of students. Expect quite a lot of experimental art 'exploring emerging concepts', although you'll sometimes find more traditional, slightly easier to understand art on show as well. It's open Wednesday to Friday 11am to 6pm and Saturday 11am to 4pm. Map p. 96.

- It's not about how big the gallery is, but what's in it. At just 3 feet square, the aptly named **Three Foot Square Gallery** is the ultimate hole-in-the-wall art show at the main entrance to COFA on Greens Road, Paddington. It is open 24 hours and is illuminated at night. Map p. 96.

Eva Breuer Art Dealer FREE Seriously cashed-up art buyers and investors get their art from here, so try and make like you've got lots of dosh if you visit. If you do fool the people at the front desk, you'll be treated to some of the finest big-name Australian art to be found outside the institutional galleries.

83 Moncur St., Woollahra. 📞 **(02) 9362 0297.** www.evabreuerartdealer.com.au. Tues–Fri 10am–6pm, Sat 10am–5pm. Map p. 98.

Firstdraft FREE   Non-profit artist-run gallery where you can see the work of emerging artists. There tends to be a focus on new technology and performance and lots of video art.

116 Chalmers St., Surry Hills. 📞 **(02) 9698 3665.** www.firstdraftgallery.com. Wed–Sat noon–6pm. Train: Central. Bus: 308. Map p. 100.

★ **Glass Artists' Gallery** FREE   Gorgeous contemporary art glass by some of the best glass artists in Australia and New Zealand, as well as international artists. Beautiful, beautiful stuff.

70 Glebe Point Rd., Glebe. 📞 **(02) 9552 1552.** www.glassartistsgallery.com.au. Tues–Sat 10am–6pm, Sun 1pm–5pm. Bus: 431 or 433. Map p. 100.

Greg Wilson Gallery FREE   I love the quirky metal sculptures on show here, but there are also plenty of paintings by Greg Wilson, who discovered his passion for art after a near-fatal motorcycle accident. His work also hangs in Parliament House in Canberra, the Australian Consulate in New York and the home of Nelson Mandela in South Africa, among other places.

107A Shepherd St., Chippendale. 📞 **(02) 4998 6772.** www.gregwilsongallery.com. Tues–Sat 10.30am–5.30pm. Bus: 352. Map p. 100.

Harrington Street Gallery FREE   This is one of Sydney's longest continuously running artists' co-ops, and a good place to check out the work of some of Sydney's emerging artists. Exhibitions change monthly.

17 Meagher St., Chippendale. 📞 **(02) 9319 7378.** www.harringtonstreetgallery.com. Tues–Sun 10am–4pm. Train: Central. Map p. 100.

★ **Hogarth Galleries** FREE   This private gallery has been showing and selling high-end Aboriginal art since 1972, long before Aboriginal canvases became fashionable and valuable. If you're looking to take some art home with you, be warned that it's not cheap, but it *is* the best you'll see outside a public gallery.

7 Walker Lane (off Liverpool St. from Oxford St.), Paddington. 📞 **(02) 9360 6839.** www.aboriginalartcentre.com.au. Tours available for a fee; bookings are essential. Tues–Sat 10am–5pm. Bus: 378 or 380. Map p. 96.

Inner City Clayworkers Gallery FREE   This co-op of potters produces some stunning ceramics. The exhibitions, which often include guest potters from interstate, are almost always good, but highlight of the year is the Sydney Teapot Show (usually in August when the gallery is open daily), which is an exhibition of teapots of all kinds— functional to whimsical; elegant to bizarre.

Cnr. St Johns Rd. and Darghan St., Glebe. ℂ **(02) 9692 9717.** www.clayworkers.com. au. Thurs–Sun 10.30am–6pm. Bus: 431 or 433. Map p. 100.

Japan Foundation Gallery FREE Changing exhibitions of Japanese art, with everything from delicate ceramics and origami to anime and manga.

Shop 23, level 1, Chifley Plaza, 2 Chifley Sq., Sydney. ℂ **(02) 8239 0055.** www.jpf.org. au. Mon–Fri 11am–4pm. Train: Martin Place. Map p. 96.

Kate Owen Gallery FREE See three floors of Aboriginal art, sourced from a variety of outback communities. Kate Owen, the gallery owner, is also an artist and paints contemporary-style images of the outback, which are also on show in the gallery.

680 Darling St., Rozelle. ℂ **(02) 9555 5283.** www.kateowengallery.com. Wed–Sun 11am–6pm. Bus: 432, 433, 434 or 445. Map p. 95.

Macquarie University Art Gallery & Sculpture Park FREE Almost all of the important post-1960s Australian artists are represented in this gallery at Macquarie University, along with indigenous artworks. There are changing exhibitions and a sculpture park with almost 100 works of art spread across the entire campus. You can arrange a **free** guided tour by calling the number below. Also worth seeing is the collection of Australian art in the university library.

Macquarie University, Building E11A, Balaclava Rd., North Ryde. ℂ **(02) 9850 7437.** www.artgallery.mq.edu.au. Mon–Fri 10am–5pm. Train: Macquarie University. Map p. 99.

Manly Art Gallery & Museum FREE There's a good collection of Australian art here, including Tom Robert's *The Flower Sellers*, but the standout is the ceramics collection, which traces the development of styles and techniques in Australia since 1945. The attached museum focuses on the history of Manly and the northern beaches with lots of historical photos and is worth visiting for the displays of swimwear, surfboards and beach memorabilia. **Sunday @ the Gallery** is a program of free events held—you guessed it—every Sunday.

West Esplanade, Manly. ℂ **(02) 9976 1420.** www.manly.nsw.gov.au/gallery. Tues– Sun 10am–5pm. Ferry: Manly. Map p. 99.

Martin Browne Fine Art `FREE` This spacious, light-filled commercial art gallery has a changing program of monthly exhibitions of modern and contemporary Australian and international artists.

57 Macleay St., Potts Point. ✆ **(02) 9331 7997.** www.martinbrownefineart.com. Tues–Sun 11am–6pm. Train: Kings Cross. Map p. 96.

MOP `FREE` MOP is an artist-run gallery with three rooms of changing art installations, usually featuring a different artist in each room. It's almost always worth a look.

2/39 Abercrombie St., Chippendale. ✆ **(02) 9699 3955.** www.mop.org.au. Thurs–Sat 1–6pm, Sun and Mon 1–5pm. Bus: 352. Map p. 100.

★ **Museum of Contemporary Art** `FREE` 'Big, bold, bright, wonderful and just plain weird' is the best way to describe the eclectic range of works and the program of exhibitions in this museum dedicated to contemporary art. If you subscribe to the I-don't-know-much-about-art-but-I-know-what-I-like school, take one of the free guided tours and see if it makes any more sense.

140 George St., The Rocks. ✆ **(02) 9245 2400.** www.mca.com.au. Daily 10am–5pm, tours Mon–Fri 11am and 1pm, Sat and Sun noon and 1.30pm. Train: Circular Quay. Map p. 96.

National Art School (NAS) Gallery `FREE` Housed in the old Darlinghurst Gaol (built in 1836), the NAS Gallery exhibits group and solo shows by Australian and international artists, including the end-of-year showcase by graduating students. The annual exhibition of the finalists of the Blake Prize (a national competition for the best artwork exploring the religious and spiritual in art, usually showing in September/October) is definitely worth seeing.

Cnr. Forbes and Burton sts., Darlinghurst. ✆ **(02) 9339 8744.** www.nas.edu.au. Mon–Sat 10am–4pm. Bus: 378, 380. Map p. 96.

NG Art Gallery `FREE` This is a commercial gallery specialising in contemporary Australian art. The work is not cheap, but it certainly doesn't hurt to look.

Upstairs, 3 Little Queen St., Chippendale. ✆ **(02) 9318 2992.** www.ngart.com.au. Tues–Fri 11am–10pm, Sat 9am–10pm. Train: Central, then 10-min. walk. Bus: 352. Map p. 100.

★ **Object Gallery** `FREE` The latest in cutting-edge Australian craft and design, with everything from weird and wonderful, but definitely not wearable, clothes to fine jewellery, furniture and industrial design, depending on the exhibition of the day.

417 Bourke St., Surry Hills. ℂ **(02) 9361 4511.** www.object.com.au. Tues–Sun 10am–6pm. Bus: 378 or 380, walk from Taylor Square. Map p. 96.

★ **Outré Gallery** `FREE`   Half shop, half gallery space; if you are into pop art, counter-culture and graphic design you'll love this place. It has the best contemporary pop art in the city with everything from original artworks to ceramic and vinyl toys. Exhibitions change monthly.

13A Burton St., Darlinghurst. ℂ **(02) 9332 2776.** www.outregallery.com. Tues–Sat 11am–6pm, Sun noon–4pm. Bus: 378 or 380. Map p. 96.

Ray Hughes Gallery `FREE`   One of the city's best private contemporary art galleries with changing exhibitions, focusing on Australian, New Zealand and Chinese contemporary artists and German expressionist graphics.

270 Devonshire St., Surry Hills. ℂ **(02) 9698 3200.** www.rayhughesgallery.com. Tues–Sat 10am–6pm. Bus: 301, 302 or 303 from Castlereagh St (near King St). Map p. 96.

Tap Gallery `FREE`   There's always something weird and wonderful going on at this contemporary artist-run gallery that is dedicated to nurturing emerging artists. There's also a theatre here, so you can often catch some performance art as well. I guess it depends on your notion of what's cheap and what's not, but this place was recently voted Sydney's best gallery for art under $5000.

278 Palmer St., Darlinghurst. ℂ **(02) 9361 0440.** www.tapgallery.org.au. Daily noon–6pm. Bus: 378 or 380. Map p. 96.

The Tin Sheds Gallery `FREE`   This gallery has exhibitions of contemporary art, across all mediums, and occasionally architecture. It's affiliated with the University of Sydney, but shows work from professional artists as well as senior students. Exhibitions usually change every three weeks.

Faculty of Architecure, 148 City Rd., The University of Sydney. ℂ **(02) 9351 3115.** Tues–Sat 11am–5pm, Bus: 370, 423,424, 426. Map p. 100.

Urban Uprising `FREE`   Urban Uprising takes art off the streets and hangs it on the walls. Gritty, realistic and confronting are some of the ways to best describe the brand of urban art that is on show here.

314 Crown St., Darlinghurst. ℂ **(02) 9331 6614.** www.urbanuprising.com.au. Mon–Sat noon–7pm. Bus: 378 or 380. Map p. 96.

FREE Opening Night Specials

Opening nights at commercial art galleries are a great way to see new art for free—and enjoy a free glass of wine and some nibblies while you're at it. Here are three favourite opening night hangouts. Wear black.

- There's an opening every Friday night at **China Heights Gallery** (257 Crown St., Darlinghurst; www.chinaheights.com) from 6.30pm until around 9pm (p. 117). Map p. 96.

- Exhibitions open on Tuesday nights at **Kudos Gallery** (St Sophia Hall, 6 Napier Street, Paddington; www.cofa.unsw.edu.au.) from 5 to 7.30pm; sometimes weekly, sometimes fortnightly (p. 118). Map p. 96.

- **NG Art Gallery** (Upstairs, 3 Little Queen Street, Chippendale; www.ngart.com.au) hosts Monthly openings on Tuesdays 6 to 8pm (p. 121). Map p. 100.

White Rabbit FREE   This privately owned gallery is a four-storey temple to one woman's passion for collecting contemporary Chinese art. There are more than 450 artworks on show here, all made post-2000, but, unlike most private galleries, they are not for sale.

30 Balfour St., Chippendale. © **(02) 8399 2867.** www.whiterabbitcollection.org. Thurs–Sun 10am–6pm. Train: Central, then 10-min. walk. Bus: 352. Map p. 100.

4 Street Art & Public Sculpture

Archibald Fountain FREE   In the northern section of Hyde Park is the Art Deco Archibald Fountain, a bronze Apollo surrounded by horses' heads, dolphins and tortoises that was erected in 1932 to commemorate the ties between Australia and France in World War I. It's a lovely place to be on a hot day.

Hyde Park, Sydney. Daily 24 hours. Train: St James or Museum. Map p. 96.

★ **Edge of the Trees** FREE   Take a wander around the *Edge of the Trees* sculpture in the forecourt of the Museum of Sydney to hear

Koori (Aboriginal) voices reciting the names of places that have today been swallowed up by the modern city.

Cnr. Phillip and Bridge sts., Sydney. Daily 24 hr. Train: Circular Quay. Map p. 96.

Golden Water Mouth FREE The five natural elements (gold, water, wood, fire and earth) in this arresting 10m-high sculpture in Chinatown made from a dead tree trunk are meant to bring good fortune and promote positive energy. Going on the buzz in nearby Dixon Street I'd say it works.

Cnr. George and Hay sts., Haymarket. Daily 24 hr. Train: Central. Map p. 96.

Il Porcellino FREE Rub the nose of the wild boar (a copy of the 500-year-old one in Florence, Italy) on the top of the hill outside the Sydney Hospital for good luck.

Macquarie St., Sydney. Daily 24 hr. Train: Martin Place. Map p. 96.

Newtown Street Art FREE Some of the city's most vibrant street art and murals can be found in and around the inner-west suburb of Newtown. The best place to go is along King Street and the adjoining streets and laneways to Enmore Road.

King St. and Enmore Rd., Newtown. Daily 24 hr. Train: Newtown. Map p. 100.

P&O Wall Fountain FREE Tom Bass's fountain on the wall of the P&O Building in Hunter Street has been affectionately known as 'The Urinal' since the editors of the irreverent '60s magazine, *Oz,* were photographed while pretending to use it as one. They were sued and sentenced to jail for 'obscenity and encouraging public urination', and the fountain has been infamous ever since.

55 Hunter St., Sydney. Daily 24 hr. Train: Martin Place. Map p. 96.

Passage FREE The water sculpture by Anne Graham in Martin Place consists of three bronze balls, reflection pools and fountains and an eerie mist that rises every 10 minutes from pavement grilles. According to the artist it 'creates an illusion of the space once occupied by past residents'. The fog and mist sometimes disrupts traffic on Macquarie Street if the wind is blowing the wrong way.

Martin Pl., Sydney. Daily 24 hr. Train: Martin Place. Map p. 96.

Silver Shish Kebab FREE The real name of this stainless steel column of cubes by Bert Flugelman is *The Pyramid Tower*, but everyone just calls it the 'Silver Shish Kebab'. I suspect I may be one of the few people in the city who loves it—one former Lord Mayor hated it so much he ordered it moved from its original spot in Martin Place to its current (half-hidden) location in Spring Street. I think the precariously balanced silver blocks brighten up even the greyest day.

Cnr. Pitt and Spring sts., Sydney. Daily 24 hr. Train: Circular Quay. Map p. 96

Still Life with Stone & Car `FREE`   I love people-watching around Jimmie Durham's crumpled red Ford Festiva convertible that has a huge boulder inside it. It appears to have been left abandoned in the middle of a roundabout and listening to out-of-towners surmise theories on how and what possibly could have happened is priceless! It's part of a sculpture trail in Walsh Bay (p. 127).

Cnr. Hickson Rd. and Pottinger St., Walsh Bay. Daily 24 hr. Train: Circular Quay. Map p. 96.

Sydney Olympic Park `FREE`   The former industrial wasteland and site of the 2000 Olympics has one of the largest collections of urban art in the country. There are more than 50 pieces of public art on show here, providing a unique record of the cultural history of the Sydney Olympic Park, with works reflecting the early industrial uses of the site through to the Olympic Games. Favourites include Robert Owen's *Discobulus*, a 7m-wide discus; *The Sprinter*, a 12m-high, 3.5 tonne, 3-D steel athlete that once adorned the top of Sydney Tower in the lead up to the Olympics (where quite frankly, it looked very silly, but here it looks good) and *Games Memories*, an installation of poles incorporating Olympic memorabilia, visual art, AV presentations and the names of volunteers at the 2000 Sydney Olympics.

Australia Ave., Sydney Olympic Park. ✆ **(02) 9714 7888.** www.sydneyolympicpark. com.au. Daily during daylight hours. Train: Sydney Olympic Park. Map p. 95.

Tank Stream Fountain `FREE`   I confess to finding this fountain festooned with Australian frogs, snakes, lizards and turtles a little twee, but I'm fascinated by what it represents. The Tank Stream was the original fresh water source used by the convicts and their gaolers when the colony was first established, but today it has completely disappeared underground and is now just part of the stormwater drainage system. This fountain commemorates what Sydney was like before it was Sydney.

Cnr. Alfred and Pitt sts., Circular Quay. Daily 24 hr. Train: Circular Quay. Map p. 96.

5 Walking Tours

City of Sydney Historical Walking Tours FREE The City of Sydney website has a series of excellent themed walking tours that you can download and follow under your own steam. The tours take around two hours to walk and each brochure (which you can download in PDF format or pick up from Community Centres, libraries or the Sydney Visitor Centre on the corner of Argyle and Playfair streets in The Rocks) includes a map with numbered points of interest along the way.

Various places. www.cityofsydney.nsw.gov.au and search for 'historical walking tours'. Map p. 96.

I'm Free Walking Tour FREE A three-hour guided walking tour of central Sydney and The Rocks that takes in most of the main attractions along the way. The tours are free, but the guides do work for tips, so pay whatever you think the tour is worth. You don't need to book, and they go whatever the weather—look for the guides wearing a fluorescent green T-shirt at the meeting spot at the anchor in Town Hall Square.

Town Hall Square, George St., Sydney. www.imfree.com.au. Tues, Thurs and Sat 10.30am. Train: Town Hall. Map p. 96.

MP3 Walking Tours Tour Sydney at your own pace with your MP3 player by downloading a podcast from www.walkingtours.com.au. There are five tours to choose from (Centennial Park, Darlinghurst, Paddington, Watsons Bay and Woolloomooloo) with a few more in the pipeline. Each tour takes around 2½ hours to walk and the well-researched stories behind the places you visit are brought to life through the voices of actors. You can download an MP3 file and print a map from the website, or if you prefer, they will burn the tour on a CD for you and post it to you.

www.walkingtours.com.au. Tours are $9.95 each. MC, V.

★ **Royal Botanic Garden Tours** FREE The extraordinarily knowledgeable and passionate volunteer guides will lead you on a 90-minute guided walk through the Royal Botanic Gardens (p. 131) each day at 10.30am, for free. You can also join a one-hour guided walk at 1pm from March to November. Both tours depart from the information counter at the Palm Grove Centre.

Royal Botanic Gardens, Mrs Macquaries Rd., Sydney. ℂ **(02) 9231 8134.** Train: Martin Place or Circular Quay. Map p. 96.

Walsh Bay Heritage & Sculpture Walks `FREE` Take a self-guided wander around the heritage finger wharves of Walsh Bay on the western side of The Rocks, following the story of the area and the people who worked and lived there on story boards and artefacts on display. Juxtaposed against all this gritty industrial heritage is a modern sculpture trail with supersized bright art installations from some of Australia's best-known artists, including Brett Whiteley. You can download maps and guides from the website.

Walsh Bay. www.walshbaysydney.com.au. Train: Circular Quay, then a 5-min. walk. Map p. 96.

Writers Walk `FREE` Keep an eye out for the bronze plaques embedded in the footpath on both the eastern and western arms of Circular Quay. Each of 50 discs has a quote about Sydney by famous writers from home and abroad.

Circular Quay. Train: Circular Quay. Map p. 96.

6 Bushwalks

Sydney is one of the few cities in the world where you can head into the bush, without leaving the city limits. Many of the walks also boast amazing cliff-top and harbour views.

★ **Bronte to Bondi Coastal Walk** `FREE` One of the best urban walks in the world, it's almost entirely along the cliff-top from Bronte Beach to Bondi Beach (p. 134).

Bronte Rd., Bronte. Allow around 90 min. Bus: 378 to Bronte Beach. Map p. 98.

Cape Bailey Coastal Walk `FREE` This is where then Lieutenant James Cook first stepped ashore on the continent in 1770. The Cape Bailey Track is a 12.5km walk from Cook's Landing Place Park around the Kurnell Peninsula towards Cronulla in the Botany Bay National Park. Drop in to the Kurnell Discovery Centre for a display that looks at the first contact between Aboriginal people and the crew of Cook's ship, the *Endeavour*. Other highlights include the Cape Bailey Lighthouse, lots of sea birds and wildflowers in spring.

Botany Bay National Park, Kurnell. Allow 3–4 hr. Train: Cronulla, then bus 67 to Kurnell. Map p. 98.

★ **Federation Cliff Walk** `FREE` This 5km walkway from Dover Heights on the northern side of Bondi to Diamond Bay just south of

Watsons Bay at the tip of South Head continues on from the Bronte to Bondi Coastal Walk (p. 250).

Lola Rd., Dover Heights. Allow around 90 min. Bus 389 to North Bondi. Map p. 98.

Frenchmans Bay Walk `FREE` Days after Cook and company arrived, French explorer Comte de Lapérouse showed up and you can do a beautiful coastal walk along the bay that was named in his honour, following around the headland now known as Cape Banks. Return the way you came, or loop back beside the golf course.

Anzac Pde., La Perouse. Allow around 2 hr. Bus: 394 to La Perouse. Map p. 98.

★ **Hermitage Foreshore Walk** `FREE` This is a delightful and easy stroll through Sydney Harbour National Park's native bushland to Rose Bay with great harbour views along the way.

Greycliffe Ave., Vaucluse. Allow around 30 min. Bus: 325 to Neilsen Park. Map p. 98.

★ **Manly Scenic Walkway** `FREE` A 9.5km coastal walking trail from The Spit Bridge to Manly (p. 246). Highlights include beaches, an historic lighthouse, Aboriginal sites, pockets of subtropical rainforest and sweeping views of the harbour and city skyline.

Avona Cres. (under The Spit Bridge), Seaforth. Allow 3–4 hours. Bus: any to Manly or Northern Beaches from Wynyard (get off just before The Spit Bridge). Map p. 99.

Mosman Foreshore & Bradleys Head Walk `FREE` This is a 10km walk with a steep section about a third of the way along, although you can break it up into two shorter walks if you wish. The first 2km section from Cremorne to Mosman hugs the shoreline of a deep inlet known as Mosman Bay, which was once a whaling station. From Mosman Wharf (you can return to the city via ferry from here) the walk leads up a steep section of suburban streets up over Curraghbeena Point (climb the steps opposite the wharf, then follow Trumfield Lane into McLeod Street) then plunges back into bushland to trace the foreshore around Bradleys Head and around to Chowder Bay (p. 94) and has some fantastic city and Opera House views along the way.

Milson Rd., Cremorne. Allow 3–4 hr. Ferry: Cremorne (or Mosman). Map p. 98.

★ **North Head Walk** `FREE` Explore the former quarantine station (now called Q Station), built in 1832 and the first point of arrival for immigrants until 1984. You can learn about their stories at the visitor centre down at the wharf. Tours are expensive (though well worth a splurge, particularly if you're partial to ghost stories), but you can wander around the grounds for free. Look for the engravings in the cliffs beside Quarantine Beach, where hundreds of internees scratched their names and the name of the ship they arrived on into the sandstone. Take a detour to Collins Beach (p. 140) to see if you can spot some little penguins, then climb the hill to the School of Artillery (p. 102). At the top of the headland is the 20-minute Fairfax Walk, where you'll get great views across the harbour to South Head and the city.

North Head Walk: East Esplanade, Manly; ferry Manly; allow 2 hr. Q Station: North Head Scenic Dr, Manly; $\textcircled{C}$ **(02) 9977 5145**; www.qstation.com.au; ferry to Manly, then bus 135 to Q Station, though it is not a frequent service. Map p. 99.

Palm Beach FREE   It's a bit of steep slog in sections, but the walk along Palm Beach and around Barrenjoey Head, past the lighthouse is well worth doing on a sunny day. Depending on which way you do the circuit you'll have Pittwater on one side, and Palm Beach on the other.

Ocean Rd., Palm Beach. Allow 90 min. Bus: 190. Map p. 101.

7 Parks & Gardens

Bicentennial Park Wetlands FREE   Follow the boardwalk at Bicentennial Park and explore a rare pocket of wetland surrounded by urban development. Created to celebrate Australia's Bicentenary in 1988, the 100-hectare parkland was once an old rubbish dump, but its rebirth included the conservation of a wetland on the Parramatta River and it's now a haven for birdlife and part of Sydney Olympic Park. There are **free** barbecues, picnic areas, playgrounds, pathways and cycling paths, as well as access to the wetlands, salt marsh and bird hides.

Australia Ave., Sydney Olympic Park. Train: Sydney Olympic Park. Map p. 95.

Cadi Jam Ora FREE   Also called the *First Encounters Garden*, these gardens showcase the many Aboriginal uses of native plants. The site was once an important ceremonial site and the scene of many of the first (and often tragic) encounters between Europeans and the local Cadigal people. A 52m 'storyline' tells the Aboriginal history of Sydney from The Dreaming to the present, compiled from more than 40 interviews with local Aboriginal people. Take a self-guided tour or take a tour with an Aboriginal guide.

Royal Botanic Gardens, Mrs Macquaries Rd., Sydney. To book a tour $\textcircled{C}$ **(02) 9231 8134.** Tour prices on request. MC, V. Train: Martin Place or Circular Quay. Map p. 96.

★ **Centennial Park** FREE   This grand, 189-hecatre park was dedicated by Sir Henry Parkes (the 'father of Federation') in 1888 as part
of the centenary celebrations and was also the site of the inauguration
of Australian Federation in 1901. The 10 ponds are popular picnic
spots and the 3.6km Grand Drive is a favourite spot to walk, run,
cycle or rollerblade. It's one of the few inner-city parks in the world
where you can go horse riding. To book a horse ride or lesson, contact the **Centennial Parklands Equestrian Centre**. FINE PRINT Centennial Park's opening hours are sunrise to sunset. All vehicles must
leave the park before sunset or pay a gate opening fee.

Bordered by Oxford St., York, Darley and Alison rds., Centennial Park. ✆ **(02) 9332
2809.** www.centennialparklands.com.au. Centennial Parklands Equestrian Centre:
✆ **(02) 9332 2809.** www.cpequestrian.com.au. Prices vary. Bus: 339, 352, 355, 371,
372, 373, 374, 376, 377, 378 or 380. Map p. 98.

Hyde Park FREE   Named after London's Hyde Park, this pocket of
green that covers two large city blocks in the middle of the CBD was
originally a racecourse. In the southern section you'll find the Art
Deco War Memorial, built in 1934 as a tribute to those who died in
World War I (p. 103). In the northern section is the flamboyant
Archibald Fountain (p. 123). The two features are linked by an impressive fig-lined avenue. On the western side of the park, near the corner
of Elizabeth and Market streets is a giant chess set. It's free to play, but
you'll have to negotiate playing time with the group of old men who
are there rain, hail or shine. It's great street theatre just to watch.

Bordered by Park, College, Liverpool and Elizabeth sts., Sydney. Train: St James or
Museum. Map p. 96.

★ **Paddington Reservoir Garden** FREE   One of Sydney's newest
gardens is also one of its best-kept secrets; this sunken garden was
planted at the bottom of a reservoir that was built in 1866. It was
decommissioned in 1899, when it became a storage facility and then
a garage with a park on top—until the roof collapsed in 1990. Then it
became a graffitied grotto (the graffiti's still there, which adds to the
delightfully shadowy atmosphere) and then it was reborn as a landscaped park, complete with an ornamental pond and hanging gardens around the edges. It feels very Romanesque and otherworldly
and is a great place to hide away from the world.

Cnr. Oxford and Oatley sts., Paddington. Bus: 378 or 380. Map p. 98.

★ **The Royal Botanic Gardens & The Domain** FREE A favourite spot for a picnic or early morning walk, these gardens are home to more than a million specimens, some of which were planted by the first fleeters 220 years ago. Don't miss the Sydney Tropical Centre in the glass pyramid and the Rare and Threatened Plants Garden, which includes the recently rediscovered Wollemi Pine, previously thought to be extinct.

Mrs Macquaries Rd., Sydney. ℭ **(02) 9231 8134.** Admission free, except to the Sydney Tropical Centre: $5.50 adults, $4.50 kids, $11 for families. Train: Martin Place or Circular Quay. Map p. 96.

Tumbalong Park FREE Keeping the kids amused all day can be expensive, so Tumbalong Park is a great place to give your wallet a rest while the kids burn off some excess energy in the playground and splashing in the fountains if it's hot.

Southern section of Darling Harbour. Monorail: Darling Park. Map p. 96.

Walama (Ballast Point Park) FREE The great views across the water and Goat Island to the Harbour Bridge are just two of the reasons to go to this newly created park on Balmain Point. It was, until late 2009, an abandoned old fuel depot and, before that, a quarry for ship's ballast. The industrial heritage has been retained with some interesting art installations and, although it will be a little bare until the landscaped areas grow, it's a great spot for a time out that even most locals don't yet know about.

End of Ballast Point Rd., Birchgrove. Bus: 432 or 441. Ferry: Birchgrove. Map p. 95.

8 Free (& Dirt Cheap) Barbecues

There's nothing more 'Sydney' than a Sunday barbie. Here's some great spots to sizzle some summertime snags for free (or dirt cheap).

Balls Head Reserve FREE There are great harbour views, a playground for the kids and some lovely walking tracks—including a wheelchair-friendly track along the crest of the ridge—and free barbecues.

Balls Head Drive, Waverton. Train: Waverton. Map p. 95.

Biddigal Reserve Coin-operated barbies overlook the northern end of Bondi Beach.

Ramsgate Ave., Bondi. Bus: 380 or 389. Map p. 98.

Blackwattle Bay Park `FREE`   Take a walk around the foreshore of Glebe Point and enjoy the views of the stunning Anzac Bridge, the longest cable-stayed bridge in Australia. The gas-fired barbecues are free.

Via Cook and Oxley sts., Glebe. Bus: 431 or 433. Map p. 100.

★ **Bronte Park**   This one tops my list as the best spot in Sydney to turn a sausage. This large grassy park flanking Bronte Beach has a playground for the kids and lots of shade, lots of tables and lots of space to move, plus eight barbecues that cost just 20¢ to heat up. It gets busy, so get there early to grab the best spots.

Bronte Rd., Bronte. Bus: 378. Map p. 98.

Bundock Park `FREE`   Clovelly is more like a giant saltwater swimming pool than a beach, so it's a great place for little kids to paddle. This park is located adjacent to the beach and has free barbecues at either end.

Via Eastbourne Ave. or Clovelly Rd., Clovelly. Bus: 339. Map p. 98.

Centennial Park `FREE`   There are eight free barbecues in this enormous park, but it's popular with enormous family groups, so the best spots can be overrun with clan gatherings on weekends. Go midweek and you'll have the place practically to yourself.

Bordered by Oxford Street, York, Darley and Alison rds., Centennial Park. ✆ **(02) 9332 2809.** www.centennialparklands.com.au. Bus: 339, 352, 355, 371, 372, 373, 374, 376, 377, 378 or 380. Map p. 98.

Clyne Reserve `FREE`   If you want to have a barbecue within cooee of the city centre this tiny little park, behind Walsh Bay on the western side of The Rocks, is your best bet. There's a good playground for kids here as well.

2 Merriman St., Millers Point. Train: Circular Quay. Bus: 431. Map p. 96.

★ **Cockatoo Island**   Buy a barbecue pack from the Muster Cafe on the island or bring your own (no BYO alcohol, but you can buy it there) and cook yourself up a middle-of-the-harbour feast on the coin-operated barbecues in the camping area (p. 94).

Cockatoo Island. Ferry: Cockatoo Island. Map p. 95.

Coogee Beach `FREE`   You'll find beachside barbecues at Goldstein Reserve and in Grant Reserve at the southern end of Coogee Beach.

Goldstein Reserve: opp. Arden St., Coogee. Grant Reserve: Beach St., Coogee. Bus: 372, 373 or 374. Map p. 98.

Frenchmans Bay Reserve FREE On the shores of Botany Bay, La Perouse is a beach named for one of the great could-have-been moments in history. French explorer Comte de Lapérouse landed here days after the First Fleet in January 1788, narrowly missing out on the chance to claim the country for France. The electric barbecues are free.

Endeavour Ave., La Perouse. Bus: 394. Map p. 98.

Lane Cove National Park FREE Lane Cove River winds through a peaceful bushland valley just beyond the backyard fences of lower North Shore suburbia near Chatswood. There are more than 30 picnic grounds, but Carter Creek, Heron Flat, The Oaks and Tunks Hill all have free electric hotplates.

Fullers Rd., Lane Cove. Admission is free if you enter on foot or by bus, but is $7 per car. No credit cards. Bus: 545 from Chatswood Station. Map p. 99.

Mort Bay Park FREE There are two covered barbecue areas and a great childrens' playground in this park and it's right near the wharf, which means it has nice water views.

McKell St., Balmain. Bus: 433 or 434. Ferry: Balmain. Map p. 95.

Pyrmont Point Park FREE Check out the water views (there are glimpses of the Harbour Bridge, but mostly you look out across to Balmain) and make use of the five free barbecues.

Pirrama Rd., Pyrmont. Bus: 443 or 449. Map p. 95.

Shelly Beach FREE From the southern end of Manly Beach walk to tiny Shelly Beach, a sheltered north-facing pocket of sand that is overlooked by most visitors, but is a favourite with locals, especially those with kids. It's also a terrific snorkelling spot with lots of fish and there are six free gas barbecues and picnic facilities.

Marine Parade, Manly. Ferry: Manly. Map p. 99.

Sydney Olympic Park FREE There are plenty of spots for a free fry-up here (p. 125), with barbecues dotted all over the place. The best spots include Bicentennial Park, The Overflow, Wentworth Common, Blaxland Common and Archery Park.

Enter via Marjorie Jackson Pkwy. or Australia Ave., Sydney Olympic Park. ℂ **(02) 9714 7888.** www.sydneyolympicpark.com.au. Train: Sydney Olympic Park. Map p. 95.

Tamarama Park The northern neighbour of Bronte Beach, 'Glamarama', as it's known by locals, tends to be a bit of a scene, but it does have a barbecues that cost just 20¢.

Gaerloch Ave., Tamarama. Bus: 361. Map p. 98.

9 Life's a Beach

One of the very best ways to spend no money in Sydney is to spend a day at the beach. But, with almost 40 beaches unfurling to the north and south of the city, how do you decide where to go? Here's a quick and easy guide to a dozen of the best beaches in town, and how to get to them.

★ **Bondi Beach** FREE Sydney's most famous beach (and its busiest), it's the place to see—and be seen—and is popular with tourists and locals alike. Forget about parking and take the bus, and wear your best cossie so you can strut your stuff alongside visiting celebrities. Surf livesavers are on patrol year-round and the northern end of the beach is surfboard free. Watch out for rips and stay between the flags.

Campbell Pde., Bondi Beach. Bus: 380, 389 or 333. Map p. 98.

★ **Bronte Beach** FREE A popular family beach (kids love the playground), Bronte offers a slightly quieter alternative to nearby Bondi, and is linked to its more famous neighbour by the equally famous Coastal Walk (p. 250). This is where the rich and famous go when they don't want to be seen. Beware the notorious 'Bronte Express,' a fast-moving permanent rip that pushes swimmers up against the southern headland.

Bronte Rd., Bronte. Bus: 378. Map p. 98.

Coogee Beach FREE One of the city's safest swimming beaches, it's more laid-back and down-market in comparison to Bondi (but then, what beach isn't?); however, it still gets packed on hot summer Sundays.

Arden St., Coogee. Bus: 372, 373 or 374. Map p. 98.

Cronulla Beach FREE At a smidge under 5km long, this is Sydney's longest beach. It's also one of the only ones you can get to by train, which means it's popular with all sorts of people from all over Sydney.

The northern end, Kurnell, is accessible only by 4WD. The waves off Shark Island, a rocky ledge 100m offshore, are the biggest and most challenging in Sydney.

The Esplanade, Cronulla. Train: Cronulla. Map p. 98.

Dee Why Beach `FREE` Good for surfers, but lots of rips make it pretty average for swimmers, although some great oceanfront cafes make it great for people-watching.

The Strand, Dee Why. Bus: 178. Map p. 101.

Lady Bay Beach `FREE` If nudity offends, stay well clear of this secluded little harbour beach on the western tip of South Head near Watsons Bay. It's also known as Lady Jane Beach and clothing is strictly optional.

Cliff St., Watsons Bay. Bus: 325 or 380. Ferry: Watsons Bay. Map p. 98.

Manly Beach `FREE` Almost as iconic as Bondi, but without the rich and famous visitors. Legend has it that this is where our love affair with the beach began, when local lad William Goscher defied the law by swimming during daylight, which was just not the done thing back in 1902, sparking a craze for sea-swimming that has never abated. There's good surfing year-round. The beach is known by three names: Queenscliff at the northern end, North Steyne in the middle and South Steyne at the southern tip.

North Steyne, Manly. Ferry: Manly. Map p. 99.

Surf Safe & Sun Smart

For most visitors, the most dangerous thing they encounter in Sydney is the surf: *always* swim or surf at patrolled beaches and *always* swim between the red-and-yellow flags, which mark the safest areas for swimming. If you do get caught in a rip (a fast-moving current) and feel yourself being pulled out to sea, swim across the current, not against it, as most rips are long and narrow. Stay calm and raise your arm above your head to attract the attention of surf lifesavers—it's the signal that you need help. And always wear lots of sunscreen—skin cancer is one of the country's biggest killers.

Narrabeen Beach FREE A good beach for bodysurfing and sunbaking near the dunes in the northern corner. The lagoon entrance is a good swimming spot, especially for kids. **Sydney Lakeside Holiday Park** (p. 49) is one of the only caravan parks beside a beach in Sydney.

Ocean St., Narrabeen. Bus: 183 or 185. Map p. 101.

Newport Beach FREE Some of the country's best surfers have honed their skills here, including two-time world champion Tom Carroll. It's a bit of a hike, but it's nice and uncrowded—go midweek and you'll pretty much have the beach to yourself. Climb Bilgola headland for knockout views south to Manly and north to, well, forever.

Barrenjoey Rd., Newport Beach. Bus: 187 or 188 (from Wynyard). Map p. 101.

Palm Beach FREE The most northerly of the city's beaches is overlooked by some of Sydney's most expensive real estate, where a week's rent in the middle of summer can set you back $30,000. But the nice thing about 'Palmy' is you don't have to be rich to jump on a bus and stake out some golden sand. If it's good enough for Nicole Kidman, it's good enough for you! If you're a fan of TV soap *Home and Away* you'll know it as Summer Bay. Nudies hang out at the end of the beach near Barrenjoey Head (the one with the lighthouse).

Ocean Rd., Palm Beach. Bus: 190 (from Wynyard). Map p. 101.

★ **Parsley Bay & Shark Beach** FREE I've put these two sheltered harbour beaches together because they are only a few minutes' walk apart. Both are flanked by shady parklands (**Parsley Bay Reserve** and **Nielsen Park,** respectively) and seem to be the secret playground of the lucky locals. Go and spoil their fun by rolling out a picnic blanket and staking some of their territory as your own. Both beaches have shark-proof swimming areas and are great for small kids.

Parsley Bay: Horler Ave., Vaucluse. Shark Beach: Greycliffe Ave., Vaucluse. Bus: 325. Map p. 98.

Tamarama Beach FREE I could be mean and say that the reason you don't see many swimmers in the water is that they are too busy looking fabulous to risk getting wet and ruining their 'do, but it may be that it is regarded as the state's most dangerous patrolled beach. It's halfway along the Bronte to Bondi Coastal Walk (p. 250).

Gaerloch Ave., Tamarama. Bus: 361. Map p. 98.

10 Harbour & Ocean Pools

Andrew (Boy) Charlton Pool   In the heart of the Botanic Gardens with views across the Woolloomooloo side of the harbour, this is one of the few outdoor pools that are heated. Named after the Australian swimming legend of the 1920s, Andrew 'Boy' Charlton, it is believed to be the birthplace of the Australian crawl (freestyle) swimming stroke. Not surprisingly, laps are the order of the day and it's popular with the before- and after-work crowd.

Mrs Macquaries Rd., The Domain. ℂ **(02) 9358 6686.** Admission $5.70 adult, $3.90 kids. MC, V. Daily 6am–7pm (8pm daylight saving) Sept–early May. Train: Martin Place, then walk to the Royal Botanic Gardens. Map p. 98.

Bondi Baths   Sydney's most famous ocean pool is home to the Bondi Icebergs, a group of cold-water swimmers who have been known to add ice to the water in the middle of winter for added chill (p. 250). The pool is open to the public in winter and summer, but the ice is strictly optional for non-members. FINE PRINT The pool is closed for cleaning every Thursday.

1 Notts Ave., Bondi. ℂ **(02) 9130 4804.** Admission $4.50 adults, $2.50 kids. MC, V. Mon–Fri 6am–6.30pm, Sat and Sun 6.30am–6.30pm. Bus: 380 or 389. Map p. 98.

Bronte Baths FREE   Built into the rock at the southern end of Bronte Beach in 1887 by the local council to cater to the new 'sea bathing' fad, it was originally men only on Sunday and public holidays, and while the rules and fashions may have changed, the original irregular-shaped structure remains largely intact. It can be a little challenging in choppy seas. FINE PRINT The pool is closed for cleaning (usually at low tide) and when the weather is rough.

Bronte Rd., Bronte. Admission free. Daily 24 hr. Bus: 378. Map p. 98.

★ Clovelly Beach FREE   It's not exactly a pool, but it's not really a beach either. This deep bay is a great place to do some serious lap swimming. Wear a snorkel and mask for a free wildlife show while you're working out. If you prefer a more traditional pool, the 25m Geoff James Pool has marked lanes alongside the bay.

End of Clovelly Rd., Clovelly. Admission free. Daily 24 hr. Bus: 339. Map p. 98.

Dawn Fraser Baths   The oldest pool and swimming club in Australia, the Victorian-era Elkington Park Baths were renamed in honour of the gold medal champion, a Balmain girl who learnt to swim and trained here (Dawn still lives in Balmain). At low tide there is a small sandy beach that is great for kids.

Fitzroy Ave., Balmain. ⓒ **(02) 9555 1903.** Admission $3.60 adults, $2.50 kids. No credit cards. Daily 7.15am–6.30pm (6.45am–7pm daylight saving) from October long weekend (usually first weekend in October) to Easter Monday. Bus: 433. Map p. 95.

★ **MacCallum Pool** `FREE`   Every single one of the these harbourside and ocean pools has a great view, but if I had to pick the best it would be this 1920s lap pool. It's long and only two lanes wide, but it has knockout views of the Opera House, Harbour Bridge and city skyline. No wonder sidestroke's so popular here. The timber deck is the place to soak up the winter sun. `FINE PRINT` The pool is closed for cleaning once a week for approximately six hours (usually on a Thursday or Friday).

Milson Rd., Cremorne. Admission free. Daily 24 hr. Ferry: Cremorne Point. Map p. 98.

McIvers Baths `FREE`   Also known as Ladies or Womens Baths, this 20m ocean pool perched on a cliff face at Coogee is reserved for women and children only—and has been since 1876. It is the last remaining women-only seawater pool in Australia and has an exemption under the New South Wales Anti-Discrimination Act. The track to the pool is steep, but the pool is well screened so it's great for those who like their privacy.

Grant Reserve, Beach St., Coogee. Admission free. Daily 24 hr. Bus: 372, 373, 374. Map p. 98.

Mona Vale Ocean Pool `FREE`   This is a very photogenic 25m rock pool in the middle of the beach on the rock shelf between Bongin Bongin Bay and Mona Vale Beach. It can be dangerous when the ocean is rough, but the waves crashing against the pool make for some great photos. There's also a toddlers' pool.

Surfview Rd., Mona Vale. Admission free. Daily, with lights for night swimming. Bus: L60, 151, 155 or 156. Map p. 101.

Newport Rock Pool `FREE`   Students of photography will recognise this rock pool at the southern end of Newport Beach as the backdrop for Max Dupain's iconic beach photographs taken from the 1930s to the '50s. It has a natural rock floor.

Calvert Pde., Newport. Admission free. Daily 24 hr. Bus: 187 or 188 (from Wynyard). Map p. 101.

North Curl Curl Rock Pool FREE It's a bit of a hike to get to this pool, also known as Dee Why Head Rock Pool, but it's worth it. The tidal pool underneath the tip of the headland has two rocky islands in the middle of the pool and one side is formed by a rock shelf, so it feels kind of wild and unkempt.

Huston Pde., North Curl Curl. Admission free. Daily 24 hr. Bus: 136 from Manly or 176 from Wynyard. Map p. 101.

North Narrabeen Rock Pool FREE Another fabulously photogenic pool at the entrance to Narrabeen Lagoon, this one has a wooden boardwalk that seems to float between two pools, enclosing a 50m lap pool within a larger 70m pool. It was built in the 1930s and is one of the largest rook pools in Sydney.

Narrabeen Park Pde., Narrabeen. Admission free. Daily 24 hr. Bus: 183 or 185. Map p. 101.

> **Look at That!**
>
> Swimming goggles are a must-have accessory at ocean and harbour pools, as saltwater can sting your eyes and even the cleanest sea water can be murky sometimes.

★ **North Sydney Olympic Pool** I always get distracted by the grinning face at the entrance to Luna Park and the massive overhead arches of the Harbour Bridge; however, other (better) swimmers have set 86 world records at this pool. It's heated and there are also regular yoga and pilates classes.

4 Alfred St. South, Milsons Point. Admission $5.50 adults, $2.80 kids. MC, V. Mon–Fri 5.30am–9pm, Sat and Sun 7am–7pm. Train: Milsons Point. Map p. 98.

Victoria Park Pool It's not a harbour pool, but it still beats any indoor pool in my book. It's open all year round and is heated, but if you want to do laps during the busy early morning time slots you'll need to book a lane. There's also a gym.

City Rd. (cnr. Parramatta Rd.), Camperdown. ☎ **(02) 9298 3090.** Admission $4.80 adults, $3.10 kids. Gym admission $13.20. MC, V. Mon–Fri 6am–7.15pm, Sat and Sun 7am–5.45pm during winter; Mon–Fri 5.45am–7.45pm, Sat and Sun 7am–5.45pm during summer. Bus: 412, 413, 422, 423, 426, 428, 438, 440, 461, 480 or 483. Map p. 100.

Wylies Baths Another historic rock pool, this one was built in 1907 by Henry Alexander Wylie, a champion long-distance and underwater swimmer whose daughter, Wilhelmina, won a silver medal in the 1912 Olympics, the first time women were allowed to compete in the swimming events. (Her best friend Fanny Durack won gold.)

Neptune St., Coogee. 🕿 **(02) 9665 2838.** Admission $3 adults, 50¢ kids. No credit cards. Daily 7am–5pm (7pm daylight saving). Bus: 372, 373 or 374. Map p. 98.

11 Free Wildlife Encounters

Cabbage Tree Bay Aquatic Reserve FREE   Cabbage Tree Bay is an aquatic reserve and is home to a fantastic array of marine life. Protected, north-facing Shelly Beach is another one of the Sydney's favourite snorkelling spots with a huge variety of fish, including stingrays and wobbegong sharks (which don't bite unless provoked) and other small sharks. You can also often see seahorses and leafy sea dragons around the shark net on the beach beside Manly Wharf on the other side of the wharf. FINE PRINT Blue-ringed octopuses have been seen in the bay. Do not touch them; they are deadly and there is no antivenene.

Marine Parade, Manly. Ferry: Manly. Map p. 99.

Clovelly's Blue Groper FREE   Clovelly Beach or, more correctly, the narrow cleft in the rocks beyond the beach, is one of Sydney's most popular snorkelling spots. You won't see sharks (which is a good thing, as this is one of my favourite swimming spots), but you will see plenty of fish and maybe even an octopus or two. Star attraction is Bluey, a friendly male blue groper. Trivia buffs take note: the blue groper is the official fish of New South Wales. Male blue gropers can grow up to 1.2m long and are bright blue. (Funny, that!)

Clovelly Rd., Clovelly. Bus: 339. Map p. 98

Collins Beach FREE   Sydney's northern harbour, near Manly, is home to the only breeding colony of little penguins (sometimes called fairy penguins) on mainland New South Wales. They are highly endangered, and the population of the colony is currently only around 50 to 60 pairs. The best place to see them is at Collins Beach on North Head and around the old Quarantine Station (now called Q Station).

Collins Beach Rd., North Head. Ferry: Manly, then bus 135. Map p. 99.

★ **Flying Foxes** FREE   Watching the thousands of grey-headed flying foxes (commonly called fruit bats) as they swarm above the arch of the Sydney Harbour Bridge at sunset on their way out to hunt is an activity that is unique to Sydney. I think the best place to watch the nightly performance is with a cocktail in hand at the **Opera Bar** beneath the Opera House, but anywhere around Circular Quay with a good view of the bridge is ideal.

Opera Bar: Lower Concourse, Sydney Opera House. ℂ **(02) 9247 1666.** Check www. bom.gov.au for sunset times. Train: Circular Quay.

Possum Prowl Nothing can stop you from grabbing a torch and doing this on your own for free, but you'll just find yourself stumbling around in the dark. Why not fork out $12 and join a ranger-led twilight Spotlight Prowl in Centennial Park, where the khaki-clad guide points out the nocturnal inhabitants? You're guaranteed to see lots of possums and other critters, it's a sure-fire hit with kids and it's half the price of a ticket to the zoo. Bookings are essential; see the website for dates of the next tour. BYO torch.

Robertson Rd. gates, Centennial Park. ℂ **(02) 9339 6699.** www.centennialparklands. com.au. Admission $12.50. MC, V. Bus: 339, 352, 355, 371, 372, 373, 374, 376, 377, 378 or 380. Map p. 98.

Snakes Alive `FREE` Every Sunday afternoon the Snake Man thrills onlookers with his venomous-snake-handling demonstration in the snake pit on the point La Perouse, and has done since the early days of the 20th century. (Of course, it hasn't always been the same person!) The half-hour show is free, but any donation is gratefully accepted—he deserves *some* danger money after all. More than one Snake Man has overlooked a snake bite received during the show and not lived to tell the tale.

The Point, Anzac Parade, La Perouse. Most Sundays 1.30–4.30pm. Bus: 394. Map p. 98.

Whale Watching `FREE` The eastern seaboard of Australia is part of a main whale migration route and Sydney's many cliff-tops and headlands are perfect vantage points for free, land-based whale watching. In late May, June and July humpback whales head north to their breeding grounds in Hervey Bay, followed by southern right whales from July through September. By November, the whales begin to return and you can see them on their southern migration right through until early December. They can come quite close to the shoreline and it's not uncommon for a few curious cetaceans to enter Sydney

Harbour each year. In the past few years Sydneysiders have been avidly following the annual progress of one whale in particular, a white humpback known as Migaloo (you can track his movements at www.migaloo.com.au). The best whale-watching spots include North and South Head, Cape Solander (overlooking Botany Bay) and Barrenjoey Head, although any cliff-top spot is good. Don't forget your binoculars!

North Head: North Head Scenic Dr., Manly; Bus 135; ferry Manly. South Head: anywhere on the South Head Heritage Trail; bus 324 or 380. Cape Solander: Captain Cook Dr., Kurnell; train Cronulla, then bus 67 to Kurnell. Barrenjoey Head: Ocean Rd., Palm Beach; bus 190.

12 Sporty Sydney

Sydneysiders love their sport. In summer it's cricket, in winter it's footy (which, means rugby league in Sydney, not soccer) or Aussie Rules (AFL) which is what they play in Victoria (and just about everywhere else but Queensland). Here's when you check out some first-class sporting action, without the first-class price tag.

★ **Barefoot Bowls** I love a sport you can play in bare feet and not get wet. Barefoot bowls is a variation on the traditional lawn bowls that is played by sensibly shod senior citizens. It is played while wearing no shoes, often with a beer in hand, and is one of the fastest, growing sports in Sydney. It's a team sport, so get an even-numbered group of friends and head to any number of bowling clubs around the city. The added bonus is that these clubs serve dirt-cheap food and drinks as well. Good spots to kick your shoes off include the **Waverley Bowling & Recreation Club,** which has barefoot bowling sessions every day for $10 (which includes tuition if you've never played before), and **Paddington Bowling Club** or **Warringah Bowling Club** on Sunday afternoons.

Waverley Bowling Club: 163 Birrell St., Waverley; ✆ **(02) 9389 3026**; MC, V; bus 360, 361, 278 or 380; map p. 98. Paddington: 2 Quarry St., Paddington; ✆ **(02) 9363 1150**; admission $12; MC, V; bus 389; map p. 98. Mosman: 74–82 Bradleys Head Rd., Mosman; ✆ **(02) 9969 4313**; admission $15; MC, V; bus 228, 238 or 247; map p. 98.

Beach Volleyball FREE We've all played hit-and-giggle beach volleyball on holidays, but if you want to see some of Australia's

Olympic beach volleyball players in action head to **Maroubra Beach** on a Saturday afternoon or **Dee Why Beach** (p. 135) on Tuesday, Wednesday and Thursday evenings.

Maroubra Beach: Marine Pde, Maroubra; bus 376, 377, 395 or 396; map p. 98. Dee Why Beach: The Strand, Dee Why; bus 136 or 176; map p. 101.

Bocce `FREE`   Bocce (similar to petanque) is yet to really take off in Sydney, but if you are keen to bowl a few over you can play all day for free at the Gazebo Wine Garden, with a tournament kicking off at 4pm for those who think they can really play. `FINE PRINT` You can also get $15 jugs of Sangria all day on Sunday here, which may cause you to overestimate your playing ability.

Gazebo Wine Garden: 2 Elizabeth Bay Rd., Elizabeth Bay. ✆ **(02) 9357 5333.** www. gazebowinegarden.com.au. AE, MC, V. Sun noon–midnight. Train: Kings Cross. Map p. 96.

Crab Racing `FREE`   They say Australians will bet on just about any-thing that moves. For proof just head to either of these pubs to see the crowd go ballistic at the weekly crab races. It's free to watch, but a couple of dollars buys you a hermit crab, give it a name and enter a heat and you might just win something (but probably not much—the fun is in the racing). It's on at the **Friend in Hand Pub,** the **Courthouse Hotel** and **Scubar**. It can get very loud and raucous.

Friend in Hand Hotel: 58 Cowper St., Glebe; ✆ **(02) 9660 2326**; Wed 8pm; bus 431 or 433; map p. 100. Courthouse Hotel: 202 Australia St., Newtown; ✆ **(02) 9519 8273**; Thurs 7.30pm; train Newtown; map p. 100. Scubar: cnr. George St. and Rawson Pl., Sydney; ✆ **(02) 9212 4244**; train Central; map p. 96.

Cricket `FREE`   On any summer weekend you'll find ovals all around the city and suburbs resounding to the crack of the willow as another ball is hit for six (over the boundary on the full) in the Sydney Grade competition. You can usually watch one of these matches for free, and a really nice spot is **Waverley Oval,** just up the hill from Bondi Beach.

Waverley Oval: Bondi Rd., Bondi; bus 380. Map p. 98.

Golf   Most of Sydney's golf courses are either super expensive or open to members only, or both, but head instead to a public course and you play 18 holes for less than $25. Try **Bondi Golf Club** for spec-tacular ocean views on an old-style links course or weekday twilight golf (2pm in winter, 4pm in summer) on the par 70 championship course at **Moore Park Golf** for $25.

Bondi Golf Club: 5 Military Rd., North Bondi; ✆ **(02) 9130 1981;** www.bondigolf.com. au; 18 holes $22; AE, MC, V; bus 380; map p. 98. Moore Park Golf: cnr. Anzac Pde and Cleveland St., Moore Park; ✆ **(02) 9663 1064;** AE, MC, V; bus 372, 373, 374, 377, 393, 395 or 399; map p. 98.

Horse Racing `FREE`   Racing may well be the sport of kings, but you don't need a king's ransom to watch it. All mid-week race days at **Royal Randwick** and **Warwick Farm** racecourses offer free entry to all punters, which sure beats the usual $15 to $35 entry fee you'll pay on weekends or major race days (called carnival days). Whether the day stays dirt cheap depends on whether you back the right horse. `FINE PRINT` Despite being an outdoor event you are expected to dress up for the carnival races—women should wear their fanciest and most feathery hat.

Royal Randwick: Alison Rd., Randwick; ✆ **(02) 9663 8400;** bus 372, 373, 374 or 377; map p. 98. Warwick Farm: Hume Hwy., Warwick Farm; train Warwick Farm; map p. 100.

Rugby League `FREE`   Almost all of the National Rugby League (NRL) teams host one or two open training sessions each season (March to September), where you can see your footy heroes on the field for free—they'll often sign autographs afterwards. (Check your favourite team's website for details.) A premiership game will cost anywhere from $20–$45 a ticket, but you can watch footy stars in the making (and those that have just retired from the premiership comp) for less than $10 (kids under 16 are usually free or a gold coin dona-tion) in the New South Wales Cup competition at many suburban ovals. Most atmospheric matches to catch are a Bears game at **North Sydney Oval** or a Newtown Jets game at **Henson Park.**

North Sydney Oval: cnr. Miller and Ridge sts., St Leonards; train North Sydney; bus 202, 203, 205, 207 or 208; map p. 98. Henson Park: end of Centennial St. (just off Sydenham Rd.), Marrickville; bus 412, 425 or 426; map p. 100.

Sheffield Shield Cricket   There are six state teams that play in this annual competition, and many of the top Australian players also play for their state teams, so it's a great way to see some cricket stars for dirt cheap (around $7 a ticket compared to $50 to $100 for international test cricket, even more for Twenty20 tickets). Most matches have three sessions of play each day and sometimes the final afternoon sessions (usually around 4 to 6pm) are free. If you really want to see the international stars live in action for free, they sometimes open their training session to the public (see the news section in the website below for more details). Most Sydney matches are played at the **Sydney Cricket Ground.**

Sydney Cricket Ground: Driver Ave., Moore Park. Ticket prices vary, go to www. ticketek.com.au. or 🕿 **132 849.** See www.scgt.nsw.gov.au for match details. AE, MC, V. Bus: 339, 373, 374, 392 or 394. Map p. 98.

★ **Surf Lifesaving Carnivals** FREE   Being a surf lifesaver is about much more than patrolling the beach and saving damsels (and dudes) in distress. Surf sports include beach- and rescue-oriented events that include combined swimming and running and surf ski and surf boat races for all ages, including 'nippers' as young as 5 years old. Visit www.surflifesaving.com.au for more information.

The elegant Sydney town hall (p. 157) houses an excellent library in a building at its rear.

LOCAL LIVING

Sydney is by far and away the most expensive Australian city to call home—and it's not just crazy real-estate prices that make this a city that's unkind to the wallet. Sydney has always been a beautiful place to spend up big, and there are plenty of tempting ways to break the budget on a daily basis. But the thing is, you don't *have* to. Local councils provide everything from great free toy and music libraries to fitness facilities for the frugal—and even free dog obedience classes. Universities and colleges are another great source of affordable services, and student clinics and salons are a great way to get specialised health and beauty treatments for next to nothing, or certainly for dirt cheap compared with normal prices.

LIVING CITY CENTRE & REDFERN

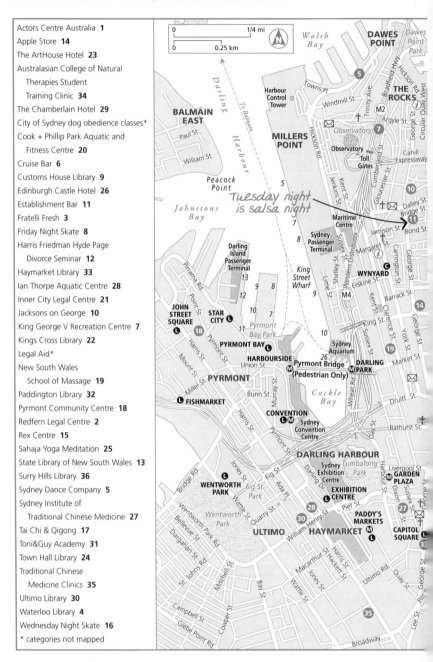

Tuesday night is salsa night

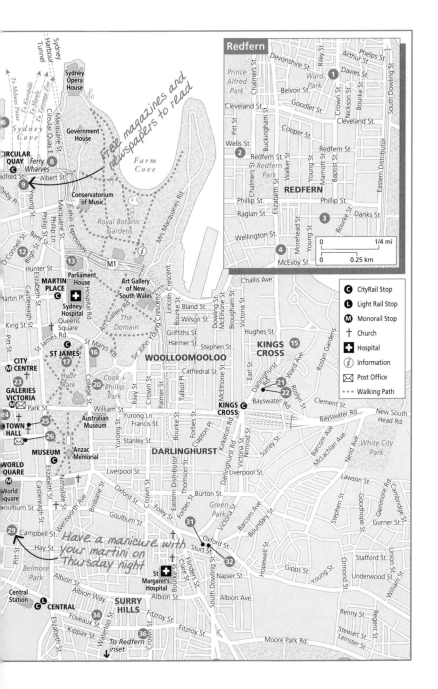

Redfern

Devonshire St.
Prince Alfred Park
Ward Park
Riley St.
Arthur St.
Phelps St.
Davies St.
Chalmers St.
Belvoir St.
Goodlet St.
Crown St.
Nickson St.
Bourke St.
South Dowling St.
Cleveland St.
Cooper St.
Cleveland St.
Pitt St.
Wells St.
Buckingham St.
Redfern St.
Redfern St.
Young St.
Marriott St.
Baptist St.
Eastern Distributor
Chalmers St.
Redfern Park
Walker St.
REDFERN
Phillip St.
Elizabeth St.
Phillip St.
Raglan St.
Morehead St.
Bourke St.
Danks St.
Wellington St.
McEvoy St.

0   1/4 mi
0   0.25 km

Free magazines and newspapers to read

Sydney Harbour Tunnel
To Milsons Point
To Kirribilli
To Manly
To Taronga Zoo
Sydney Opera House
Government House
Macquarie St.
Circular Quay E.
Sydney Cove
CIRCULAR QUAY
Ferry Wharves
Alfred St.
Albert St.
Conservatorium of Music
Cahill Expressway
Royal Botanic Gardens
Farm Cove
Mrs Macquaries Rd.
O'Connell St.
Bent St.
Phillip St.
Phillip Ln.
Macquarie St.
Young St.
Hunter St.
MARTIN PLACE
Parliament House
M1
Martin Pl.
Castlereagh St.
Sydney Hospital
Hospital Rd.
Art Gallery of New South Wales
King St.
St James Rd.
Queens Square
The Domain
Art Gallery Rd.
Lincoln Crescent
Sir John Young Crescent
Bland St.
Dowling St.
McElhone St.
Brougham St.
Victoria St.
Bourke St.
Wilson St.
Griffiths St.
Harmer St.
Stephen St.
Challis Ave.
Hughes St.
KINGS CROSS
Roslyn Gardens
Pitt St.
St Marys Rd.
ST JAMES
CITY CENTRE
Hyde Park
College St.
Cook + Phillip Park
Riley St.
Crown St.
Palmer St.
Talbot Pl.
Cathedral St.
WOOLLOOMOOLOO
Earl St.
Darlinghurst
Ward Ave.
GALERIES VICTORIA
Park St.
TOWN HALL
William St.
Australian Museum
Yurong Ln.
Francis St.
Forbes St.
Clapton Pl.
Bourke St.
KINGS CROSS
Bayswater Rd.
Roslyn St.
Clement St.
Bayswater Rd.
New South Head Rd.
MUSEUM
Anzac Memorial
Stanley St.
DARLINGHURST
Kirketon Rd.
Darlinghurst Rd.
Victoria St.
Nimrod St.
Surrey St.
Barcom Ave.
McLachlan Ave.
Neild Ave.
White City Park
WORLD SQUARE
World Square
Elizabeth St.
Castlereagh St.
Goulburn St.
Liverpool St.
Nithsdale St.
Brisbane St.
Oxford St.
Crown St.
Foley St.
Eastern Distributor
Forbes St.
Thomson St.
Burton St.
Green Park
Liverpool St.
Victoria St.
Barcom Ave.
Boundary St.
Hopewell St.
Lawson St.
Stephen St.
Goodhope St.
Glenmore Rd.
Cambridge St.
Gurner St.
Wentworth Ave.
Goulburn St.
Oxford St.
Foley St.
Oxford St.
Sturt St.
Napier St.
Gipps St.
Young St.
Ormond St.
Stafford St.
Underwood St.
Union St.
William St.
Have a manicure with your martini on Thursday night
Campbell St.
Hay St.
Pitt St.
Belmore Park
Albion St.
Albion Way
Flinders St.
Clare St.
St Margaret's Hospital
Albion St.
Albion Ave.
Renny St.
Stewart St.
Regent St.
Leinster St.
Central Station
CENTRAL
Elizabeth St.
Foveaux St.
SURRY HILLS
Fitzroy St.
Fitzroy St.
Moore Park Rd.
Kippax St.
Waterloo St.
Crown St.
To Redfern inset

C CityRail Stop
L Light Rail Stop
M Monorail Stop
† Church
✚ Hospital
ⓘ Information
✉ Post Office
••• Walking Path

LIVING INNER WEST

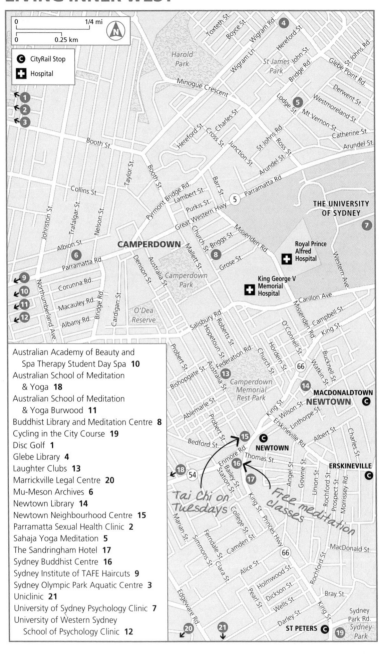

Australian Academy of Beauty and
  Spa Therapy Student Day Spa **10**
Australian School of Meditation
  & Yoga **18**
Australian School of Meditation
  & Yoga Burwood **11**
Buddhist Library and Meditation Centre **8**
Cycling in the City Course **19**
Disc Golf **1**
Glebe Library **4**
Laughter Clubs **13**
Marrickville Legal Centre **20**
Mu-Meson Archives **6**
Newtown Library **14**
Newtown Neighbourhood Centre **15**
Parramatta Sexual Health Clinic **2**
Sahaja Yoga Meditation **5**
The Sandringham Hotel **17**
Sydney Buddhist Centre **16**
Sydney Institute of TAFE Haircuts **9**
Sydney Olympic Park Aquatic Centre **3**
Uniclinic **21**
University of Sydney Psychology Clinic **7**
University of Western Sydney
  School of Psychology Clinic **12**

LIVING EASTERN SUBURBS

CityRail Stop
Golf Course

Brasserie Bread **9**
Bunnings Warehouse **5**
Fuss Beauty College
    Student Salon **1**
Kingsford Legal Centre **7**
Laughter Clubs **2**
Randwick College
    Massage Clinic **4**
Sahaja Yoga Meditation **3**
University of New South Wales
    Optometry Clinic **8**
University of New South Wales
    Psychology Clinic **6**

Cheap massages—nice!

Have a free eye test

1 Free & Dirt Cheap Classes

Actors Centre Australia FREE Twice a year the Actors Centre Australia (ACA) offers free two-hour acting workshops. Spaces are limited to 250 people and they book out fast, but if you miss out there's always a $25 drop-in class ($20 for members). You can't book these, so arrive at least 30 minutes before classes start to register. Check the website for timetables.

41 Devonshire St., Surry Hills. ✆ **(02) 9310 4077.** www.actorscentre.com.au. Bus: 301 or 352. Map p. 148.

Apple Store FREE Yes, there is a catch to the series of free computer workshops run by the Apple Store, which is (surprise, surprise) that you'll only learn about Apple products. But hey, if you want to learn how to do really cool things with your iPhone, or master the software that comes with your Mac, these free courses are great. Better still, there's often a live music session with well-known musicians thrown in for free! See the website for details.

LIVING NORTH SIDE

367 George St., Sydney. ℂ **(02) 8083 9400.** www.apple.com/au/retail/sydney/. Mon–Wed, Fri and Sat 8am–8pm, Thurs 8am–9pm, Sun 10am–6pm. Train: Martin Place or Wynyard. Map p. 148.

The ArtHouse Hotel This gorgeous city pub was, 150 years or so ago, a school of arts. It was one of the first places in Sydney where the public could get an affordable education and, keeping this tradition alive, you can join a dirt-cheap life-drawing class in Dome Restaurant & Bar every Monday night for just $3. As an added incentive, there are $6 drink specials available as well.

275 Pitt St, Sydney. ℂ **(02) 9284 1200.** www.thearthousehotel.com.au. Mon 6–8.30pm. Train: Town Hall. Map p. 148.

Brasserie Bread `FREE` There's nothing better than sitting back with a coffee while the kids make a mess in someone else's kitchen. There are two one-hour baking classes every Saturday, where the kids will learn how to make and bake two items, which they get to take home—if they last that long. Bookings are essential.

1737 Botany Rd., Banksmeadow. ✆ **1300 966 845.** www.brasseriebread.com.au. Sat 10am and noon. Bus: 309. Map p. 151.

Bunnings Warehouse `FREE` Bunnings Warehouse, one of the country's largest home and hardware chains, offers free do-it-yourself (DIY) workshops on all sorts of home improvement subjects, from how to build a timber deck to garden design. It also holds regular kids' classes (usually art and craft or kindergarten gardening) and the occasional ladies' DIY nights, where you can pick up all manner of handy home hardware hints. Most classes and workshops are on weekends and stores are all over Sydney—check the website for the closest store to you.

www.bunnings.com.au.

City of Sydney dog obedience classes `FREE` Does your dog rule your life? Learn how to get Rover to do want you want at one of the City of Sydney free dog obedience classes. They are held at various times throughout the year in St Peters, Rushcutters Bay, Surry Hills and Glebe. Places fill up fast, so bookings are essential. `FINE PRINT` The course is only open to residents from the City of Sydney Council local government area and those residents of council areas on the city's border. The courses run over six consecutive weeks and are open to dogs between five months and 10 years of age.

Various venues. Call ✆ **(02) 9256 9333** or visit www.cityofsydney.nsw.gov.au for details. Map p. 148.

Fratelli Fresh `FREE` Learn how to cook Italian food from the experts. Fratelli Fresh, one of Sydney's most popular (and upmarket) food providores, offers free cooking classes at the Danks Street store with the chefs from Cafe Sopra (p. 70), one of the classiest Italian cafes in town. These classes are popular and fill up fast, so book ahead (see the website for details).

7 Danks St., Waterloo. ✆ **(02) 9699 3161.** www.fratellifresh.com.au. Tues, Wed and Thurs, 4–5pm. Bus: 301. Map p. 148.

Mu-Meson Archives `FREE` It's not so much a class as a get-together, although you'll find plenty of crafty folk ready to give you a few tips at Stitch'N'Bitch, a meeting of like-minded knitters held at Mu-Meson

Archives. Entry is free, but you are expected to bring a plate of food, a drink and a handicraft to keep you busy. Check the website for details.

Cnr. Trafalgar St. and Parramatta Rd. (behind King Furniture Building), Annandale. www.mumeson.org. Bus: 412, 413, 438, 436, 437 or 440. Map p. 150.

The Sandringham Hotel `FREE` Every second Monday the upstairs bar at The Sando Hotel swaps rock and roll for naked ladies (and men) with a free life-drawing session.

387 King St., Newtown. ✆ **(02) 9557 1254.** www.sando.com.au. Every second Mon 8pm. Train: Newtown. Map p. 150.

Sydney Dance Company Sydney Dance Company is one of the country's best professional dance companies. You'll pay top dollar to see the dancers perform at the Opera House, Sydney Theatre or CarriageWorks, but you can dance with them for a surprisingly small amount. Sixty dance classes are offered each week and all are taught by professional dancers and choreographers. Classes run on a casual basis, which means you don't have to sign up for a 10-week course. All types of dance styles are taught, from classical ballet and 'Broadway jazz' to Latin, tap and hip-hop, and classes cater to all levels. Classes cost $18 (or $15 if you buy a 10-class pass, valid for 12 months).

Sydney Dance Company Dance Studios, The Wharf, Pier 4, Hickson Rd., Walsh Bay. ✆ **(02) 9258 4818.** www.sydneydancecompany.com. Train: Circular Quay. Bus: 430, 431 or 433. Map p. 148.

2 Free Books, Newspapers & Magazines

Libraries are a great place to get your hands on the latest bestseller for free (membership is always free, but you will need proof of address). Another bonus is that the Internet is often free or dirt cheap. Here are some of the libraries in the city centre and inner suburbs.

Customs House Library `FREE` This has the largest range of local and international newspapers in any Australian public library and a ground floor 'magazine salon' that feels more lounge than library.

31 Alfred St., Sydney. ✆ **(02) 9242 8595.** Mon–Fri 10am–7pm, Sat–Sun 11am–4pm, closed public holidays. Train: Circular Quay. Map p. 148.

Glebe Library `FREE` This is a good place for preschoolers, who love the toy section. It has a selection of more than 200 toys you can borrow for up to three weeks, as well as puzzles. Of course, they also have the requisite collections of books, CDs DVDs and magazines available for loan.

186 Glebe Point Rd. (cnr. Wigram Rd.), Glebe. ℭ **(02) 9298 3060.** Mon and Wed 10am–7pm, Tues, Thurs and Fri 10am–6pm, Sat 10am–4pm. Bus: 431 or 433. Map p. 150.

Haymarket Library `FREE`   Haymarket Library has the largest Chinese-language book collection of any public library in Australia. Daily newspapers are also available in English, Chinese and Vietnamese—and it has Indonesian- and Thai-language books, as well.

744 George St., Haymarket. ℭ **(02) 8019 6477.** Mon–Fri 8.30am–6pm, Sat 10am–4pm. Train: Central. Map p. 148.

Kings Cross Library `FREE`   Go here to borrow books, CDs, DVDs and magazines, as well as good selection of daily newspapers. It's in the same building as the Kings Cross Neighbourhood Centre.

Level 1, 50–52 Darlinghurst Rd., Kings Cross. ℭ **(02) 9246 4530.** Mon and Tues 10am–7pm, Wed–Fri 10am–6pm, Sat 10am–4pm, Sun 11am–4pm. Train: Kings Cross. Map p. 148.

Manly Library `FREE`   The Manly Library has books, CDs, DVDs, magazines, toys and jigsaw puzzles for loan. Once a month there is a free 'Baby Bounce & Rhyme' session with songs and rhymes aimed at tiny tots aged 2 to 18 months (see the website for dates).

Market Pl., Manly. ℭ **(02) 9976 1720.** www.manly.nsw.gov.au/Library.html. Mon–Wed 9.30am–8pm, Thurs and Fri 9.30am–5pm, Sat 9.30–4pm, Sun 1–4pm. Ferry: Manly. Map p. 152.

Newtown Library `FREE`   The Newtown Library is a bit of local land-mark and community hub. It has a good selection of books, CDs, DVDs and magazines for loan, as well as daily newspapers and Inter-net and email access.

8–10 Brown St., Newtown. ℭ **(02) 8512 4250.** Mon and Wed 10am–7pm, Tues 10am–6pm, Thurs and Fri 10am–5pm, Sat and Sun 11am–4pm. Train: Newtown. Map p. 150.

Paddington Library `FREE`   Go here to borrow books, CDs, DVDs and magazines. However, there's a catch: if you want to borrow any-thing you'll need to be a member of the Woollahra Library and Infor-mation Service. There's an online form available at www.woollahra.nsw.gov.au.

Paddington Town Hall, 247 Oxford St., Paddington. ℭ **(02) 9391 7988.** Mon, Tues, Thurs and Fri 10am–6pm, Wed noon–8pm, Sat 10am–4pm. Bus: 378 or 380. Map p. 148.

FREE Once Upon a Time there Was Free Storytelling...

These half-hour storytelling sessions are aimed at preschoolers (kids aged 3 to 5) and are free, but kids must be accompanied by a parent or guardian (in other words, it is not a free babysitting service). See the library listings for address details unless otherwise noted.

- **Customs House Library:** Wednesday at 11am.
- **Glebe Library:** Tuesday at 10.30am.
- **Rex Centre:** Wednesday at 10.30am at the Rex Centre (Level 1, 58A Macleay Street, Potts Point, adjacent to Baroda Street and the playground in Fitzroy Gardens; map p. 148).
- **Newtown Library:** Monday at 11am.
- **Paddington Library:** Thursday at 3.30pm and Friday at 10.30am.
- **Surry Hills Library:** Thursday at 11am.
- **Ultimo Library:** Thursday at 11.30am.
- **Waterloo Library:** Friday at 11am.

Stanton Library FREE   This library not only has books, CDs, DVDs and magazines for loan, but also lots of literary events (p. 226), as well as daily book clubs (times vary), word processing and e-mail facilities and a really good selection of journals and local newspapers.
234 Miller St., North Sydney. ℭ **(02) 9936 8400.** www.northsydney.nsw.gov.au. Mon–Thurs 9am–9pm, Fri 9am–6pm, Sat and Sun 10am–5pm. Train: North Sydney. Map p. 152.

State Library of New South Wales FREE   You can't actually borrow books from the State Library of New South Wales, but it's a great place to read and research and there's free Wi-Fi. The Shakespeare Room, a delightfully medieval room modelled on Cardinal Wolsey's closet at Hampton Court Palace and lined with books on and by Shakespeare, is open on Tuesday from 10am to 4pm, and is a perfect place to hide away with a good book.

Macquarie St., Sydney. ℂ **(02) 9273 1414.** www.sl.nsw.gov.au. Mon–Thurs 9am–8pm, Fri 9am–5pm, Sat and Sun 10am–5pm, closed public holidays. Train: Martin Place. Map p. 148.

Surry Hills Library FREE This brand new library specialises in books on fashion and design, but also has more general books and magazines, CDs, DVDs and toys for loan and free Wi-Fi. There are 16 public computers available (for free, unless you want to e-mail) and if you are a member, there are even free computer training classes.

405 Crown St., Surry Hills. ℂ **(02) 8374 6230.** Mon, Wed and Fri 10am–6pm, Tues and Thurs 10am–8pm, Sat and Sun 10am–4pm. Bus: 301 or 352. Map p. 148.

Town Hall Library FREE This has lots of paperbacks for loan and a good magazine and newspaper section. It's a handy library to use if you work in the city because you can request and borrow from the 500,000 items held at the other library branches, then pick them up and return them here, rather than at your local branch.

Level 1, Town Hall House, 456 Kent St., Sydney. ℂ **(02) 9242 8555.** Mon–Fri 8am–6pm. Train: Town Hall. Map p. 148.

Ultimo Library FREE The Ultimo Library has books, CDs, DVDs and magazines for loan, plus daily newspapers in English and Chinese.

Ultimo Community Centre, 40 William Henry St., Ultimo. ℂ **(02) 9298 3110.** Mon, Tues, Thurs and Fri 10am–6pm, Wed 10am–7pm, Sat and Sun noon–4pm. Light rail: Paddy's Markets. Map p. 148.

Waterloo Library FREE Waterloo Library has books, CDs, DVDs, magazines and toys for loan, plus newspapers in English and Russian. This library also holds the Koori Collection, some 1,250 items on Australian Aboriginal–related subjects such as politics, land rights, sport and the history of the arrival of the first Europeans.

Waterloo Town Hall, 770 Elizabeth St., Waterloo. ℂ **(02) 9288 5688.** Mon–Thurs 10am–6pm, Fri 10am–5pm, Sat 11am–4pm. Bus: 343 or 355. Map p. 148.

3 Beauty & Bodywork

Australasian College of Natural Therapies Student Training Clinic You can get the full range of massages at the student clinic for not a whole lot of cash ($26 to $35), but you can also get some fabulous spa treatments, such as body scrubs and hydro baths at half the price you'd pay in a swish day spa. Also on offer are dirt-cheap facials, pedicures and waxing packages.

57 Foveaux St., Surry Hills. ✆ **(02) 9218 8855.** www.acnt.edu.au. Mon and Fri 8.30am–5pm, Tues–Thurs 8.30am–7.30pm, Sat 8am–5pm, Sun 9am–4pm. Train: Central. Map p. 148.

Australian Academy of Beauty and Spa Therapy Student Day Spa   Heavily discounted spa and beauty treatments are provided by academy students in a purpose-built student salon day spa. It actually feels more like a day spa and less like a learning centre, unlike some student salons. Call for appointment times.

Level 2, 18–22 George St. (under Fitness First), North Strathfield. ✆ **(02) 9764 5849.** www.australianacademyofbeautytherapy.com. Train: North Strathfield. Map p. 150.

The Chamberlain Hotel `FREE`   There are free manicures on offer every Thursday night at the Chamberlain Hotel, but they come with a wonderful catch: you have to have a martini while you get your nails done. Manicures & Martinis is a fun girls' night out—other drinks are available if martinis aren't to your taste.

428 Pitt St., Haymarket. ✆ **(02) 9288 0888.** www.chamberlainhotel.com.au. Thurs from 5pm. Train: Central. Map p. 148.

Ella Baché Student Salon   Enjoy cut-price beauty treatments, such as facials, aromatherapy massage, lash tinting and perming, waxing and permanent hair removal, body wraps and masks, as well as fake tanning, manicures and pedicures. Check (and book) online for opening times and great deals, such as 90-minute facials that normally cost $145 for a bargain basement price of $67. They also have a great range of treatments for men, including facials and massage.

Level 2, 77 Berry St., North Sydney. ✆ **(02) 9432 5077.** www.collegensw.ellabache.com.au. Train: North Sydney. Map p. 152.

Fuss Beauty College Student Salon   The students of this private beauty college do all the standard beauty treatments—manicures, pedicures, facials, make up, spray tans and waxing—in the student salon for half the price you'd pay elsewhere. When $78 gets you a two-hour 'detox overhaul' with an aromatherapy massage, mud body wrap and head massage, how can you resist? If you're game, they also do laser hair removal and skin treatments. Bookings are essential.

Shop 2, 161 New South Head Rd., Edgecliff. ✆ **(02) 9326 2204.** www.fuss.com.au. Mon–Fri 9.30am–4.30pm, Thurs 5.30–8.30pm. Train: Edgecliff. Map p. 151.

Nature Care Student Clinic   Ninety minutes of sweet-smelling bliss for just $45? That's a bargain. This student clinic offers a range of aromatherapy, massages and other natural therapies, such as homeopathy, kinesiology and energetic healing ('re-establishing the natural flow between mind, body and spirit') for $28 to $45 depending on the treatment. See the website for treatment schedules and bookings are essential.

52 Nicholson St., St Leonards. ℭ **(02) 9906 1566.** www.naturecare.com.au. Mon, Thurs and Fri 9am–8.30pm, Tues and Wed 12.30–8.30pm, Sat 9am–6pm. Train: St Leonards. Map p. 152.

New South Wales School of Massage   You might not get all the soothing rainforest music, soft candlelight or fancy decor, and you might be sharing the treatment room with half a dozen others and there might be a bit of chat going on, but who cares when you're getting a one-hour massage for just $25. The student clinic offers relaxation, Swedish, deep-tissue and sports massage, shiatsu, aromatherapy, pregnancy massage and reflexology on Thursday morning and all day Saturday. Bookings are essential.

Level 1, 225 Clarence St., Sydney. ℭ **(02) 9262 2654.** www.schoolofmassage.com. au. Train: Town Hall. Map p. 148.

Randwick College Massage Clinic   The massage clinic at this TAFE college is staffed by students and has a range of one-hour massages available (relaxation, remedial and sports) for just $25 (if you're a student you can save an extra $5). The clinic is open during college semesters between February and December (but it's closed for most of July) and massages can be booked for Tuesday and Friday afternoons and most of Thursday.

Building B, room B1.29, Randwick TAFE, cnr. Darley Rd. and King St. (opp. Centennial Park), Randwick. ℭ **(02) 9469 8738.** www.sit.nsw.edu.au/randwick/. Bus: 339, 372,373, 374, 376 or 377. Map p. 151.

Sydney Institute of TAFE Haircuts   Many of the TAFE colleges that teach hairdressing often require heads of hair to practise on, which means you can get a dirt-cheap haircut. There's no specific time or date, but contact the college to find out if and when they need people.

www.sit.nsw.edu.au. Try Petersham College: 27 Crystal St., Petersham; ℭ **(02) 9335 2339.** Sutherland College (Gymea): cnr. Hotham Rd. and the Kingsway, Gymea; ℭ **(02) 9710 5015.** Ultimo College: Harris St., Ultimo; ℭ **(02) 9217 5131.** Map p. 150.

Toni&Guy Academy A cut, colour and blow dry at any Toni&Guy Salon can cost more than $350, but let the supervised students from the Toni&Guy Academy do it and a cut will set you back $25—a colour just $35. And the chance to legitimately call yourself a model for the day—well, that's priceless! Check the website for student styling times, but they are available most days. (Look under 'models required'.) FINE PRINT While the cut is cheap, you will need to spend some time there. Your stylist will be learning, so there will be quite a bit of discussion with supervisors along the way, so allow a couple of hours.

255C Oxford St., Paddington. ℂ **(02) 9380 2299.** Bus: 378 or 380. Map p. 148.

4 Health & Wellbeing

DIRT-CHEAP GYMS

Cook + Phillip Park Aquatic and Fitness Centre This is more than just a great pool in the middle of the city; there's also a cardio room and gym and a great range of fitness classes. It's run by the YMCA, which keeps prices very affordable compared to private gyms. A casual visit to the pool is $6 and it's $16.50 for access to all the fitness facilities, including the pool, and classes.

4 College St., Sydney. ℂ **(02) 9326 0444.** www.cookandphillip.org.au. Mon–Fri 6am–10pm, Sat and Sun 7am–8pm. Train: St James. Map p. 148.

Ian Thorpe Aquatic Centre The Ian Thorpe Aquatic Centre has everything you'd find in a swish super-expensive exclusive gym club, but without the super-expensive price tag, thanks to the YMCA. There's a 50m indoor pool, sauna, steam room, spa, fitness centre, spin studio, cafe . . . the list goes on. It costs just $6 to use the pool (plus an extra $10 if you want to use the gym) and good-value 20-visit passes are available.

458 Harris St., Ultimo. ℂ **(02) 9518 7220.** www.itac.org.au. Mon–Fri 6am–8.45pm (pool) and 10pm (gym), Sat–Sun 6am–8pm. Light rail: Exhibition Centre. Map p. 148.

King George V Recreation Centre You get access to state-of-the-art sports and fitness facilities for just $13.50 a visit, including fitness classes.

Cumberland St., The Rocks. ℂ **(02) 9244 3600.** Main Centre: Mon–Fri 6.30am–9pm, Sat–Sun 10am–4pm; Fitness Centre: Mon–Thurs 6.30am–8.30pm, Fri 6.30am–7pm, Sat 10am–4pm. Train: Circular Quay. Map p. 148.

Pyrmont Community Centre   Forget signing up for long-term con-
tracts when you know you'll only go to the gym every now and again.
A casual visit to this fully equipped gym in the community centre is
just $7 ($6 if you're a local resident) and that includes the lunchtime
fitness classes.

Cnr. John and Mount sts., Pyrmont. ℂ **(02) 9298 3130.** Mon–Thurs 9am–9pm, Fri
9am–6pm, Sat 10am–4pm. Light rail: John St Square. Map p. 148.

Sydney Olympic Park Aquatic Centre   Follow in the wake of champions at the venue of the 2000 Sydney Olympics, where 15 world
records and 38 Olympic records were set in the water over the two-
week period. The competition pool is now open to the public for lap
swimming and there is also a leisure pool, Splasher's Water Playground (p. 256) and fitness centre. See website for specific times for
lap swimming and waterslide operating times.

Olympic Blvd., Sydney Olympic Park. ℂ **(02) 9752 3666.** www.aquaticcentre.com.
au. Mon–Fri 5am–9pm, Sat and Sun 6am–8pm (7pm in winter). Adult $6.80, kids
$5.50, pool only; $16.50 for gym and adult fitness classes. Train: Sydney Olympic Park.
Map p. 150.

DOCTORS & NURSES

Parramatta Sexual Health Clinic `FREE`   Affiliated with the University of Sydney, this teaching clinic offers free treatment, diagnosis,
follow-up, education and counselling for sexual health, sexually
transmissible diseases and HIV/AIDs. The clinic also has facilities for
colposcopy, contraception advice, pregnancy testing and counselling. Visits on Thursday are by appointment only (you have to wait
your turn on other days) and no referral is needed.

Level 1, Jeffrey House, 162 Marsden St., Parramatta. ℂ **(02) 9843 3124.** http://stirc.
med.usyd.edu.au/clinics/pshc.php. Thurs 4–7pm. Train: Parramatta. Map p. 150.

Sydney Institute of Traditional Chinese Medicine   Save money on
acupuncture, Chinese herbal medicine and Chinese remedial massage *(Tui Na)* at the student clinic of one of Australia's leading traditional Chinese medicine colleges. Massages start at $10, $20 for
acupuncture and $15 for herbal treatments, though the actual herbs
cost extra.

Level 5, 25 Dixon St., Haymarket. ℂ **(02) 9281 1173.** www.sitcm.edu.au. Mon and
Thurs 2–6.30pm, Tues, Wed and Fri 9am–6.30pm, Sat 9am–1.30pm. Train: Central.
Map p. 148.

Traditional Chinese Medicine Clinics The College of Traditional Chinese Medicine at University of Technology has two supervised student clinics that charge next to nothing and are open to the public. One specialises in acupuncture and Chinese remedial massage (open Monday afternoon and all day Friday), the other in Chinese herbal medicine (open Monday and Wednesday).

Ground floor, Building 4, Harris St. (cnr. Thomas St.), Ultimo. ☎ **(02) 9514 2509.** www.science.uts.edu.au/centres/tcm/clinics.html. Train: Central. Map p. 148.

Uniclinic It's a bit of a trek to get there (the clinic is on the Campbelltown campus), but this University of Western Sydney (UWS) training clinic offers supervised naturopathy, osteopathy, podiatry, traditional Chinese medicine and acupuncture and remedial and relaxation massage to the general public for $20 or $30 per consultation. All treatments are carried out by students and all are supervised by qualified clinicians and staff. No referral is needed, though you will need to make an appointment.

Level 3, Building 24, UWS Campbelltown Campus, Narellan Rd., Campbelltown. ☎ **(02) 4620 3700.** www.uws.edu.au. Train: Macarthur, then a 10-min. walk. Map p. 150.

University of New South Wales Optometry Clinic FREE A teaching facility for optometry students at the University of NSW operates a number of specialised clinics for all sorts of vision problems, as well as a general clinic. The service is available to anyone and eye examinations are carried out by supervised senior students and are free. See the website for appointment times.

Level 1, Rupert Myers Building, UNSW Kensington Campus (off Barker St.). ☎ **(02) 9385 4624.** www.optom.unsw.edu.au. Bus: 392, 394, 396, 397, 399 or L94 from Circular Quay. Map p. 151.

University of New South Wales Psychology Clinic This psychology clinic is staffed by psychologists enrolled in the Master of Psychology (Clinical) postgraduate program at the University of New South Wales, and while they can't provide treatment for people who are acutely psychotic, suicidal or in immediate crisis, they do provide clinical psychological services to adults, children and families who are experiencing psychological, emotional or behavioural problems. Sessions cost $50, which is at least half the price you pay at most psychological practices.

8th floor, Mathews Building, UNSW Kensington Campus (off Botany St). © **(02) 9385 3042.** http://clinic.psy.unsw.edu.au. Bus: 392, 394, 396, 397, 399 or L94 from Circular Quay. Map p. 151.

University of Sydney Psychology Clinic   The University of Sydney Psychology Clinic offers adult, child and family therapy sessions for $10. It's a teaching and research clinic and all treatments and assessments are undertaken by Intern Clinical Psychologists under the supervision of highly experienced Clinical Psychologists and Clinical Neuropsychologists. It's a good way to see a shrink without shrinking your bank balance. You don't need a referral, but appointments are essential.

Transient Building F12, Fisher Rd. (cnr. Physics Rd.), University of Sydney, Camperdown. © **(02) 9351 2629.** www.psych.usyd.edu.au/clinic. Mon–Fri 9am–5pm. Bus: 412, 413, 422, 423, 426, 428, 438, 440, 461, 480 or 483. Map p. 150.

University of Western Sydney School of Psychology Clinic   The University of Western Sydney offers a full range of psychology services, including obsessive-compulsive disorder (OCD) and anxiety disorders, behavioural medicine and child psychology, provided by postgraduate interns enrolled in Masters Degrees of Clinical and Forensic Psychology. Interns operate in pairs and all services are provided under the supervision of the staff of the School of Psychology. There is a one-off fee of $50 for all services provided, irrespective of the type of service (assessment or therapy) or the number of appointments during the course of treatment.

Building 24, UWS Bankstown Campus, Bullecourt Ave., Milperra. © **(02) 9772 6686.** www.uws.edu.au/psychology/. Wed–Fri. Train to Bankstown, then bus: 900 or 922. Map p. 150.

FIT & ACTIVE FOR FREE

Cycling in the City Course FREE   The City of Sydney runs free cycling courses throughout the year. Each course takes roughly half a day and teaches the essential skills of low-risk and responsible riding and is, according to the people who run the course, not for beginners; rather, it's 'designed for people who can already ride, but want confidence to ride on city streets'. Check the website for course dates and BYO bike.

CARES Facility, Sydney Park, Sydney Park Rd., Alexandria. © **(02) 9265 9333.** www.cityofsydney.nsw.gov.au and search for 'cycling'. Train: St Peters. Map p. 150.

Salsa Lessons

Sydney loves to shimmy and shake, but there's nothing worse than a clumsy cha-cha-cha or a rusty rumba, so head to one of these free or dirt-cheap dance classes before you hit the floor.

● Lessons at **Cruise Bar** are not free, but they're pretty cheap. Twenty dollars will get you a group dance lesson (and a drink) from 6pm on Tuesday nights at Cruise Bar, in the Overseas Passenger Terminal, West Circular Quay (✆ **(02) 9251 1188;** www. cruisebar.com.au; map p. 148).

● **FREE** They're dancing in the streets in Manly, or at least sashaying down the wharf end of **The Corso,** Outside Manly Town Hall (✆ **(02) 9976 1721;** www.manly.nsw.gov.au; map p. 152). Join a free salsa or waltz lesson each Thursday night from 6pm during the summer months.

● **FREE** Take advantage of the free group salsa lessons at **Establishment Bar** on Tuesday at 8pm before the dance party kicks off at the Establishment at 252 George Street, Sydney (✆ **(02) 9240 3000;** map p. 148). No partner is needed—but it's not a bad place to find one!

Disc Golf FREE   You might know it as frisbee golf, but whatever you call it, it's a lot of fun. For those that haven't played before, it's a bit like golf, but without a club and with a frisbee in place of a golf ball. The aim of the game is to complete each hole by getting your disc into a basket in the least number of throws. It's on every weekend and it's free, although the desperately disc-less will have to fork out a small fee to hire equipment.

Newington Armory, Jamieson St., Sydney Olympic Park. ✆ **(02) 9714 7888.** www. sydneydiscgolfclub.com or www.sydneyolympicpark.com.au. Sat and Sun 10.30am–3pm. Train: Sydney Olympic Park. Map p. 150.

Friday Night Skate FREE   Strap on your rollerblades and join like-minded skaters for a two-hour roll around the Sydney Harbour foreshore. It's not a particularly challenging skate, but you will need to be reasonably confident. There's also a free Wednesday night city skate that meets around 8.45pm at the steps of the Land Titles Office. The first Wednesday of the month is Virgin Skate, not so much for beginners as for first-timers to the weekly roll. The terrain gets harder each Wednesday until the last session of the month—Mission Skate—which is a bit extreme.

Visit www.sydneyfreeskate.com for details. Friday night skate: Meet at the Opera House end of Circular Quay at 8pm Friday. Train: Circular Quay. Wednesday night skate: Land Titles Office, cnr. Art Gallery, St Mary's and Prince Albert rds., opp. Hyde Park, Sydney. Train: St James. Map p. 148.

FREE MEDITATION & YOGA

Australian School of Meditation and Yoga `FREE` The folks at the Australian School of Meditation & Yoga promise that you can 'experience inner peace and lasting happiness by reawakening your natural spiritual consciousness and becoming self-realised' after attending a few of their free meditation classes. All that peace and quiet can't hurt though, and at least it's free, so what does it matter if lasting happiness takes a few sessions?

Visit www.asm.org.au for details. Woodstock Burwood Community Centre: 22 Church St. (off Fitzroy St.), Burwood; ✆ **(02) 9758 8913;** second Sun of the month 4.30–5.30pm; train Burwood; map p. 150. Reverse Garbage Community Centre: 142 Addison Rd., Marrickville; ✆ **(02) 9758 8913;** last Sun of the month 3.30–5.30pm; bus 428; map p. 150.

Buddhist Library and Meditation Centre `FREE` This not-for-profit library and mediation centre runs a series of free lectures on Tuesday evenings, designed to teach the basic principles of Buddhism and meditation. Outside of the course, which usually runs over four consecutive weeks, are weekly meditation classes (Tuesday 7pm, Wednesday 7.30pm, Friday 6pm) and a Saturday morning yoga class (10am). All classes are free, but donations are accepted.

90–92 Church St., Camperdown. ✆ **(02) 9519 6054.** www.buddhistlibrary.org.au. Mon–Fri 12.30–5pm (7pm Tues). Bus: 435, 436, 437, 438, 440, 461 or 480. Map p. 150.

Laughter Clubs `FREE` Guaranteed to make you feel good—or at least put a smile on your face—laughter yoga combines laughter with yogic breathing, although it may just give you a fit of the giggles. Check the website for details.

www.laughteryoga.org. Bondi Laughter Club: Bondi Pavilion, Queen Elizabeth Dr., Bondi Beach; Sun 10am; bus: 380 or 389; map p. 151. Newtown Laughter Club: Memorial Park, cnr. Federation Rd. and Australia St., Camperdown; Sat 10am; Train: Newtown. Map p. 151.

Tai Chi on the Cheap

Tai chi might look slow and easy, but it's harder than you think—and it's more of a workout than it looks. Join a class or two and get the basics right. Although similar to Tai Chi, Qigong is a more meditative exercise movement. Learn both at one of the free classes.

● Join the Tuesday Tai Chi class outside the **Newtown Neighbour-hood Centre** (1 Bedford St., Newtown, opp. Newtown Station; ℃ **(02) 9516 4755;** www.newtowncentre.org; map p. 150) for just $5 ($2.50 if you are unwaged). Bookings are essential.

● **FREE** There are free Tai Chi and Qigong classes every Wednes-day from 7 to 8.15am in Hyde Park near the Archibald fountain (℃ **(02) 9661 9328;** www.larryfriedberg.com; map p. 148).

Manly Library Stretch, Breathe and Meditate **FREE** Learn to relax and find your inner calm in this half-hour stretching and guided breathing and meditation class run by the Australian School of Meditation & Yoga on the second Saturday of the month (except in June). It's free, although any donations are gratefully accepted.

Manly Library Meeting Room, Market Pl., Manly. ℃ **0415 919 965.** www.asm.org.au. Second Sat of the month 3.30–5pm. Ferry: Manly. Map p. 152.

Sahaja Yoga Meditation **FREE** According to founder of Sahaja Yoga, Shri Mataji Nirmala Devi, 'Sahaja Yoga is different from other yogas because it begins with self-realisation', which really just means that this type of yoga is more about meditation and mental silence than any downward-facing dogs or warrior poses. There are free one-hour yoga and meditation meetings held at various locations around Sydney.

Visit www.sahajayoga.com.au for details. City centre: level 6, 110 Bathurst St., Sydney; ℃ **0413 542 273;** Fri 12.30pm; map p. 148. North Sydney: Stanton Library, 234 Miller St., North Sydney; ℃ **(02) 9499 9646;** Mon 12.30pm; map p. 152. Bondi Junction: 33 Spring St., Bondi Junction; ℃ **0422 798 498;** Mon 11.15am; map p. 151. Paddington: Paddington Public School, Oxford St., Paddington; ℃ **(02) 9328 6624;** Wed 7.30pm; map p. 151. Glebe: 123 Wigram Rd., Glebe; ℃ **(02) 9566 4021;** Thurs 7pm; map p. 150.

Sydney Buddhist Centre Meditation Classes FREE This is a good place to go if you're curious about meditation, but wary of signing up for a full course before giving it a go. The Saturday morning drop-in class is designed for people who have no previous meditation experience. You don't need to book and all it costs is a small donation.

24 Enmore Rd., Newtown. ✆ **(02) 9519 0440.** www.sydneybuddhistcentre.org.au. Sat 10.20–11.30am. Train: Newtown. Map p. 150.

5 Free Advice

Harris Freidman Hyde Page Divorce Seminar FREE Learn everything you've ever wanted to know about *untying* the knot, but were too afraid to ask. The free one-hour divorce seminar every Tuesday (times vary) is popular, so you'll need to reserve a place.

Level 10, 25 Bligh St., Sydney. ✆ **(02) 9231 2466.** www.hfhp.com.au. Train: Wynyard or Martin Place. Map p. 148.

Inner City Legal Centre FREE You can make an appointment with a volunteer lawyer to get free legal advice, information and referrals on Tuesday evening for general legal matters or employment law, and on Wednesday night for family and employment law matters or gay, lesbian or transgender legal advice.

50–52 Darlinghurst Rd., Kings Cross. ✆ **(02) 9332 1966.** www.iclc.org.au. Tues and Wed 6–8pm. Train: Kings Cross. Map p. 148.

Kingsford Legal Centre FREE University of New South Wales students from the Law Faculty boost their study of the operation of the legal system by working for clients of the legal centre for free. Appointments can be made for Tuesday and Thursday evenings.

Ground floor, Law Building, University of New South Wales, Anzac Parade, Kensington. ✆ **(02) 9385 9566.** www.law.unsw.edu.au. Bus: 391, 392, 393, 394, 395, 396, 397, 398 or 400. Map p. 151.

Kirribilli Neighbourhood Centre Legal Advice FREE Make an appointment for a free 20-minute interview with a professional solicitor on a range of matters including credit and debt, family law, criminal matters, motor vehicles, wills and small business. Bookings are essential.

16 Fitzroy St., Kirribilli. ✆ **(02) 9922 4428.** www.kncsydney.org. Tues 6–7pm. Train: Milsons Point.

FREE Free Futures

Why waste good money on some dodgy clairvoyant or palm-reading shyster when you can get it for free? And if you don't like what they have to say, you can always drown your sorrows at these two pubs . . .

● **Edinburgh Castle Hotel:** Every Tuesday from 6.30 to 8.30pm there's a resident tarot card reader who will expose what destiny has in store for you (294 Pitt Street, corner Bathurst Street, Sydney; ℂ **(02) 9264 8616;** www.edinburghcastlehotel.com.au; map p. 148). It's free—though if you are told what you want to hear it might be worth a decent tip!

● **Jacksons on George:** Free psychic readings on Wednesday nights from 7pm at 176 George Street, Sydney (ℂ **(02) 9247 2727;** www.jacksonsongeorge.com.au; map p. 148).

Legal Aid FREE   Legal Aid is primarily set up to provide legal services and representation for those that can't ordinarily afford legal help. You can get face-to-face advice on a number of issues without the need to apply or being means tested, although sessions are usually limited to 20 minutes before being referred to another lawyer or applying for a grant.

Visit www.legalaid.nsw.gov.au or call ℂ **1300 888 529** for information. Map p. 148.

Marrickville Legal Centre FREE   Face-to-face legal advice sessions on Tuesday and Thursday covering victims' compensation, discrimination, credit and debt, consumer complaints, family law (children's matters only), motor vehicle accidents (property damage), employment and fines. Appointments are essential.

338 Illawarra Rd., Marrickville. ℂ **(02) 9559 2899.** www.mlc.asn.au. Tues and Thurs 6.30–8.30pm. Train: Marrickville. Map p. 150.

Redfern Legal Centre FREE   Receive specialist credit and debt advice on Monday and Thursday evenings and assistance for women experiencing domestic violence, as well as more general legal issues. *Note:* they do not provide advice in conveyancing, commercial law and immigration law. Appointments are essential.

73 Pitt St., Redfern. ℂ **(02) 9698 7277.** www.rlc.org.au. Train: Redfern. Map p. 148.

Grandma Takes a Trip (p. 195) is a must for retro clothing aficionados.

SHOPPING

It can be all too easy to find yourself in a spending frenzy in Sydney, a city that is home to some of the best brand-name and designer shopping in the country. However, there are ways you can shop 'til you drop *without* breaking the bank, as long as you stay away from the big department stores and high-end boutiques. Instead, head to inner-city suburbs such as Newtown, Surry Hills and Alexandria, one of the big outlet centres in the outer suburbs or spend the weekends browsing the many markets. Or, save your hard-earned dollars for the twice-yearly city-wide sales, which begin on Boxing Day (December 26) and run through to the end of January and again from late June to mid-July.

Shopping hours are usually from 8.30am to 5.30pm Monday to Wednesday and Friday, 9am to 5pm Saturday and 8.30am to 9pm on Thursday. Most city and shopping centre stores are also open from around 10am to 4pm on Sunday.

1 Dirt-Cheap Shopping Zones

Alexandria for Factory Outlets   The traditional home of Sydney's rag trade has always been Surry Hills and Redfern, but rising real-estate prices have seen many factories and warehouses converted into plush apartments and a good few shops have relocated to nearby Alexandria. You'll find most of them on **Botany Road, McEvoy Street** and **Bourke Road.**

Train: Green Square. Map p. 178.

Cabramatta for Fabrics   Catch a train out to 'Cabra' (Sydney's Little Saigon) and pick up some great cut-price fabrics, Chinese fashion, jade jewellery, dirt-cheap kitchenware and items to sort out your feng shui while you're there (not to mention some of the cheapest, tastiest pho in town at Pho 54; p. 260). The best shops are on **Freedom Plaza, Park Road** and **John Street.**

Train: Cabramatta.

Chinatown for Chinoiserie   If you're looking for cheap Chinese *any-thing*—be it brand-new 'antiques', kitchenware, paper lanterns, silk cushions, herbal medicines, made-in-China underwear and socks, Hello Kitty handbags, Asian groceries or pork buns—head to Chinatown, which is bordered by **Hay, Harbour, Liverpool** and **Castlereagh streets. Dixon Street** is a pedestrianised shopping mall and there are plenty of bargains in **World Square, Paddy's Markets, Market City, Dixon Court** and any number of arcades that cut through the city blocks.

Train: Central. Map p. 177.

Glebe for Books   Glebe's always been a bit bookish. A slightly more gentrified version of neighbouring Newtown, it's full of students and academics, which might be why there are so many great bookshops catering especially to second-hand, rare and out-of-print books. The university end of **Glebe Point Road** is home to a heap, plus there are cafes in case you can't wait to turn those pages.

Bus: 431, 433 or 434. Map p. 174.

Newtown for Recycled and Retro   Grimy and grungy, the inner-city suburb of Newtown is Sydney's beating heart of all things recycled, re-used and retro—and I'm not just talking about the people on the street. Maybe it's all the starving students, artists, musicians and poets, or maybe it's the suburb's proud working-class roots, but if you're looking to pick up a cheap, slightly soiled bargain with a heap of street cred, this is the place to go. **King Street** and **Enmore Road** are the two main strips, with most of the good stuff to be found west of Newtown Station, where second-hand clothing and furniture shops predominate.

Train: Newtown. Bus: 352, 370, 422, 423, 426 or 428. Map p. 174.

Paddington for Designer Fashion   You might wonder why Padding-ton, with its famous **Oxford Street** 'Style Mile' of high-end designer stores, gets a mention in a guidebook dedicated to all things free and dirt cheap. Well, it's actually home to a number of great consignment stores where, if you really *must* have that label, at least it's cheap. Who cares if it's been worn before? It's still Dior, *daaarling*. Padding-ton is also home to one of the city's best fashion markets (p. 182).

Bus: 352, 378, 380 or 389.

Surry Hills for Vintage and Art   Another of my favourite inner-city neighbourhoods, Surry Hills is a vibrant place packed with galleries and boutiques full of cool streetwear, quirky gifts and cutting-edge design. The yuppies have started to move in, so it's not as cheap and cheerful as it once was, but there are still some great finds, particu-larly on the streets that spear off **Crown** and **Bourke streets.**

Bus: 301, 302, 303, 339, 352, 374, 376, 378, 380 or 391. Map p. 177.

2 Charity & Thrift Shops

Anglicare Depot   This church-based charity has 14 shops around Sydney, all offering pre-loved clothing and small household items. But the real bargains are to be found at the Summer Hill sorting ware-house, where clothes are priced by the kilo and the more you buy the cheaper it gets: $5 for the first kilo, $2.50 for each kilo thereafter. Clothes are piled high, so be prepared to do some digging.

105 Carlton Cres., Summer Hill. ℂ **(02) 9798 8206.** MC, V. Train: Summer Hill. Map p. 174.

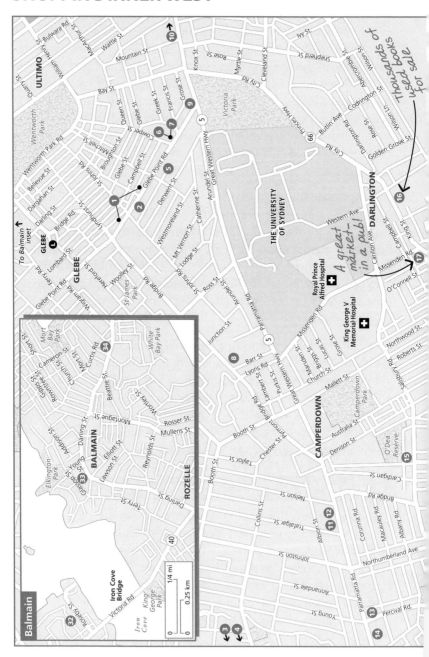

thousands of
used books
for sale

A great
market—
in a pub!

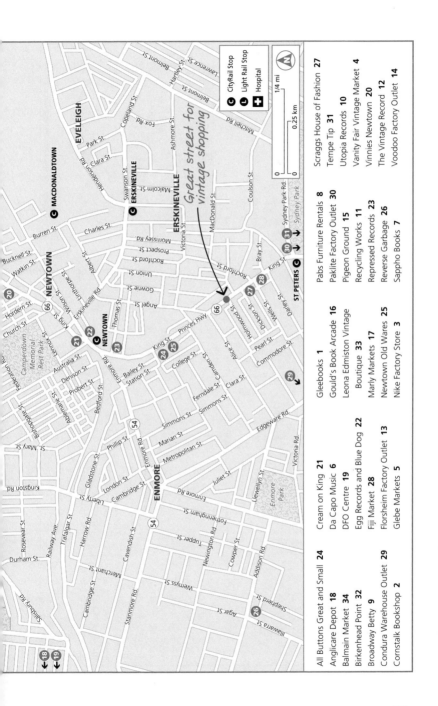

Great street for vintage shopping

Legend

- CityRail Stop
- Light Rail Stop
- Hospital

0 — 1/4 mi
0 — 0.25 km

All Buttons Great and Small **24**
Anglicare Depot **18**
Balmain Market **34**
Birkenhead Point **32**
Broadway Betty **9**
Condura Warehouse Outlet **29**
Cornstalk Bookshop **2**

Cream on King **21**
Da Capo Music **6**
DFO Centre **19**
Egg Records and Blue Dog **22**
Fiji Market **28**
Florsheim Factory Outlet **13**
Glebe Markets **5**

Gleebooks **1**
Gould's Book Arcade **16**
Leona Edmiston Vintage Boutique **33**
Marly Markets **17**
Newtown Old Wares **25**
Nike Factory Store **3**

Pabs Furniture Rentals **8**
Paklite Factory Outlet **30**
Pigeon Ground **15**
Recycling Works **11**
Repressed Records **23**
Reverse Garbage **26**
Sappho Books **7**

Scraggs House of Fashion **27**
Tempe Tip **31**
Utopia Records **10**
Vanity Fair Vintage Market **4**
Vinnies Newtown **20**
The Vintage Record **12**
Voodoo Factory Outlet **14**

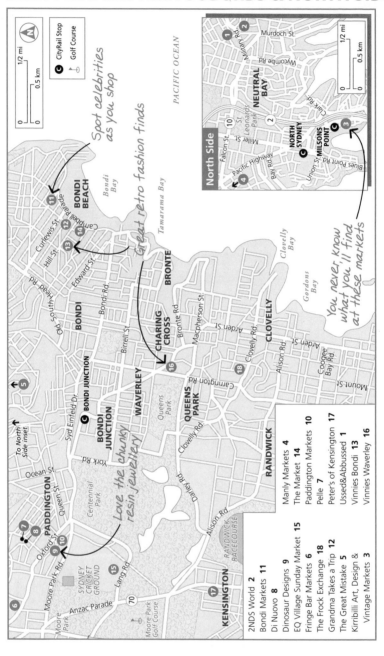

North Side

Spot celebrities as you shop

Great retro fashion finds

You never know what you'll find at these markets

Love the chunky resin jewellery

PACIFIC OCEAN

Bondi Bay

Tamarama Bay

Bronte

BONDI BEACH

BONDI

Clovelly Bay

Gordons Bay

Clovelly

CHARING CROSS

WAVERLEY

QUEENS PARK

RANDWICK

BONDI JUNCTION

PADDINGTON

KENSINGTON

2NDS World **2**
Bondi Markets **11**
Di Nuovo **8**
Dinosaur Designs **9**
EQ Village Sunday Market **15**
Fringe Bar Markets **6**
The Frock Exchange **18**
Grandma Takes a Trip **12**
The Great Mistake **5**
Kirribilli Art, Design & Vintage Markets **3**

Manly Markets **4**
The Market **14**
Paddington Markets **10**
Pelle **7**
Peter's of Kensington **17**
Ussed&Abbussed **1**
Vinnies Bondi **13**
Vinnies Waverley **16**

CityRail Stop
Golf Course

NEUTRAL BAY
NORTH SYDNEY
MILSONS POINT

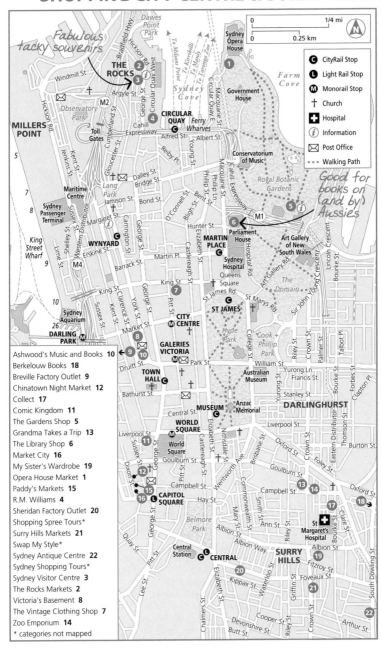

Fabulous tacky souvenirs

THE ROCKS ②③

Good for books on (and by) Aussies

C	CityRail Stop
L	Light Rail Stop
M	Monorail Stop
†	Church
✚	Hospital
ⓘ	Information
✉	Post Office
···	Walking Path

Ashwood's Music and Books 10
Berkelouw Books 18
Breville Factory Outlet 9
Chinatown Night Market 12
Collect 17
Comic Kingdom 11
The Gardens Shop 5
Grandma Takes a Trip 13
The Library Shop 6
Market City 16
My Sister's Wardrobe 19
Opera House Market 1
Paddy's Markets 15
R.M. Williams 4
Sheridan Factory Outlet 20
Shopping Spree Tours*
Surry Hills Markets 21
Swap My Style*
Sydney Antique Centre 22
Sydney Shopping Tours*
Sydney Visitor Centre 3
The Rocks Markets 2
Victoria's Basement 8
The Vintage Clothing Shop 7
Zoo Emporium 14
* categories not mapped

SHOPPING ALEXANDRIA & REDFERN

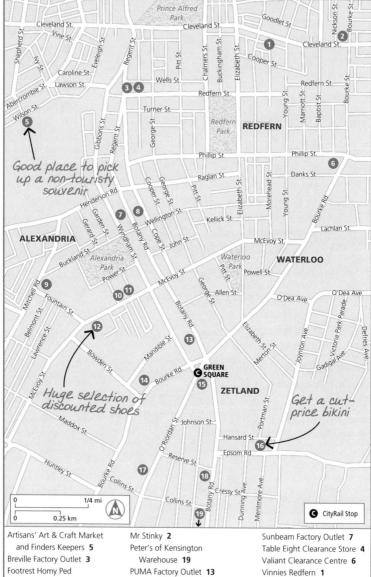

Good place to pick up a non-touristy souvenir

Huge selection of discounted shoes

Get a cut-price bikini

Artisans' Art & Craft Market and Finders Keepers **5**	Mr Stinky **2**	Sunbeam Factory Outlet **7**
Breville Factory Outlet **3**	Peter's of Kensington Warehouse **19**	Table Eight Clearance Store **4**
Footrest Homy Ped Factory Outlet **8**	PUMA Factory Outlet **13**	Valiant Clearance Centre **6**
The Handbag and Shoe Factory Outlet **11**	The Remnant Warehouse **18**	Vinnies Redfern **1**
Mitchell Road Auction Centre **9**	Seafolly **10**	World Kitchen Factory Outlet **17**
	Shoes 2000 Factory Warehouse **12**	Yardware Factory Outlet **15**
	Sportscraft and Saba Outlet **14**	Zimmermann **16**

Recycling Works   This huge warehouse of second-hand furniture donates a goodly dollop of their profits to a range of charities or worthy appeals, depending on who needs it most at the time.

45 Parramatta Rd. (btw. Trafalgar and Nelson sts.), Annandale. ✆ **(02) 9517 2711.** MC, V. Bus: 413, 436, 437, 438 or 440. Map p. 174.

Salvos Stores   The Salvation Army has Salvos Stores in almost every suburb of Sydney, where you'll find a treasure trove of good-quality pre-loved clothing, furniture, books, toys and manchester. The stuff is always dirt cheap, but shop Monday through Wednesday for $1 and $3 clothing specials. The biggest and best is lovingly known as the **Tempe Tip** (not to be confused with a real rubbish tip), which has just about anything and everything you could ever want to buy for a nominal amount. It's a great spot to go for furniture if you're frugal.

4 Bellevue St., St Peters. ✆ **(02) 9519 1513**. www.salvosstores.salvos.org.au. MC, V. Train: Sydenham. Map p. 174.

Vinnies   Like the Salvos, the St Vincent de Paul Society has donated clothing and homewares stores all over the city, and there are a few that have some seriously chic and stylish vintage fashions. Try the **Bondi** and **Newtown** stores or **Waverley**, which also has a lot of pre-loved designer and high-end label clothes. For retro furniture try **Waverley** or **Redfern.**

Bondi: 60 Hall St, Bondi; ✆ **(02) 9300 0585;** bus: 380 or 389. Map p. 176. Newtown: 187 King St, Newtown; ✆ **(02) 9557 1996;** train: Newtown. Map p. 174. Waverley: 253 Bronte Rd., Waverley; ✆ **(02) 9387 7088;** bus 378. Map p. 176. Redfern: 317 Cleveland St, Redfern; ✆ **(02) 9387 7088;** bus: 372. Map p. 178. www.vinnies.org.au. MC, V.

3 Factory Outlet Centres

Birkenhead Point   There are more than 135 big-name fashion brand factory outlet and clearance stores here, including Country Road, Jigsaw, Marcs, Spotlight, Birkenhead Surf Factory Outlet, Morrissey, Table Eight, Fleur Wood, Insport, French Connection (FCUK), David Jones Warehouse and Kathmandu.

Roseby St., Drummoyne. ✆ **(02) 9812 8800.** www.birkenheadpoint.com.au. Most shops take AE, MC, V. Bus: 500 from Town Hall. Map p. 174.

Outlet Shopping Tours

Buy enough stuff on sale and you'll have saved more than what you spend on a full- or half-day bus tour that visits some of the more popular fashion factory outlets scattered around the inner-city suburbs—and you'll have had a whole heap of fun along the way.

- **Shopping Spree Tours** (© **1300 558 353;** www.shoppingspree.com.au; MC, V) cost $75 for a full day and also include lunch, though they only run on Fridays.

- **Sydney Shopping Tours** (© **1800 673 709;** www.sydney shoppingtours.com.au; MC, V) cost $49 for half-day and $69 for full-day tours (the full day includes lunch).

★ **DFO Centre**   There's a Direct Factory Outlet (DFO) mega-mall in almost every major city on the east coast. Sydney's is at Homebush, where you'll find 90 stores (everything from fashion and sportswear to manchester and furniture) offering up to 70% off normal retail prices, although often it's the stuff that nobody wanted last year.

Cnr. Homebush Bay Dr. & Underwood Rd., Homebush. © **(02) 9748 9800.** www.dfo.com.au. Most shops take AE, MC, V. Train: Strathfield, then bus 525. Map p. 174.

Market City   East meets west in this shopping centre above Paddy's Markets in Chinatown, so expect lots of cheap Chinese imports and speciality stores as well as some good streetwear, more than 30 factory outlets of top fashion brands and great yum cha in the food hall.

Cnr. Hay and Thomas sts., Haymarket. www.marketcity.com.au. Most shops take AE, MC, V. Train: Central. Monorail: Paddy's Markets. Map p. 177.

4 Markets

Artisans' Art & Craft Market FREE   Local artists and designers show and sell their sculpture, design, ceramics, glass, craft and Indigenous art.

Eveleigh Railyards, 243 Wilson St. (next to CarriageWorks), Darlington. © **(02) 9209 4220.** First Sun of the month 10am–4pm. Train: Redfern. Map p. 178.

Balmain Market `FREE`   This tiny market sells mainly bric-a-brac and second-hand clothes, with a sprinkling of art and homewares—plus, there's good food inside the hall.

St Andrews Church, cnr. Darling St. and Curtis Rd., Balmain. ℭ **(02) 9555 1791.** www.bondimarket.com.au. Sat 8.30am–4pm. Bus: 442. Map p. 174.

★ **Bondi Markets** `FREE`   The best place for vintage and retro clothing or to snag a piece from a future fashion designer. It's also where you're most likely to find celebrities slinking around the stalls, hiding behind their sunglasses.

Bondi Beach Public School, Campbell Parade, Bondi. ℭ **(02) 9315 8988.** www.bondimarkets.com.au. Sun 10am–5pm. Bus: 380 or 389. Map p. 176.

Chinatown Night Market `FREE`   Go to one of Sydney's only regular night markets for good, cheap made-in-China fashion, jewellery, ornaments and masseurs.

Dixon Street Mall, Haymarket. Fri 4–11pm. Train: Central. Map p. 177.

EQ Village Sunday Market `FREE`   You'll find a mix of jewellery and accessories, skin-care products, toys, homewares and clothing under the cover of the market umbrellas.

Lang Rd. (next to the SCG), Moore Park. www.entertainmentquarter.com.au. Sun 10am–4pm. Bus: 339, 355, 372, 373, 374, 376, 377, 391, 392, 394, 395, 396, 397 or 399. Map p. 176.

Finders Keepers `FREE`   They are only on twice a year, but the Finders Keepers markets are definitely worth going to if you like design and art. More than 60 emerging artists and designers from around Australia converge at CarriageWorks for the market, which is usually held in May and December.

CarriageWorks, 245 Wilson St., Darlington. www.thefinderskeepers.com. Train: Redfern. Map p. 178.

★ **Glebe Markets** `FREE`   Glebe Markets are alternative with lots of second-hand clothes, books and music and slightly out-there arts and crafts. There's a big grassy area that's great for kids to run around and there's usually some entertainment.

Glebe Primary School, Glebe Point Rd., Glebe. www.glebemarkets.com.au. Sat 10am–4pm. Bus: 431 or 433. Map p. 174.

Kirribilli Art, Design & Vintage Markets `FREE` You never know what you might find among the art, jewellery, fashion and various unique pieces here. It's affiliated with a vintage market (antiques, collectables and vintage clothing) in neighbouring Bradfield Park, called Kirribilli Vintage Quarter Market.

Burton St. Tunnel, Milsons Point. Second Sun of the month 9am–3pm. Train: Milsons Point. Map p. 176.

Manly Markets `FREE` Jewellery, paintings, photography, sculptures, homemade body care products and souvenirs. The markets have recently expanded and now include a weekly farmers market in Short Street Plaza each Saturday from 9am to 1pm.

Sydney Rd. (beach end), Manly. ✆ **(02) 9231 7011.** www.manlymarkets.com.au. Sat and Sun 10am–5pm. Ferry: Manly. Map p. 176.

Opera House Market `FREE` Here you'll find arts and crafts from Sydney-based artists. Some of it's tacky and touristy, some of it's not, but it's worth a look if only because it is in such a beautiful spot.

Opera House Forecourt, Sydney. Sun 10am–5pm. Train: Circular Quay. Map p. 177.

★ **Paddington Markets** `FREE` These markets have long been a launching pad for most of Australia's, and certainly Sydney's, famous fashion designers. It's the place to find quality contemporary art, craft and fashion, sold to you by the artists and craft makers themselves. Go early, as it gets very crowded by early afternoon.

Paddington Uniting Church, Oxford St., Paddington. ✆ **(02) 9331 2923.** www.paddingtonmarkets.com.au. Sat 10am–4pm. Bus: 378 or 380. Map p. 176.

Paddy's Markets `FREE` There's been a market here since 1834, although back then it was all about hay, grain and cattle (hence the

---

`FREE` Stuff for Free

There's a lot of truth in the old saying 'one person's trash is another's treasure' and every local council generally has a couple of scheduled pick-up days each year when householders can leave any unwanted bits of furniture and other bulky items outside for removal. It can be a great way to source free furniture; check your local council's website for scheduled pick-up days and get ready to load the truck!

Shopping Sippers

We all know drink driving is a big no-no, as is DWT (driving while texting), but no-one says you can't drink and *shop* at these markets that are held in pubs. Just don't let the alcohol cloud your better judgement or you could spend more than you bargained for.

- ● FREE Find cheap designer threads in the heart of Paddington's exclusive shopping strip at the **Fringe Bar Markets** at 106 Oxford Street (www.thefringe.com.au). What's not to love about that? Head there on Saturday between 10am and 5pm.

- ● FREE Newtown's best boho, vintage and soon-to-be fashionable designs are for sale at the **Marly Markets** at the Marlborough Hotel (145 King Street; ℂ **(02) 9519 1222**) on the first Saturday of the month from 11am to 4pm.

name of the surrounding suburb: Haymarket). These days there are close to 1000 stalls that sell everything from fresh produce to cheap fashion and accessories, electrical goods and souvenirs.

Hay St., Haymarket. Wed–Sun 9am–5pm.Train: Central. Light Rail and monorail: Paddy's Markets. Map p. 177.

The Rocks Markets FREE   There is some tourist tat here, but the quality of the art, craft, jewellery and homewares on sale is mostly pretty good and it can be a great place to pick up a non-touristy—or touristy, if that's what you like—souvenir.

Northern end of George St., The Rocks. Sat and Sun 10am–5pm. Train: Circular Quay. Map p. 177.

Surry Hills Markets FREE   It's all about second-hand and handmade items at this monthly market in the park.

Cnr. Crown and Little Collins sts., Surry Hills. First Sat of the month. Bus: 301, 302, 303 or 352. Map p. 177.

Vanity Fair Vintage Market   This is the city's biggest vintage market with retro clothing, vintage jewellery, fashion accessories, art, linen, lace and homewares. Most of the stallholders are dealers, so the stuff tends to be high quality (less trash, more treasure), but it's also a little higher in price than other second-hand markets around town.

Leichhardt Town Hall, cnr. Norton and Marion sts., Leichhardt. www.vanityfairmarkets. com. Second weekend of every month. Adults $4, kids $2, two-day ticket $6/$3. No credit cards. Bus: 370, 440 or 445. Map p. 174.

5 Bargain Shopping from A to Z

ANTIQUES

The Market   This is not to be confused with the weekly Bondi Markets (p. 181); in this case, the cavernous hall is packed to the rafters with second-hand furniture and old wares.

2 Jacques Ave., Bondi. ✆ **(02) 9365 1315.** MC, V. Bus: 380 or 389. Map p. 176.

Mitchell Road Auction Centre   If you really want to nab a bargain, go to the Monday auction, but if you can't get there then the store is a good second best. Prices vary from super-cheap to positively pricey, but it stocks everything from Victoriana to 20th-century design.

76 Mitchell Rd., Alexandria. ✆ **(02) 9310 7200.** www.mitchellroadauctions.com. MC, V. Train: Erskineville. Map p. 178.

★ **Newtown Old Wares**   I guess it depends on your definition of antiques, but this place specialises in furniture and homewares from 'deco to disco', blurring the line between antique and retro. It's one of my favourite shops for the high tacky factor alone.

439 King St., Newtown. ✆ **(02) 9519 6705.** No credit cards. Train: Newtown. Map p. 174.

Sydney Antique Centre   Some of the stuff here is hideously expensive, but you can sometimes find a real bargain in one of the 50 'stores' that are under the one big roof. There's antique furniture, porcelain, glass, jewellery, clocks, watches, kitchenware, lights, Asian goods, rugs, sports memorabilia, bottles, books, dolls and collectables.

531 South Dowling St., Surry Hills. ✆ **(02) 9361 3244.** www.sydantcent.com.au. Most stores take MC, V. Bus: 339, 372, 374, 376, 391, 393 or 395. Map p. 177.

BEACHWEAR

Seafolly   Factory seconds, samples and discontinued lines of the popular Seafolly swimwear range for both adults and kids are sold at this warehouse store. Most are around half the price of what you'd pay in retail stores, but sometimes you can score up to 80% off.

111–117 McEvoy St., Alexandria. ℭ **(02) 9690 1955.** MC, V. Train: Green Square. Map p. 178.

Zimmermann   A teeny, weeny Zimmermann bikini usually sells for more than $200, but you can often pick one up at this outlet store for a much more reasonable $70. Other gear usually sells for around 60% to 80% off normal prices. If that doesn't make you feel good on the beach, nothing will.

48–56 Epsom Rd., Zetland. ℭ **(02) 9697 9988.** www.zimmermannwear.com. AE, MC, V. Train: Green Square. Bus: 345, 348 or 370. Map p. 178.

BOOKS

Berkelouw Books   It's not only the extensive range of new, rare and second-hand books that make this bookstore a favourite with bookworms, it's also the late opening hours: until 11pm most nights; midnight on Friday and Saturday.

19 Oxford St., Paddington. ℭ **(02) 9360 3200.** www.berkelouw.com.au. AE, MC, V. Bus: 378 or 880. Map p. 177.

Comic Kingdom   You can spend hours arguing about whether comics constitute books, but, really, what difference does it make when you can spend hours browsing the thousands of classic comics, weird LPs, dog-eared paperbacks and pop-culture mags at this temple to geekdom. Prices start at just 50¢; $5 can buy you hours of illustrated pleasure.

71 Liverpool St., Sydney. ℭ **(02) 9267 3629.** www.comickingdom.com.au. MC, V. Train: Town Hall. Map p. 177.

Cornstalk Bookshop   If you are after a ripping murder mystery or books on or by Australians, this is the place to go. Specialising in antiquarian, rare and out-of-print books on Australiana and detective fiction, this place sells books that you can't get anywhere else.

112 Glebe Point Rd., Glebe. ℭ **(02) 9660 4889.** www.cornstalk.com.au. MC, V. Bus: 431 or 433. Map p. 174.

★ **Gleebooks**   Gleebooks is the best bookshop in Sydney, as far as I'm concerned. Not only does it stock a huge range of titles, but it hosts regular author events, book signings, readings and other literary events. The original Gleebooks up the road (at 191 Glebe Point Road) specialises in children's, antiquarian and second-hand, so it's the place to go to get a great bargain.

49 and 191 Glebe Point Rd., Glebe. ℂ **(02) 9660 2333.** www.gleebooks.com.au. AE, MC, V. Bus: 431 or 433. Map p. 174.

★ **Gould's Book Arcade**   Gould's is a cavernous temple to second-hand and out-of-print books, covering just about any topic—though the owner, Bob Gould, has a passion for Australian history and politics and the art section is huge.

32 King St., Newtown. ℂ **(02) 9519 8947.** www.gouldsbooks.com.au. No credit cards. Train: Newtown. Map p. 174.

Sappho Books   There are four rooms of second-hand books here with more than 30,000 titles on hand. As the name would suggest, there's a strong female author and lesbian section, but you'll find just about any type of book except airport thrillers, cheap romances and trash. There's also a lovely little cafe in the courtyard out the back where you'll often find a jazz trio on Sunday afternoon.

51 Glebe Point Rd., Glebe. ℂ **(02) 9552 4498.** www.sapphobooks.com.au. MC, V. Bus: 431 or 433. Map p. 174.

FABRICS

All Buttons Great and Small   This place likes to brag that it has an 'extravagant' collection of buttons, and it does. If you're after buttons—of any kind—this is the place to go.

419A King St., Newtown. ℂ **(02) 9550 1782.** www.allbuttons.com.au. AE, MC, V. Train: Newtown. Map p. 174.

Fiji Market   It might seem a little odd to visit what is primarily a spice shop if you're on the hunt for affordable fabric, but Newtown's Fiji Market is so much more than it looks from the outside. Importing all things Indian, there is a great range of fabrics, saris, sarongs and bangles—of course, they might all smell a bit spicy, but that's half the attraction of shopping here.

591 King St., Newtown. ℂ **(02) 9517 2054.** No credit cards. Train: St Peters. Map p. 174.

The Remnant Warehouse   You'll find thousands of small lengths of material and leftovers perfect for crafts and patchwork, fashion and costume designers. There's also a good range of fashion and designer fabrics, and lots of accessories and haberdashery items.

494 Botany Rd., Alexandria. ℂ **(02) 9698 7855.** www.theremnantwarehouse.com. au. MC, V. Bus: 309 or 348. Map p. 178.

FASHION

Di Nuovo   Recycled designer fashion from Australia and overseas at up to half the price you would pay for the same thing brand new. Everything's sold on consignment and stock changes every two months.

92 William St., Paddington. ℂ **(02) 9361 4221.** www.dinuovo.com.au. AE, MC, V. Bus: 378 or 380. Map p. 176.

The Frock Exchange   A favourite with Sydney's fashionistas, this little corner store in Clovelly sells recycled designer label fashions without the expensive price tags (think Marc Jacobs, Prada and Collette Dinnigan). It's part of the high-end Belinda chain, which means you can sometimes pick up brand new never-worn items at sale prices.

221 Clovelly Rd., Clovelly. ℂ **(02) 9664 9188.** www.thefrockexchange.com.au. MC, V. Bus: 339. Map p. 176.

The Great Mistake   Turn your fashion faux pas into someone else's fashion find. But it's not just fashion mistakes on sale; savvy shoppers use it to turn over their wardrobe on a seasonal basis. Good-quality recycled fashion is sold on consignment and stock changes daily, although the best time to go is early February and August when new stock arrives from other stores at greatly reduced prices. Popular labels found here include Country Road, Fletcher Jones, Sportscraft, Aywon, Trent Nathan, Sportsgirl, Covers, Weiss, Adele Palmer/Jag, Carla Zampatti and Simona.

Shop 8, 3–9 Spring St., Chatswood. ℂ **(02) 9412 1070.** www.greatmistake.com.au. MC, V. Train: Chatswood. Map p. 176.

Leona Edmiston Vintage Boutique   Leona Edmiston is one of the country's top designers, producing gorgeously glamorous frocks, shoes and accessories. She's a favourite of style queens such as Nicole Kidman, Kylie Minogue, Helena Christensen and Elle Macpherson. Her clothes are usually well out of our price range, but her vintage store in Balmain sells past-season collections and samples at prices that are eminently more affordable.

483 Darling St., Balmain. ℂ **(02) 9810 3046.** www.leonaedmiston.com. AE, MC, V. Bus: 433. Map p. 174.

Fashion Auction

Recessionista fashionistas can pick up some fashion bargains at the regular fashion auctions held at The Entertainment Quarter (EQ) on Lang Road in Moore Park (✆ **(02) 8117 6700;** no credit cards). There's often a small reserve on the stock, but there are some amazing bargains to be had on some seriously good labels. Unfortunately, you can't try on the clothes before you bid and it's cash only, but you can check out the brands online the Friday before the auction, which is always held on a Sunday at 1pm, and view the clothes in real life for an hour before the first hammer falls. Visit the website for more details and next auction dates: www.entertainmentquarter.com.au.

Sportscraft and Saba Outlet   There are two bargain-filled levels at this factory outlet store. Downstairs tends to be mainly homewares and manchester, but go upstairs for elegant clothing from two of the country's best brand names at around 75% off retail prices.
Cnr. Bourke Rd. and Bowden St., Alexandria. ✆ **(02) 9319 4615.** AE, MC, V. Train: Green Square. Map p. 178.

Table Eight Clearance Store   Table Eight does great high-street fashion and office wear, as well as a good range of leisure wear. There are clearance stores in the Birkenhead Point outlet centre and DFO in Homebush, but if they are too far out of the way, head to the Redfern store, where you can find samples, overruns and stock cuts for 70% off.
164–166 Redfern St., Redfern. ✆ **(02) 9318 0886.** www.t8clearance.com. AE, MC, V. Train: Redfern. Map p. 178.

Ussed&Abbussed   There's no fear of leaving your credit card used and abused after a shopping spree at this store, which sells last season's designer jeans, clothes and accessories at up to 80% off normal retail prices. Despite the name, nothing has been pre-loved: it's all new stock.
Shop 1, 7 Parraween St., Cremorne. ✆ **(02) 9909 2827.** MC, V. Bus: 169, 172, 175, 176, 179, 180, 202, 207, 227, 228, 229 or 230. Map p. 176.

FURNITURE, HOMEWARES & ELECTRICAL

2NDS World   Just about every gas and electrical appliance you could desire, from flat-screen TVs to whitegoods, juicers, hairdryers and phones, is available here. Some are seconds, some are superseded models, some are just on sale, but they are all cheaper than what you'll find in chain and department stores.

237 Military Rd., Cremorne. ℂ **(02) 9904 1101.** www.2ndsworld.com.au. MC, V. Bus: 168, 169, 171, 172, 183, 244, 246, 248, 247 or 249. Map p. 176.

Breville Factory Outlets   Need a new electric razor? Or perhaps an electric jug, hairdryer, rice cooker—or any other small electrical appliance? Then head to one of these factory outlets and enjoy big savings on Breville, Kambrook, Ronson and Philishave factory seconds. They are all in good working order and comply with all safety regulations, but choose carefully—there's a no return or refund policy.

Pyrmont: 46 Wattle St., Pyrmont; ℂ **(02) 9660 8217;** AE, DC, MC, V; bus 443, 449 or 501. Redfern: 180 Redfern St., Redfern; ℂ **(02) 9318 2370;** AE, DC, MC, V; train Redfern. Map p. 177.

Pabs Furniture Rentals   The ex-rental furniture for sale may have been used, but the rental stock is turned over very quickly, so it's not dated and it's usually still in pretty good condition. There's everything from televisions to fridges to sofas.

5 Pyrmont Bridge Rd., Camperdown. ℂ **1800 201 020** (toll free in Australia). www.pabs.com.au. AE, DC, MC, V. Bus: 412, 413, 436, 437, 438 or 440. Map p. 174.

Peter's of Kensington   A massive warehouse-sized retail shop selling all manner of kitchenware and cooking gadgets, luggage, toys and nursery items—even cosmetics. Shoppers will be pleased to know that there is almost always a sale of some type on, and it's a great place to buy wedding gifts. The retail store is at Kensington, but there's also a warehouse in Alexandria that is open only on weekends, where you'll save even more cash.

Kensington: 57 Anzac Pde., Kensington; ℂ **(02) 9662 1099;** AE, MC, V; bus 390, 391, 392, 394, 396, 397, 398 or 399. Alexandria: 6 Bradford St., Alexandria; AE, MC, V; bus 309, 310 or 357. www.petersofkensington.com.au. Map p. 176.

Sheridan Factory Outlet   Bedroom and bathroom fashion at dirt-cheap prices is the name of the game here. The factory outlets sells discontinued stock and slightly imperfect items—but at prices this low, who cares if there is a tiny dye run on your bottom sheet or a slightly dodgy hem on your $20 queen-sized bath towel? There's also a store at DFO in Homebush.

Shop 5, 17–51 Foveaux St., Surry Hills. ℂ **(02) 9212 1813.** AE, DC, MC, V. Train: Central. Map p. 177.

Sunbeam Factory Outlet You can get up to 50% off household appliances at this factory outlet. Some are discontinued lines, others are perfectly fine but the box is torn or dirty and most items come with a 12-month replacement warranty.

110–120 Botany Rd., Alexandria. ℂ **(02) 9318 9000.** AE, MC, V. Bus: 355. Map p. 178.

Valiant Clearance Centre Go here for high-quality modern designer furniture at up to 75% off the retail price. Most of the stock is either ex-rental or ex-display so, other than being a little shop-worn, it's perfect.

Level 1, 863 Bourke St. (cnr. Philip St.), Waterloo. ℂ **(02) 9310 1666.** AE, MC, V. Bus: 301. Map p. 178.

Victoria's Basement Why would you pay full price for china, cookware, glassware, tableware, dinnerware, kitchen gadgets, giftware or collectables when they are always on sale at Victoria's Basement? Big-name brands include Waterford, Wedgwood, William James, Scanpan, Avanti and Portmeirion and they are often half the recommended retail price.

Basement, Queen Victoria Building, George St. (btw. Park and Market sts.), Sydney. ℂ **(02) 9261 2674.** www.victoriasbasement.com.au. AE, MC, V. Train: Town Hall. Map p. 177.

World Kitchen Factory Outlet Collect some bakeware, dinnerware, kitchen tools, cookware and cutlery from leading brands such as CorningWare, Pyrex, Corelle, Baker's Secret and OXO at up to 70% off retail prices at this factory outlet.

29–31 O'Riordan St., Alexandria. ℂ **(02) 9317 1061.** www.worldkitchen.com.au. AE, MC, V. Train: Green Square. Map p. 178.

Yardware Factory Outlet Give your backyard a makeover with some stylish new outdoor furniture from this factory outlet, where you can get up to 75% off factory seconds, ex-display models, sample stock and discontinued models.

6 O'Riordan St., Alexandria. ℂ **(02) 9310 2666.** www.yardware.com.au. AE, MC, V. Train: Green Square. Map p. 178.

MUSIC

Ashwood's Music and Books Go here for second-hand CDs, LPs, DVDs, videos and books. Sheet music (some of it dating back to the early 1900s) is available for between $1 and $5. If you're a vinyl junky you'll love this place.

129 York St., Sydney. ✆ **(02) 9267 7745.** MC, V. Train: Town Hall. Map p. 177.

Da Capo Music   More than 50,000 second-hand and antiquarian music books, scores and sheet music. It's a great place to finally get your hands on those hard-to-find music items; it's a very popular spot with collectors.

Upstairs, 51 Glebe Point Rd., Glebe. ✆ **(02) 9660 1825.** www.dacapo.com.au. AE, MC, V. Bus: 431 or 433. Map p. 174.

Egg Records   There's a great range of second-hand and independent music on vinyl and CDs, film and memorabilia at this quirky little store in Newtown. Pop next door after you've finished buying to browse the range of vintage posters at **Blue Dog:** they're proudly 'keeping Newtown Weird'.

Egg Records: 3 Wilson St., Newtown; ✆ **(02) 9550 6056;** www.eggrecords.com.au. MC, V. Blue Dog: 9 Wilson St, Newtown. Train: Newtown. Map p. 174.

Repressed Records   Second-hand CDs, vinyl and lots of grunge rock clothing are available here. It's good place to go for independent music recordings.

356 King St., Newtown. ✆ **(02) 9557 6237.** www.repressedrecords.com. MC, V. Train: Newtown. Map p. 174.

Reverse Garbage

It's the ultimate in recycling. Reverse Garbage (✆ **(02) 9569 3132;** www.reversegarbage.org.au; MC, V) is a not-for-profit co-op that sells all sorts of stuff that has been dumped (think computer bits, industrial discards, off-cuts, fabrics, bits of plastic and even bathroom sinks), er . . . sorry, I mean donated by all sorts of companies and individuals who no longer have a use for it. It's popular with arty types who use the bits in their work or even theatre sets and stage costumes. Big bits (such as filing cabinets, store mannequins or metal drums) are sold on an individual basis, but the small things you can buy by the sack: $20 for a hessian bagful. It's at at 8/142 Addison Road, Marrickville.

Swap 'til You Drop

If you're a strong believer in the reduce, re-use, recycle credo, you'll love these fashion swapping events.

- Once a month the Clothing Exchange hosts a fashion swap meet called **My Sister's Wardrobe** upstairs at 10A Fitzroy Place (off Crown Street) in Surry Hills (www.clothingexchange.com.au; no credit cards), attracting everything from designer wear to quality basic garments from local high street stores. Your clothes will swapped for 'buttons', which you can then use to purchase new clothes. Obey the golden rule and do unto others . . . bring only what you would be prepared to take home! This is not about dumping tattered gear for new threads—everything you take to swap will need to be in near-perfect condition and clean—but it's a fun way to pick up some new clothes for the price of the entry fee ($20 if you book online; $25 at the door). Entry includes a glass of wine. Map p. 177.

- **Swap My Style** events are similar to those hosted by the Clothing Exchange, but you also have the option to swap one-on-one as well as browsing the racks. Everything must be less than two years old and have a minimum item value of $100. It's the perfect place to free your wardrobe of all those 'it will look great once I've lost five kilos' pieces and shoes that were a size too small but you bought them anyway. Check the website for details of the next event, which is usually held at night in a swish bar, such as **The Loft** (upstairs at Kings Street Wharf, 3 Lime Street) or **Ivy** (320–330 George Street). You'll need to register online (www.swapmystyle.com.au; no credit cards); entry fees vary from $25 to $50, depending on the venue, and include glass of bubbly.

The Vintage Record If you believe iPods are a passing fad and that vinyl is—and always will be—king, get yourself to The Vintage Record for a veritable vinyl feast with one of the city's biggest collection of old-fashioned black plastic discs.

31A Parramatta Rd., Annandale. ✆ **(02) 9550 4667.** www.thevintagerecord.com. MC, V. Bus: 412, 413, 436, 437, 438, 440, 461, 480 or 483. Map p. 174.

Utopia Records   This is one for the heavy metal fans, with all things metal, including a great range of second-hand CDs and vinyl.

233 Broadway, Ultimo. ✆ **(02) 9571 6662.** www.utopia.com.au. MC, V. Bus: 412, 413, 431, 433, 436, 437, 438, 440, 461, 480 or 483. Map p. 174.

SHOES & BAGS

Condura Warehouse Outlet   Here you'll find fashionable handbags for every occasion—from beach to office to sparkly evening bags—as well as hats, gloves, scarves and belts.

10 Gerald St., Marrickville. ✆ **(02) 8595 6999.** www.condura.com.au. MC, V. Train: Sydenham. Map p. 174.

Footrest Homy Ped Factory Outlet   Homy Peds may not be the sexiest shoes around, but they sure are made for walking, which makes them a traveller's (and shopper's) best friend in my book. Besides, they are much more stylish than they used to be. Buy them here, rather than at your local chemist, and you'll save a packet.

115A Botany Rd., Waterloo. ✆ **(02) 9310 3320.** AE, MC, V. Train: Redfern. Map p. 178.

The Handbag and Shoe Factory Outlet   As the name implies, you can get all manner of brand-name shoes and handbags here on the cheap (all items are at least half price).

Shop 3, 111 McEvoy St., Alexandria. ✆ **(02) 9699 3449.** MC, V. Bus: 305 or 370. Map p. 178.

Paklite Factory Outlet   Paklite makes great luggage and you can get samples, discontinued lines and end-of-line items at between 30 and 70% off retail prices from their factory store (only open on Friday).

First Floor, 82 Bellingara Rd., Miranda. ✆ **(02) 9522 8911.** MC, V. Train: Miranda. Map p. 174.

Pelle   This place sells second-hand European designer footwear and accessories. I know that some people might find the idea of walking around in someone else's shoes a bit off-putting, but everything sold in the shop is in mint condition.

90 William St., Paddington. ✆ **(02) 9331 8100.** www.pelleshoes.com.au. MC, V. Bus: 378 or 380. Map p. 176.

Shoes 2000 Factory Warehouse   It tends to specialise in work boots and school shoes, but don't let that put you off if you're looking for some strappy sandals or shiny stilettos—it's home to one of the largest selections of fashionable shoes, sandals, boots and sports shoes in Sydney, all at discounted prices. Some styles are on sale here before they get to the shops.

135–139 McEvoy St., Alexandria. ℂ **(02) 9319 6422.** MC, V. Bus: 305 or 370. Map p. 178.

Florsheim Factory Outlet   This shoe store doubles as the Florsheim Factory Outlet. Popular with well-dressed men and lawyer-types, these high-quality men's leather dress shoes sell here for between 10% and 50% less than what you'd get them for in the shops. There's also a small range of women's shoes.

264 Parramatta Rd., Stanmore. ℂ **(02) 9569 4787.** AE, DC, MC, V. Bus: 412, 413, 436, 437, 438, 440, 461, 480 or 483. Map p. 174.

SPORTSWEAR

Nike Factory Store   Why pay good money for Chinese-made fakes when you can buy the real thing for a song at the factory door? Just do it!

130 Parramatta Rd., Auburn. ℂ **(02) 9648 4791.** AE, MC, V. Train: Auburn. Map p. 174.

PUMA Factory Outlet   You'll find almost the entire range of PUMA sportswear at discounted prices at this factory outlet in Alexandria. They sell a good mix of current season and clearance stock, as well as a few discontinued lines and samples.

1/290 Botany Rd., Alexandria. ℂ **(02) 9690 2700.** AE, MC, V. Train: Green Square. Map p. 178.

UNDERWEAR

Voodoo Factory Outlet   You'd be mad to pay full price for hosiery when you can buy it direct from the factory for around 30% less. It stocks lots of brands (Voodoo, Kolotex, Kayser, Kicks, Wicked and Sheer Relief) as well as bras and knickers by Bonds, Berlei and Playtex and a range of socks.

320 Parramatta Rd., Stanmore. ℂ **(02) 9560 7336.** AE, MC, V. Bus: 413, 435, 436, 437, 438, 461, 480 or 483. Map p. 174.

VINTAGE

Broadway Betty   Broadway Betty is dark and dingy, and it's also next door to a brothel. If you're game enough to make it through the door and do some digging you'll find a treasure trove of glitzy party frocks and vintage shoes.

259 Broadway, Glebe. ℂ **(02) 9571 9422.** AE, MC, V. Bus: 412, 413, 431, 433, 436, 437, 438, 440, 461, 480 or 483. Map p. 174.

Cream on King   This recycled retro store is all about the '70s, '80s and '90s. Unlike many of the other vintage clothes stores in Newtown staff have done the digging for you, so you don't need to impersonate a ferret to find something worth taking home. (Although that does mean you pay a little more.)

317 King St., Newtown. ℂ **(02) 9565 2955.** MC, V. Train: Newtown. Map p. 174.

★ **Grandma Takes a Trip**   A huge range of clothing and accessories from the '50s through '80s is available here, all imported from the UK, US and Europe. The Bondi store has a great collection of retro swimwear.

Surry Hills: 263 Crown St., Surry Hills; ℂ **(02) 9356 3322;** bus 378 or 380; map p. 177. Bondi: 79 Gould St., Bondi; ℂ **(02) 9130 6262;** bus 380 or 389; map p. 176. www. grandmatakesatrip.com.au. MC, V.

Mr Stinky   There's nothing stinky at all about the range of classic clothing from the '60s, '70s and '80s. If you like brightly coloured polyester this could well become your favourite store.

482–484 Cleveland St. (cnr. Bourke St.), Surry Hills. ℂ **(02) 9310 7005.** MC, V. Bus: 372, 393 or 395. Map p. 178.

Pigeon Ground   This place is half record store, it's half clothing store and *all* vintage. I shop here just for the great range of handmade accessories such as the Vinyl Richie bangles made from melted records and other quirky bits of recycled jewellery.

102 Salisbury Rd., Camperdown. ℂ **(02) 9557 6364.** www.pigeonground.com. MC, V. Bus: 412. Map p. 174.

Scraggs House of Fashion   Great retro fashion, but even better retro accessories at this tiny shop down the St Peters end of King Street. Be prepared to sort through the racks for the best stuff.

559 King St., Newtown. ℂ **(02) 9550 4654.** MC, V. Train: St Peters. Map p. 174.

The Vintage Clothing Shop This is the place to go if you're looking for some vintage glam, with lots of sparkly '20s flapper frocks, ball gowns and heirloom-quality jewellery. It may not be as cheap as some of the grungier vintage stores you'll find in Newtown and Surry Hills, but if you looking for a special occasion ensemble it's much cheaper (and more stylish) than buying new. If you're not hooked on white you could well find the perfect wedding dress here.

Shop 7, St James Arcade, 80 Castlereagh St., Sydney. ℂ **(02) 9238 0090.** www.thevintageclothingshop.com. MC, V. Train: St James. Map p. 177.

Zoo Emporium Walk through the doors of Zoo Emporium and you're back in the '70s and '80s with racks of retro street fashion on display.

180b Campbell St. (off Crown St.), Surry Hills. ℂ **(02) 9380 5990.** AE, MC, V. Bus: 378 or 380. Map p. 177.

6 Non-Touristy Souvenirs

Artisans' Art & Craft Market Pick up a unique handmade piece of made-in-Sydney art to take home on at these monthly markets at Eveleigh Railyards.

Eveleigh Railyards, 243 Wilson St. (next to CarriageWorks), Darlington. First Sun of the month 10am–4pm. Train: Redfern. Map p. 178.

Collect The retail arm of the not-for-profit Object Gallery is the place to find beautiful (but not always cheap) unique ceramics, collectable glass, homewares and jewellery.

417 Bourke St., Surry Hills. ℂ **(02) 9361 4511.** www.object.com.au. AE, MC, V. Bus: 378 or 380. Map p. 177.

Dinosaur Designs A Paddington Markets success story, these colourful homewares and chunky jewellery made from resin are all handmade and very, very covetable. They now have a shop in New York, but nothing beats buying wares from their concept store next door to the churchyard market where it all began.

339 Oxford St., Paddington. ℂ **(02) 9361 3776.** AE, MC, V. Bus: 378 or 380. Map p. 176.

The Gardens Shop What better way to remember Sydney than planting a living souvenir in your garden? The Gardens Shop inside the Royal Botanic Gardens sells a range of native Australian seeds (check your country's customs regulations about importing seeds before you buy). They also have a great range of Australian native bush foods, cosmetics based on Australian plant species and beautiful stationery, cards and prints featuring exquisite drawings of Australian plants.

Royal Botanic Gardens, Mrs Macquaries Rd., Sydney. ℂ **(02) 9231 8125.** MC, V. Train: Martin Place or Circular Quay. Map p. 177.

The Library Shop   The bookshop at the State Library of New South Wales has one of the best collections of books on, and by, Australians and is a great place to pick up a book that is a cut above the usual published-for-tourists picture books. There also a good range of limited-edition prints, photographs and some lovely Sydney-centric greeting cards, many of which look great framed. They also have an extensive range of beautifully illustrated classic Australian kids' books.

Macquarie St., Sydney. ℂ **(02) 9273 1414.** www.sl.nsw.gov.au. MC, V. Train: Martin Place. Map p. 177.

R.M. Williams   A pair of iconic hand-crafted elastic-sided R.M. Williams boots don't come cheap, but they make a fantastic non-touristy souvenir, and they last *forever*. There are a number of outlets across the city, but the one in The Rocks is pretty central.

71 George St, The Rocks. ℂ **(02) 9247 0204.** AE, MC, V. Train: Circular Quay. Map p. 177.

The Best Non-Touristy Touristy Souvenir for Under $6

Don't leave Sydney without a couple of 'Coathanger' coathangers. The **Sydney Visitor Centre** (cnr. Argyle and Playfair streets, The Rocks; ℂ **(02) 9240 8788;** www.sydneyvisitorcentre.com; MC, V) stocks my all-time favourite Sydney souvenir: Harbour Bridge (also known as 'The Coathanger') clothes hangers. You can't get much more Sydney than that!

They also have some natty trays for your freezer that make ice blocks in the shape of Australia, Australian-animal-shaped cookie cutters and a whole range of inexpensive Australian novelties that you won't find in most souvenir shops.

Street theatre (p. 215) is a great source of free entertainment.

ENTERTAINMENT & NIGHTLIFE

If Sydney was a person, it would be a good-time girl in sky-high heels. Sydney loves to party, whether it be at the world's best fireworks display on New Year's Eve or just heading to a favourite bar for a drink with friends, watching a rock band in a pub or burning up the dance floor until the sun comes up.

It pays to plan your time in Sydney to make the most of the gratis entertainment that's on offer. You'll often catch free classical music in the city at lunchtime, whereas Sunday afternoon is the best time for jazz. Tuesday is the day to see movies on the cheap, tickets to theatre matinees are more affordable than night-time performances—previews are also an excellent way to save cash—and happy hour is always the best time for a drink.

1 Muzak

CLASSICAL MUSIC

★ **Art Gallery of New South Wales** FREE   The Sunday Concert Series, performed by the students and staff of the Australian Institute of Music (AIM) at the Art Gallery of New South Wales, reflects the themes and eras of the artworks and exhibitions on display. There are concerts most Sundays from 12.30 to 1.30pm at the Old Courts on the ground level of the gallery.

Art Gallery Rd., The Domain. ✆ **(02) 9225 1700.** www.artgallery.nsw.gov.au. Train: Martin Place, then 10 min. walk. Map p. 204.

City Recital Hall Angel Place   This space was designed in a shoebox shape, which is apparently the best for listening to western classical music, and is the home of the city's best orchestras. Tickets usually cost a bomb, but the monthly Little Lunch Music concerts cost just $10 and feature some of the city's best classical artists.

2 Angel Pl. (btw. George and Pitt sts., near Martin Pl.), Sydney. ✆ **(02) 8256 2222.** www.cityrecitalhall.com. Train: Martin Place. Map p. 204.

★ **Conservatorium of Music** FREE   Part of the University of Sydney, the Conservatorium is one of the country's most prestigious music schools. You can catch the classical stars of tomorrow in concert for free at the Open Academy concerts that are held on most Saturdays at 11am. There's also a 50-minute Lunchbreak Concert Series every Wednesday at 1.10pm; entry is the price of a gold coin. For those who have a bit of cash to spend, there's the dirt-cheap Conductor Series, where you can enjoy the best ensembles—from early music to improvisational jazz—for just $15. FINE PRINT If you buy tickets to three or more concerts, the tickets price reduces to just $10 each.

Macquarie St. (opp. Bridge St.), Sydney. ✆ **(02) 9351 1438.** www.music.usyd.edu.au. Train: Circular Quay. Map p. 204.

Great Hall Organ Recitals FREE   Modelled on the great hall of Westminster Palace in London, the Great Hall at Sydney University is one of the finest examples of Victorian Gothic architecture in Australia; it's all

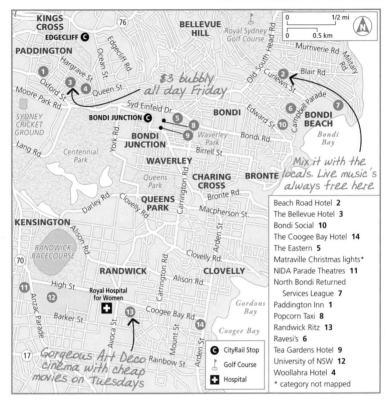

KINGS CROSS
EDGECLIFF C
PADDINGTON
76
BELLEVUE HILL
Royal Sydney Golf Course
Murriverie Rd.
Edgecliff Rd.
Ocean St.
Hargrave St.
Oxford St.
Moore Park Rd.
Queen St.
Syd Einfeld Dr.
$3 bubbly all day Friday
Blair Rd.
Old South Head Rd.
Curlewis St.
Campbell Parade
Military Rd.
BONDI
Edward St.
BONDI BEACH
Bondi Bay
SYDNEY CRICKET GROUND
BONDI JUNCTION C
Lang Rd.
Centennial Park
York Rd.
BONDI JUNCTION
Waverley Park
Bondi Rd.
Birrell St.
WAVERLEY
Queens Park
Darley Rd.
Clovelly Rd.
CHARING CROSS
BRONTE
Carrington Rd.
Bronte Rd.
Macpherson St.
Mix it with the locals. Live music's always free here
QUEENS PARK
KENSINGTON
Alison Rd.
RANDWICK RACECOURSE
70
Arden St.
Clovelly Rd.
RANDWICK
High St.
CLOVELLY
Royal Hospital for Women
Carrington Rd.
Alison Rd.
11
12
Anzac Parade
Barker St.
Avoca St.
Coogee Bay Rd.
13
Mount St.
14
Arden St.
Gordons Bay
Coogee Bay
17
Gorgeous Art Deco cinema with cheap movies on Tuesdays
Rainbow St.

0 ___ 1/2 mi
0 ___ 0.5 km
N

Beach Road Hotel **2**
The Bellevue Hotel **3**
Bondi Social **10**
The Coogee Bay Hotel **14**
The Eastern **5**
Matraville Christmas lights*
NIDA Parade Theatres **11**
North Bondi Returned Services League **7**
Paddington Inn **1**
Popcorn Taxi **8**
Randwick Ritz **13**
Ravesi's **6**
Tea Gardens Hotel **9**
University of NSW **12**
Woollahra Hotel **4**
* category not mapped

C CityRail Stop
Golf Course
Hospital

arched ceilings, carved angels and stained-glass windows. And as grand as that all is, the masterpiece is the Great Hall Organ. There are regular free recitals on Sunday afternoons, usually at 3.30pm, with a pre-recital talk at 3.10pm. See the website for the next scheduled concert.

Main Quadrangle, off University Ave., University of Sydney. ℂ **(02) 9351 2222.** www.usyd.edu.au/organ. Bus: 412, 413, 435, 438, 440, 461, 480 or 483. Map p. 210.

★ **Kirribilli Neighbourhood Centre** Check out the view of the Harbour Bridge while you soak in the music at the bi-monthly Sunday Sunset Concerts in the gallery. They're performed by the Amateur Chamber Music Society at 5pm on the first Sunday of odd-numbered months (plus in December). Tickets cost just $10 and include wine and supper.

16 Fitzroy St., Kirribilli. ℂ **(02) 9922 4428.** www.kncsydney.org. Train: Milsons Point. Map p. 202.

ENTERTAINMENT & NIGHTLIFE NORTH SIDE

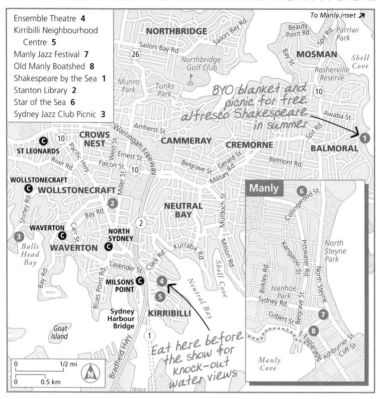

Ensemble Theatre **4**
Kirribilli Neighbourhood
Centre **5**
Manly Jazz Festival **7**
Old Manly Boatshed **8**
Shakespeare by the Sea **1**
Stanton Library **2**
Star of the Sea **6**
Sydney Jazz Club Picnic **3**

St Andrew's Cathedral FREE   St Andrew's Cathedral has a vibrant music program that includes organ recitals on Friday from 1.10 to 1.40pm; a series of recitals by some of Sydney's most talented young musicians from the Sydney Conservatorium of Music and the Australian Institute of Music on Thursday from 1.10pm; concerts by the boys in the choir from St Andrew's Cathedral School on Monday from 12.30pm (during school term); big band music (think army, police and navy) on Wednesday at 12.30pm; and the Cathedral Choir singing choral Evensong every Thursday at 5.30pm. The choristers also sing choral Matins on Wednesday at 8am—and let's not forget the cathedral's principal Sunday morning service at 10.30am. All concerts are free, although a gold coin donation is much appreciated.

St Andrew's Cathedral, cnr. George and Bathurst sts., Sydney. 🕐 **(02) 9265 1661.** www.cathedral.sydney.anglican.asn.au. Train: Town Hall. Map p. 204.

St James' Church FREE Catch a free half-hour concert at St James' every Wednesday at 1.15pm. The program is varied, with everything from the Royal Australian Navy Band to classical strings, guitar trios and organ recitals. The concerts are free, but a donation of $5 is suggested. For those with a bit more cash, the church is also home to regular baroque brass and other classical concerts with tickets selling for $25 (which includes a glass of wine). That's way less than half the price you'd pay at most other classical music venues around the city.

173 King St., Sydney. ✆ **(02) 8227 1300.** www.sjks.org.au. Train: Martin Place. Map p. 204.

St Mary's Cathedral FREE Do the names Ora Pro Nobis, Nomen Jesu Christi, St Bede or St Patrick ring any bells? They should, as they are just four of the 12 bells of St Mary's. You can get to know the bells (and the bell ringers) on a first-name basis during practice on Thursday from 6 to 8pm, or during the service ringing (Sunday from 10 to 10.30am and Wednesday from noon to 1pm). You can even learn the fine art of bell ringing yourself if you book ahead.

St Mary's Rd., Sydney. ✆ **(02) 9220 0400.** www.stmaryscathedral.org.au. Train: St James. Map p. 204.

St Stephen's Uniting Church FREE You never know who or what you'll find on stage at this Friday lunchtime concert series, but you can expect anything from a *camerata* orchestra to soloists on French horn, clarinet or baroque bassoon. The 30-minute concerts start at 1.10pm and entry is free, although a donation is appreciated.

197 Macquarie St., Sydney. ✆ **(02) 9221 1688.** www.ssms.org.au. Train: Martin Place. Map p. 204.

The University of Sydney War Memorial FREE Carillons, the largest musical instruments in existence, are the mother of all bells. To qualify as a carillon there must be at least 25 bells, and the War Memorial at Sydney University, which was built to commemorate the 197 students and staff who died in World War I, has a whopping 62. There are free recitals every Sunday afternoon (usually around 2pm). The best place to listen is in the southwest corner of the main quadrangle, which is a lovely spot for a picnic. During university term you can also catch a free recital from 1 to 2pm on Tuesday, when you can visit the clavier room and see the keyboard that actually plays the bells.

Main Quadrangle, off University Ave., University of Sydney. ✆ **(02) 9487 2386.** www.carillon.org.au/usyd/. Bus: 412, 413, 435, 438, 440, 461, 480 or 483. Map p. 210.

Arq **57**
Art Gallery of New South Wales **26**
The ArtHouse Hotel **36**
Bar Europa **30**
The Bat and Ball Hotel **6**
BBM*
Belvoir St Theatre **5**
The Beresford Hotel **65**
The Bourbon **33**
The Brag*
Brett Whiteley Studio **4**
Brooklyn Hotel **17**
Buskers*
Cafe Sydney **15**
Charlie Chans **54**
Chauvel Cinema **64**
City Recital Hall Angel Place **23**
The Clock Hotel **66**
COFA Talks **62**
Conservatorium of Music **16**
Cruise Bar **12**
Darling Harbour Hoopla and
   Jazz & Blues Festival **44**
Darlinghurst Theatre **31**
Darlo Bar **51**
Dendy Cinemas Opera Quays **13**
The Domain Concert Series **27**
Drum Media*
Edinburgh Castle Hotel **48**
El Rocco Jazz Bar **41**
Establishment Bar **18**
Fortune of War Hotel **14**
The Fringe Bar **61**
Gaelic Club **1**
The Genesian Theatre **37**
Govinda's **47**
Great Southern Bar **55**
Greater Union and Hoyts cinemas **49**
Griffin Stablemates **45**
Hyde Park **34**
Japan Foundation **19**
Jazushi **3**
Kings Cross Hotel **42**
La Cita **24**
The Mac **53**
Martin Place Bar **25**
NSW Parliament **22**
Old Fitzroy Theatre **39**
Opera Bar **11**
Paddy Maguires **60**
Palace Cinemas **58**
Pontoon **38**
Powerhouse Museum **59**

SBW Stables Theatre **46**
Scubar **63**
Slip Inn **29**
St Andrew's Cathedral **43**
St James' Church **28**
St Mary's Cathedral **32**
St Stephen's
   Uniting Church **21**
State Library of
   New South Wales **20**
Stonewall Hotel **56**
Strawberry Hills Hotel **2**
The Studio at The Sydney
   Opera House **8**
The Sugarmill **35**
Sydney Harbour Bridge **7**
Sydney Theatre Company **10**
Tap Gallery **52**
Time Out Sydney*
Two Thousand*
The Victoria Room **50**
Vivid Sydney **9**
The World Bar **40**
* categories not mapped

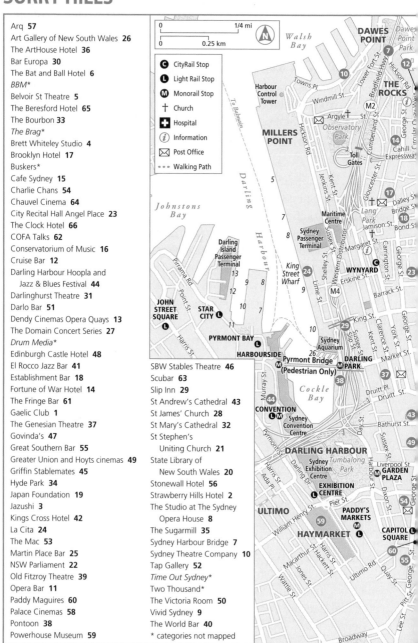

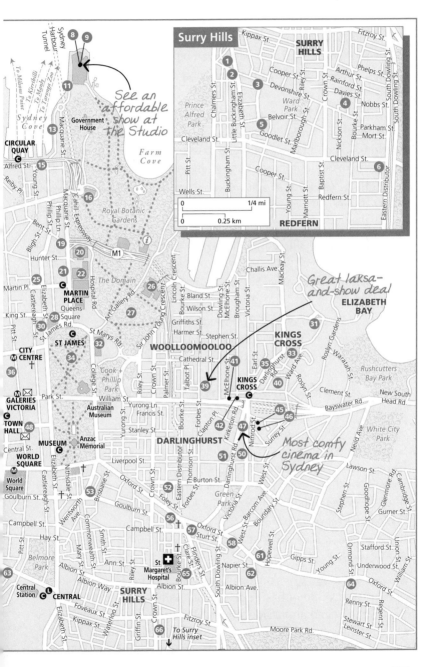

Surry Hills

SURRY HILLS

Prince
Alfred
Park

Ward
Park

REDFERN

See an
affordable
show at
the Studio

CIRCULAR
QUAY

Sydney
Cove

Government
House

Farm
Cove

Royal Botanic
Gardens

ELIZABETH
BAY

Great laksa-
and-show deal

MARTIN
PLACE

Queens
Square

KINGS
CROSS

ST JAMES

CITY
CENTRE

The Domain

WOOLLOOMOOLOO

Rushcutters
Bay Park

KINGS
CROSS

GALERIES
VICTORIA

TOWN
HALL

Cook +
Phillip
Park

Australian
Museum

DARLINGHURST

Most comfy
cinema in
Sydney

White City
Park

MUSEUM

Anzac
Memorial

WORLD
SQUARE

World
Square

Green
Park

Central
Station

CENTRAL

Margaret's
Hospital

SURRY
HILLS

Belmore
Park

To Surry
Hills inset

JAZZ

The ArtHouse Hotel FREE   There's free live jazz every Friday night from 6.15pm in the very cozy Dome Lounge, which is more like a lounge room than a bar, but with much better drinks.

275 Pitt St., Sydney ℂ **(02) 9284 1200.** www.thearthousehotel.com.au. Train: Town Hall. Map p. 204.

★ **Cafe Sydney** FREE   Listen to sophisticated jazz while overlooking the Harbour Bridge on the rooftop of Customs House. The food and drinks aren't cheap, but the jazz is free from midday every Sunday. If you're out to impress, this would be a very good place to do it.

Customs House, Level 5, 31 Alfred St., Circular Quay. ℂ **(02) 9251 8683.** www.cafe sydney.com. Train: Circular Quay. Map p. 204.

El Rocco Jazz Cellar FREE   This cozy basement bar has a free open mic and jazz and Latin jam sessions on Monday from 8pm called Bar Me. Everyone is welcome, whether you play, sing or prefer to watch.

154 Brougham St. (cnr. William St.), Potts Point. ℂ **(02) 9368 0894.** Train: Kings Cross. Map p. 204.

Fortune of War Hotel FREE   Proudly boasting that it's the oldest pub in Sydney, this atmospheric little pub has a Heritage-Listed hamper-style bar, old-fashioned tiled walls and free jazz on Sunday afternoons from 3 to 6pm.

137 George St., The Rocks. ℂ **(02) 9247 2714.** www.fortuneofwar.com.au. Train: Circular Quay. Map p. 204.

Jazushi FREE   This place offers free jazz every night of the week except Monday, dished up alongside Japanese food with a French flavour—tempura camembert anyone? Mains are $12 to $25, but are designed to share and prices can quickly add up, so if you're hungry, fill up elsewhere and just nibble on a few of the cheaper dishes and BYO wine to save cash.

145 Devonshire St., Surry Hills. ℂ **(02) 9699 8977.** www.jazushi.com.au. Train: Central. Map p. 204.

★ **Opera Bar** FREE   You can't get much more Sydney than the Opera Bar; it's one of best spots to watch the sun go down and the city light up. Grab an outside table and soak up the spectacular view while listening to very fine live jazz on a Sunday afternoon from 2 to 9pm. There's also live lounge music Monday to Saturday from 8.30pm until late. The music's always free, and while the drinks may not be the cheapest in town this is definitely one place that's worth a splurge. A balmy night at the Opera Bar—it doesn't get much finer than this.

Lower Concourse, Sydney Opera House. 𝄢 **(02) 9247 1666.** www.operabar.com.au. Train: Circular Quay. Map p. 204.

Strawberry Hills Hotel `FREE`   Free jazz from 4pm on weekends and $5 steaks (they're not the best in town, but they are among the cheapest) make this a great place to spend Saturday or Sunday afternoon.

453 Elizabeth St. (cnr. Devonshire St.), Strawberry Hills. 𝄢 **(02) 9698 2997.** Train: Central. Bus: 372. Map p. 204.

Sydney Jazz Club Picnic `FREE`   The Sydney Jazz Club is the third-oldest, continually running jazz club in the world. It holds a monthly picnic at Berry Island Reserve in Wollstonecraft on the North Shore. Confusingly, it's on the Sunday following the third Friday of every month from noon to 3pm. BYO picnic hamper and rug and there's a playground to keep kids amused.

Berry Island Reserve, end of Shirley Rd., Wollstonecraft. 𝄢 **(02) 9719 3876.** www.sydneyjazzclub.com. Train: Wollstonecraft. Map p. 202.

★ **Unity Hall Hotel** `FREE`   The Unity Hall Jazz Band gets the crowd tapping their toes in this old working-class pub in Balmain every Friday night from 9.30pm and every Sunday afternoon from 4pm.

292 Darling St., Balmain. 𝄢 **(02) 9810 1331.** www.unityhallhotel.com.au. Bus: 412, 433 or 442. Map p. 210.

★ **The Victoria Room** `FREE`   One of my favourite bars in Sydney, this place is the epitome of tasteful bordello chic—although they prefer to describe it as British Raj. Either way, think red velvet, gilt, rich wallpapers and sublime sofas. It's popular with gal-pals who flock here for a sophisticated high tea in the afternoon and cocktails once the sun sets, plus it's a great place to listen to live music at the Wednesday Night Jazz Club from 8pm.

Level 1, 235 Victoria St., Darlinghurst. 𝄢 **(02) 9357 4488.** www.thevictoriaroom.com. au. Train: Kings Cross. Bus: 311. Map p. 204.

Woollahra Hotel `FREE`   If you like your jazz a little more tribal than Dixie or a bit more samba than swing, this is the place to go. The free live Jazz Juice sessions are every Sunday from 6.30 until 9.30pm and

Thursday from 7.45 until 10.45pm. Expect everything from wild Afri-
can drumming to Afro–Cuban jazz—and wear your dancing shoes.

116 Queen St., Woollahra. ℭ **(02) 9327 9777.** www.woollahra.com.au. Bus: 380, 387
or 389. Map p. 201.

LIVE ACOUSTIC & ROCK

★ **Annandale Hotel** You'll find the full range of music, from reggae
to heavy metal, at this working-class pub that's a favourite with students. This is where you'll see the next big thing on stage every night
except Tuesday, when you can catch a cult movie at the Sinema
instead (p. 220). It'll cost around $15 to see most bands, but Wednes-
day nights are dirt cheap: see five bands for $5 at the Jäger Uprising.
The five bands play (on two stages) for 30 minutes each in a battle-of-
the-bands play-off that's worth $10,000.

17–19 Parramatta Rd., Annandale. ℭ **(02) 9550 1078.** www.annandalehotel.com.
Bus: 412, 413, 436, 437, 438 or 440. Map p. 210.

The ArtHouse Hotel FREE The beautifully refurbished 1830s
School of Arts is now the place to go for clever cocktails and free live
acoustic music on Thursday from 6.30pm and Friday from 8.30pm.

275 Pitt St., Sydney. ℭ **(02) 9284 1200.** www.thearthousehotel.com.au. Train: Town
Hall. Map p. 204.

The Bat and Ball Hotel FREE Tuesday brings Fresh Sets—that's
fancy-talk for an open-mic night—to this slightly grimy inner-city pub.
It's a good place to see up-and-comers play their stuff.

495 Cleveland St., Surry Hills. ℭ **(02) 9699 3782.** www.batandballhotel.com.au. Bus:
372, 393 or 395. Map p. 204.

FREE Trashioke

Even the most elegant man or woman has a no-taste trashbag lurking
deep within their psyche, so let it free and sing and dance at the **Edinburgh Castle Hotel** (294 Pitt St., Sydney; ℭ **(02) 9264 8616;** www.
edinburghcastlehotel.com.au) on Saturday night from 7 to 11pm. The
pub's 'wardrobe department' supplies the gear, the karaoke machine
supplies the tunes—all you have to do is supply the moves and the
'tude. Map p. 204.

Beach Road Hotel `FREE`   This pub has live rock and pop on Wednesday, Thursday and Sunday nights. Tuesday's a bit more folksy and acoustic, while Friday and Saturday nights are all about DJs and dancing. Whatever your taste, the music's always free, the dress code's casual—this is Bondi Beach, after all—and the crowd is friendly.

71 Beach Rd., Bondi. ℂ **(02) 9130 7247.** www.beachrdhotel.com.au. Bus: 380 or 389. Map p. 201.

Lansdowne Hotel `FREE`   Good pub. Cheap food. Free bands. What else can I say? Okay, so it's a little dark and the floor can get a bit sticky, but come here when it's dark and crowded and you'll hardly notice. You can catch some great indie rock played loud on Friday and Saturday nights. Wear lots of black if you don't want to stand out in the crowd.

2 City Rd., Chippendale. ℂ **(02) 9211 2325.** Bus: 426, 428, 431, 433, 438, 440 or 461. Map p. 210.

The Mac `FREE`   The proper name of this pub is The Macquarie, but everyone just calls it The Mac. The Mac likes to boast that it is 'the only dedicated house of funk in Sydney', and it has free live music every night. See the website for details of what's on.

42 Wentworth Ave., Surry Hills. ℂ **(02) 8262 8888.** www.macquariehotel.com. Bus: 301, 303 or 378. Map p. 204.

North Bondi Returned Services League (RSL) `FREE`   The Bondi Rats, as it's known to locals, serves dirt-cheap fish and chips and beer. On Saturday nights, the place rocks with free live music—unless there's a Wallabies rugby game, in which case it is invaded with rugby fans that come to watch the game on the big screen.

120 Ramsgate Ave., North Bondi. ℂ **(02) 9130 3152.** www.northbondirsl.com.au. Bus: 380 or 389. Map p. 201.

Paddy Maguires `FREE`   An Irish pub in the heart of Chinatown? It might not be the first place you'd think to go for some of the city's best live reggae music, but the Irish have always been full of surprises. Monday is reggae night, but there's also live music on Tuesday, Wednesday, Friday and Saturday. Sunday is reserved for Irish music sessions; entry is always free.

Cnr. George and Hay sts., Haymarket. ℂ **(02) 9212 2111.** www.paddymaguires.com. Train: Central. Map p. 204.

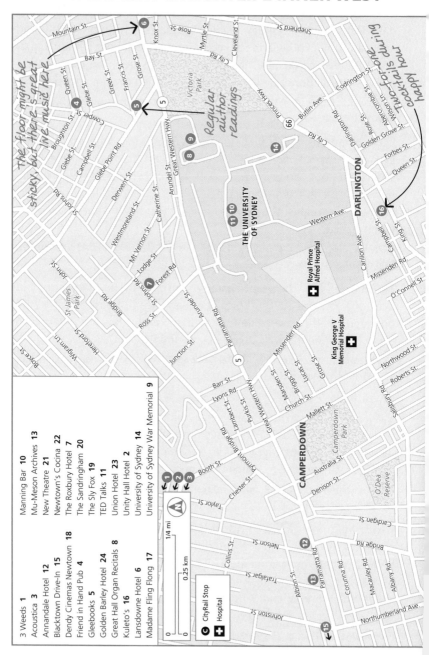

The floor might be sticky, but there's great live music here

Regular author readings

Two-for-one cocktails during happy hour

THE UNIVERSITY OF SYDNEY

Victoria Park

DARLINGTON

Royal Prince Alfred Hospital

King George V Memorial Hospital

CAMPERDOWN

Camperdown Park

O'Dea Reserve

3 Weeds **1**
Acoustica **3**
Annandale Hotel **12**
Blacktown Drive-In **15**
Dendy Cinemas Newtown **18**
Friend in Hand Pub **4**
Gleebooks **5**
Golden Barley Hotel **24**
Great Hall Organ Recitals **8**
Kuleto's **16**
Lansdowne Hotel **6**
Madame Fling Flong **17**

Manning Bar **10**
Mu-Meson Archives **13**
New Theatre **21**
Newtown's Cocina **22**
The Roxbury Hotel **7**
The Sandringham **20**
The Sly Fox **19**
TED Talks **11**
Union Hotel **23**
Unity Hall Hotel **2**
University of Sydney **14**
University of Sydney War Memorial **9**

1/4 mi
0.25 km

G CityRail Stop
✚ Hospital

EVELEIGH

Lawrence St.

Mitchell Rd
Belmont St.

Copeland St.

Fox Rd

Park St.

MACDONALDTOWN

Clara St.

Henderson Rd

Ashmore St.

Swanson St.

Malcolm St.

Sydney Park Rd

Sydney Park

Burren St.

Charles St.

ERSKINEVILLE

ERSKINEVILLE

Victoria St.

MacDonald St.

Coulson St.

Bucknell St.

Watkin St.

Albert St.

Morrissey Rd

Prospect St.

Rochford St.

Bray St.

ST PETERS

Lord St.

King St.

Rochford St.

Goodsell St.

Hordern St.

Luthorpe St.

Wilson St.

Erskineville Rd

Union St.

Gowrie St.

Angel St.

66

NEWTOWN

King St.

18

Church St.

Lennox Rd

Federation Rd

Camperdown Memorial Rest Park

NEWTOWN

Thomas St.

Princes Hwy

King St.

99

23

22

Holmwood St.

Dickson St.

Wells St.

Darley St.

New St.

Australia St.

Denison St.

Probert St.

Bailey St.

Station St.

College St.

Camden St.

Alice St.

Pearl St.

Commodore St.

John St.

21

20

Probert St.

Bishopgate St.

Albemarle St.

Bedford St.

Enmore Rd

Ferndale St.

Clara St.

Simmons St.

Simmons St.

St. Mary St.

Phillip St.

Marian St.

Edgeware Rd

54

24

Gladstone St.

London St.

Metropolitan St.

Juliet St.

Kingston Rd

Cambridge St.

Liberty St.

19

Fotheringham St.

Enmore Rd

Llewellyn St.

Enmore Park

Victoria Rd

Rosevear St.

Railway Ave.

Trafalgar St.

Harrow Rd

Cambridge St.

Cavendish St.

Stanmore Rd

ENMORE

54

Tupper St.

Newington Rd

Cowper St.

Addison Rd

Victoria Rd

Durham St.

Salisbury Rd

Merchant St.

Wemyss St.

The Sandringham `FREE` There are two live music venues inside this historic pub that has been a Sydney live music stalwart since, well, almost forever. Most bands cost between $5 and $15 at the door, but Wednesday through Sunday you'll often find the bands are free in the downstairs bar.

387 King St., Newtown. ☎ **(02) 9557 1254.** www.sando.com.au. Train: Newtown. Map p. 210.

Tea Gardens Hotel `FREE` Free live bands draw a lively and sometimes boisterous crowd to the very casual main bar of this atmospheric hotel Sunday afternoon from 5 to 8pm.

2–4 Bronte Rd., Bondi Junction. ☎ **(02) 9389 3288.** www.teagardenshotel.com.au. Train: Bondi Junction. Map p. 201.

OUTDOOR CONCERTS

Acoustica `FREE` A highlight of this annual roots, blues and folk festival in mid-April is an all-day concert in Birchgrove Park (p. 18). Beside the music there's food and market stalls and free entertainment for the kids.

Birchgrove Park, Grove St., Birchgrove. ☎ **(02) 9367 9359.** wwwacousticafestival.com. au. Bus: 441, 442 or 433. Ferry: Balmain or Birchgrove. Map p. 210.

Darling Harbour Jazz & Blues Festival `FREE` Every year on the Queen's Birthday long weekend (usually the second Monday in June) Darling Harbour hosts some of the biggest names in jazz, blues and soul, all of whom perform on four stages over the three-day weekend—and you can watch for free.

Various venues and performance spaces around Darling Harbour. www.darling harbour.com. Monorail: Darling Park. Map p. 204.

The Domain Concert Series `FREE` As part of the Sydney Festival (p. 16), The Domain hosts two of the city's largest, and most popular, free outdoor concerts each January. The line-up varies from year to year, but the first of the Saturday night extravaganzas is usually jazz and the second is classical music and opera played by the Sydney Symphony. They always attract big crowds, so get in early to get a good spot on the lawn and BYO picnic blanket. The site opens at 3.30pm, and the music kicks off at 8pm.

The Domain (btw. Art Gallery and Hospital rds.), Sydney. www.sydneyfestival.org.au. Train: Martin Place or St James. Map p. 204.

FREE Free Street Press

Sydney's free street press is your best source of info on what's on where and what's around for free or dirt cheap. Look out for *The Brag* and *Drum Media* at pubs and clubs, cooler clothing stores and music shops around the city and inner suburbs for a listing of who's playing when and where. Some more ideas are:

● *BBM:* If you're a backpacker, pick up a copy of *BBM*, which has heaps of pub and club info as well as handy work and immigration tips and contacts, although it has an unashamed British slant (*BBM* does stand for *British Balls Magazine*, after all).

● *Time Out Sydney:* Another excellent source is this monthly mag, but it costs $4. If that's too rich for you, check out the online version: www.timeoutsydney.com.au. It's almost as good.

● **Two Thousand:** Head to www.twothousand.com.au for an online source of what's hip, hot and cool in town.

Manly Jazz Festival FREE   This jazz festival on the October long weekend is a quintessential Sydney experience for any jazz lover (p. 19)—it's great to chill out by the sea while listening to jazz.

Various venues in Manly. ℂ **(02) 9976 1430.** www.manly.nsw.gov.au/manlyjazz. Ferry: Manly. Map p. 202.

2 Dance Clubs

Cruise Bar FREE   Thursday night is salsa night and there are resident DJs on Friday and Saturday nights at this waterfront bar underneath the Overseas Passenger Terminal. Take a break from burning up the dance floor and check out the view and the amazing light wall. Entry to all three nights is free.

Levels 1–3, Overseas Passenger Terminal, West Circular Quay. ℂ **(02) 9251 1188.** www.cruisebar.com.au. Train: Circular Quay. Map p. 204.

The Eastern   If the weekend seems too far away, head to the delightfully opulent Ruby Lounge or the open rooftop Pacifica on Wednesday night for a mix of R & B, electro pop and house music. It's usually

$10 to get in, but if you call ahead and ask very nicely you can get your name on the door list, which means its half price for the men and ladies get in free. Early birds can warm up first with $3 drinks from 6 to 9pm.

500 Oxford St., Bondi Junction. ✆ **(02) 9387 7828.** www.theeastern.com.au. Train: Bondi Junction. Map p. 201.

★ **Establishment Bar** FREE   This cavernous space is usually full of suits winding down and hip young things winding up, but Tuesday night is Rumba Motel, with a free salsa lesson at 8pm before the party kicks off at 9pm.

252 George St., Sydney. ✆ **(02) 9240 3000.** Train: Wynyard. Map p. 204.

La Cita FREE   Shake, shimmy and shine at the free Salsa Club dance nights at this Latin restaurant and nightclub on King Street Wharf. Entry is free on Monday, Wednesday and Thursday, and the dancing starts at 9.30pm.

9 Lime St., Kings Street Wharf. ✆ **(02) 9299 9100.** www.lacita.com.au. Train: Wynyard. Map p. 204.

Manning Bar FREE   If you find yourself in need of a disco fix at midday on a Monday, head to the balcony at Manning Bar inside the University of Sydney for Mnml Mndays, an hour of the latest underground electronic music from 1pm.

Manning Rd., University of Sydney. ✆ **(02) 9563 6000.** www.manningbar.com. Bus: 412, 413, 435, 438, 440, 461, 480 or 483. Map p. 210.

Pontoon FREE   Pontoon is in a great spot on the city side of Darling Harbour and Friday night's dance club is free. If you need to eat, all meals (think burgers and monster-sized sandwiches) are less than $10.

201 Sussex St., Cockle Bay Wharf, Darling Park. ✆ **(02) 9267 7099.** www.pontoonbar.com. Train: Town Hall. Map p. 204.

The World Bar FREE   Hitting the wall is no longer a bad thing at The Wall, an arts-based nightclub with free music every Wednesday. The Tea Room upstairs in this converted terrace is a showcase for emerging artists and the house party downstairs turns it up with some of Sydney's best DJs. I love the cocktails served in tea cups.

24 Bayswater Rd., Kings Cross. ✆ **(02) 9357 7700.** www.theworldbar.com. Train: Kings Cross. Map p. 204.

`FREE` On the Street

Sydney's **buskers** can provide hours of happy entertainment, from juggling and fire twirling to didgeridoo playing, contortionism and good old-fashioned singing and dancing, for next to nix (you can make a donation, but it's totally up to you). The best buskers are usually found performing around Circular Quay and the western foreshore towards The Rocks and are at their most active on weekends and during the summer holidays. On weekends you'll usually find a few near the markets and around Playfair Street in The Rocks and Darling Harbour is another busking hot spot. During the week you'll find a few in Pitt Street Mall, usually trying to catch the attention of the office crowds and, late at night, if you're lucky, there'll be a musician or two taking advantage of the haunting acoustics in the tunnel that runs from Central Station to George Street. Busking is also a large feature of the line up at the **Darling Harbour Hoopla** festival, the country's biggest acrobatic and street theatre carnival at Easter. Visit www.darling harbour.com.au for information. FINE PRINT If you're tempted to secure a pitch and lay out your own hat, you'll need a permit to busk in Sydney. Visit www.cityofsydney.nsw.gov.au for details.

3 Gay & Lesbian

Arq `FREE`   Arq is the place to ditch your shirt and party hard with the 'fierce and fabulous' in the biggest gay club in town. Most nights there's a hefty cover charge, but on Thursday you can catch Arqademic, starring some of Sydney's best drag queen talent, for free. Doors open at 9pm and shows start at 12.30am and 1.30am. You can also sign up for a Sunday School show and party (doors open 9pm) for just $5.

16 Flinders St., Darlinghurst. ℂ **(02) 9380 8700.** www.arqsydney.com.au. Bus: 378 or 380. Map p. 204.

★ **The Sly Fox** `FREE`   Popular with the girls (maybe it's the $8 cocktails, or maybe it's just the crowd . . .) this gay pub in Enmore has a great live music scene alternating from house and dance to rock and pop. Monday is comedy night and there are free bands on Thursday night. The one night you shouldn't miss is the Tuesday night Bingay, a hilarious and naughty version of the old folks' favourite game. It's free, but it's also (justifiably) popular, so you might want to book a seat. Doors open at 8pm.

199 Enmore Rd., Enmore. ℂ **(02) 9557 1016.** Train: Newtown. Map p. 210.

Stonewall Hotel FREE   The Stonewall Hotel has something for everyone—no matter what your taste—with DJs, drag performances, male dancers and live entertainment seven nights a week. Expect a youngish and enthusiastic crowd. Friday and Saturday nights have a $5 cover, but entry is free every other night. The best value is to be found at the free cabaret show on Sunday at 8pm.

175 Oxford St., Darlinghurst. ℂ **(02) 9360 1963.** www.stonewallhotel.com. Bus: 378 or 380. Map p. 204.

4 Theatre

★ **Belvoir St Theatre**   This is the place to see contemporary and ensemble drama with a hard-edged and sometimes radical bent—and it's where you can see some of Australia's finest actors on stage. Many Australian playwrights got their first break at the downstairs theatre, which is usually much cheaper than the upstairs theatre. Ticket prices for upstairs productions are $56 and downstairs are $29, but sign up to the online newsletter and you can get preview tickets for $34 and $10 respectively. Or, if you a have a student card, a student rush ticket for $25. Tuesday night is pay-what-you-can (minimum $10) for the downstairs shows. FINE PRINT Student rush tickets are available for Tuesday 6.30pm and Saturday 2pm performances from 10am on the day; they're subject to availability.

25 Belvoir St., Surry Hills. ℂ **(02) 9699 3444.** www.belvoir.com.au. Train: Central. Map p. 204.

Darlinghurst Theatre   This intimate little theatre leans towards showing avant-garde first-time productions with good local talent. Preview tickets save you $10 (they're $27, rather than $37).

19 Greenknowe Ave., Potts Point. ℂ **(02) 8356 9987.** www.darlinghursttheatre.com. Train: Kings Cross. Map p. 204.

Ensemble Theatre   A smallish theatre with a good line-up of modern classics and Australian drama by the second-longest-running theatre company in Australia. The actual theatre was once a boatshed. It's worth getting here early to have dinner at the restaurant, which has knock-out water views ($54 for two courses). Full-price tickets are $54 to $63, but previews can save you between $6 and $15, depending on the night (you'll make the biggest saving on Saturday night).

78 McDougall St., Kirribilli. ℂ **(02) 9929 0644.** www.ensemble.com.au. Train: Milsons Point. Map p. 202.

The Genesian Theatre   This tiny little theatre in an old church in the middle of the city has a great $45 meal deal: a two-course feed at the nearby Forbes Hotel, plus a ticket to the current show. The playbill usually lists plays by Shakespeare, Noel Coward, Oscar Wilde, Agatha Christie and other perennial favourites.

420 Kent St., Sydney. ℂ **1300 306 776.** www.genesiantheatre.com.au. Train: Town Hall. Map p. 204.

New Theatre   What was once the left-wing political Workers' Theatre is now an independent theatre company with an eclectic program, although most works still tend to have a cutting political edge. It's a good place to catch gay drama. Full-price tickets are pretty cheap at $22 to $30, but check the website for details of $10 previews. Most (but not all) productions also offer one Sunday pay-what-you-can (minimum $10) performance.

542 King St., Newtown. ℂ **(02) 9519 3409;** tickets 1300 306 776. www.newtheatre. org.au. Train: Newtown. Map p. 210.

NIDA Parade Theatres   NIDA is Australia's National Institute of Dramatic Arts and almost all of Australia's acting superstars were trained here. You can catch the next Mel Gibson, Cate Blanchett or Toni Collette strutting their stuff at one of the four NIDA Parade Theatres. Ticket prices vary, but it's a lot cheaper seeing the performers now than when they are really famous.

215 Anzac Pde., Kensington. ℂ **(02) 9697 7600.** www.nida.edu.au. Bus: 392, 394, 396, 397, 399 or L94 from Circular Quay. Map p. 201.

★ **Old Fitzroy Theatre**   This tiny theatre is hidden away in the back room of a 100-year-old pub and is the home of the Tamarama Rock Surfers, who are dedicated to performing the work of emerging young

Australian playwrights. The beer, laksa and show (BLS) packages are hard to beat at $35. Bargain hunters can also scoop up a good deal with Cheap Tuesday tickets for $17 or a $25 BLS package (tickets are normally $21 to $29) and late sessions for $16. See the website for more details.

129 Dowling St., Woolloomooloo. ℭ **1300 438 849.** www.oldfitzroy.com.au. Train: Kings Cross. Map p. 204.

SBW Stables Theatre   This is the original home of the Nimrod Theatre, one of the birthplaces of contemporary Australian theatre. The tradition continues with the resident Griffin Theatre Company, a not-for-profit organisation committed to developing emerging playwrights. Tickets range from $33 to $44, but under-30s can get a ticket for $26 from Tuesday to Thursday and any age group can get a $15 Monday Rush ticket on Monday nights after 6pm. Check the website for preview dates, when all seats sell for $33.

10 Nimrod St., Kings Cross. ℭ **1300 306 776.** www.griffintheatre.com.au. Train: Kings Cross. Map p. 204.

Shakespeare by the Sea FREE   A professional performance of Shakespeare for free? Sounds too good to be true, but it is (although a $20 donation to pay the actors is appreciated). A different play is performed each year in the park by the beach at Balmoral (near Mosman on the North Shore), with shows on Friday, Saturday and Sunday from mid-January to early March. BYO picnic and blanket.

$10 Preview Special

Buy a ticket to any B Sharp preview performance at the downstairs theatre at the **Belvoir St Theatre** (p. 216) and you're entitled to a $10 ticket for a preview of any production at the **Darlinghurst Theatre** (p. 216), the **Old Fitzroy Theatre** (p. 217) or a **Griffin Stablemates** (13 Craigend St., Kings Cross; ℭ **(02) 9332 1052;** www.griffintheatre.com. au) production. Simply show your preview ticket stub when booking or mention the deal over the phone and present your stub to collect your ticket on the night. This deal is fully reciprocal amongst the four theatre companies, but tickets are subject to availability.

The Esplanade (off Raglan St.), Balmoral. 📞 **(02) 9969 0824.** www.shakespeare-by-the-sea.com. Bus: 238 or 257. Map p. 202.

Star of the Sea   Suburban theatres often offer great value for decent semi-amateur productions. This theatre in Manly is a part of Stella Maris College, where theatre students work alongside professionals, and there is a good program of local professional theatre company productions. Tickets range from $10 to $30.

Cnr. Collingwood St. and Iluka Ave., Manly. 📞 **(02) 9977 5144.** www.staroftheseatheatre.com.au. Ferry: Manly. Map p. 202.

The Studio at the Sydney Opera House   No visit to Sydney is complete without a visit to the city's most famous building, the Sydney Opera House. Opened by Queen Elizabeth in 1973, the World-Heritage-Listed building has seven performance venues. The 'House' puts on more than 1500 performances in front of almost 1.3 million people each year, on average, making it one of the world's busiest performing arts centres. Tickets to most shows cost anywhere from $60 to $250, but those looking for a dirt-cheap night should check the website for previews (expect to pay about half the advertised ticket price), and ask about student or under-27s pricing. If nothing's available and you're determined to catch a show in one of the world's most famous song and dance halls, check out what's on in The Studio, the smallest performance space inside the house, where tickets to most performances are usually less than $30 and the shows tend to be less mainstream, more quirky and/or more provocative.

Bennelong Point. 📞 **(02) 9250 7111;** tickets (02) 9250 7777. www.sydneyoperahouse.com. Train: Circular Quay. Map p. 204.

Sydney Theatre Company   This theatre company might be under the artistic direction of actress Cate Blanchett, but that doesn't mean she treads the boards in *every* show (although she usually appears in at least one each year). The two theatres in which the company performs, Wharf 1 and Wharf 2, are housed on an old wooden wharf and show an eclectic mix of drama, from one-person shows to edgy productions of Shakespeare. Tickets are usually $70 to $130, but check the website for previews, which usually save you around 25%. Theatre buffs love the free backstage briefs held in the week prior to the opening of each production at The Wharf, where you can learn all about the play from the actors, directors, designers and playwrights.

Piers 4/5 and 6/7, Hickson Rd., Walsh Bay. ☎ **(02) 9250 1999.** www.sydneytheatre.
org.au. Train: Circular Quay. Bus: 430, 431 or 433. Map p. 204.

Tap Gallery   This artist-run gallery has a small theatre space with a
policy that allows anyone with a show who thinks it's worth staging
to use the space. Don't expect mainstream productions here. If you're
in the front row you'll be close enough to touch the actors, but tickets
are great value at $20 to $25, and most shows offer a pay-what-you-
can Tuesday ($12 minimum).

278 Palmer St., Darlinghurst. ☎ **(02) 9361 0440.** www.tapgallery.org.au/theatre.
html. Bus: 378 or 380. Map p. 204.

5 Flicks for Next to Nix

Annandale Hotel FREE   This pub is better known for its live rock,
but those in the know head there on Tuesday for Sinema, when the
main bar is transformed into a movie theatre and you can catch a cult
movie at 7.30pm for free (although a $5 donation is suggested to
cover expenses).

17–19 Parramatta Rd., Annandale. ☎ **(02) 9550 1078.** www.annandalehotel.com.
Bus: 412, 413, 436, 437, 438 or 440. Map p. 210.

Art Gallery of New South Wales FREE   The Art Gallery presents a
regular free program of films in conjunction with major exhibitions
and in conjunction with Art After Hours—they can range from rarely
screened classics to documentaries, shorts and experimental films.
Check the website for details of what's on and when; films are usually
screened on Wednesday and Sunday.

Art Gallery Rd., The Domain. ☎ **(02) 9225 1700.** www.artgallery.nsw.gov.au and
www.artafterhours.com.au. Daily 10am–5pm. Train: Martin Place, then a 10-min.
walk. Map p. 204.

The ArtHouse Hotel   Get a group of girlfriends together and get
yourselves to Cinem-Attic for the $25 dinner-and-movie deal. It's def-
initely chick-flick-centric (think *Moulin Rouge* and *Romeo + Juliet*).
It's on every second Wednesday in the cozy and comfy Attic Bar.
Bookings are essential and you can buy your tickets online.

275 Pitt St., Sydney. ☎ **(02) 9284 1211.** www.thearthousehotel.com.au. Train: Town
Hall. Map p. 204.

★ **The Beresford Hotel** FREE   Monday night is movie night, when
free cult and classic films are shown in the beer garden—as long as

it's not raining. You can also get a special movie night meal: (very good) pasta and a glass of wine or beer for just $15. BYO cushion; movies start at 7pm.

354 Bourke St., Surry Hills. ✆ **(02) 9357 1111.** www.theberesford.com.au. Bus: 372, 373, 378 or 380. Map p. 204.

Blacktown Drive-In   Sydney's last remaining drive-in movie theatre has an early bird movie session that costs just $25 per car. That means you can catch a new-release movie for just $5 if there are five of you and you have your own car. Movies tend to be family-oriented, so go to the later double movie session for more grown-up flicks. The movie might be dirt cheap, but the huge dose of nostalgia that comes with it is definitely priceless!

Cricketers Arms Rd., Blacktown. ✆ **(02) 9622 4170.** www.greaterunion.com.au. Map p. 210.

Chauvel Cinema   Named after one of Australia's greatest filmmakers and housed in the former ballroom of Paddington Town Hall (what other cinema can boast a barrel-vaulted ceiling and fully sprung floor?), the Chauvel screens a selection of art-house and classic movies as well as hosting regular film festivals. The Palace Movie Club deal applies, and Sunday classics are $12. Check the website for details of Cinemateque membership, which could have you watching movies on a Monday night for less than $2 a show.

Cnr. Oxford St. and Oatley Rd., Paddington. ✆ **(02) 9361 5398.** www.chauvelcinema. net.au. Bus: 378 or 380. Map p. 204.

Behind the Scenes

It's not free, but it's certainly dirt cheap compared to the backstage tours at the Sydney Opera House that cost $150 (and include breakfast). The 75-minute guided tour of **The Wharf** and **Sydney Theatre** provides an insight into theatre production and gives a rare look at what happens behind the scenes at the Sydney Theatre Company. Tours are held on the first and third Thursday of every month at 10.30am and cost $8 per person. Bookings are essential; go to www. sydneytheatre.org.au or call ✆ **(02) 9250 1777.**

Cheapskate Tuesday

The two mainstream cinema chains, **Hoyts** (www.hoyts.com.au) and **Greater Union** (www.greaterunion.com.au)—which both have cinemas in George Street in the city and throughout the suburbs—offer $10 tickets to all sessions on Tuesday, saving $6.50 on the normal ticket price. Better still, see a movie at the **Chauvel Cinema** (p. 221) or **Dendy Cinemas** (below) on Tuesday for $9 and save up to $7.50. See map p. 204 and websites for details of cinema locations and screening times.

Darlo Bar `FREE` Cult '60s and '70s classics are shown for free on the rooftop of the Darlo Bar every Tuesday night at 8pm (later in summer)—plus, there's free popcorn!

Cnr. Liverpool St. and Darlinghurst Rd., Darlinghurst. ✆ **(02) 9331 3672.** www.darlo bar.com.au. Bus: 311. Map p. 204.

Dendy Cinemas This is another cinema chain that offers cheap tickets on Tuesday. The Newtown and Opera Quays cinemas focus on arthouse and 'quality' movies, rather than the Hollywood blockbusters.

Opera Quays: 2 East Circular Quay; ✆ **(02) 9247 3800;** train Circular Quay. Map p. 204. Newtown: 261 King St., Newtown; ✆ **(02) 9550 5699;** train Newtown. www.dendy. com.au. Map p. 210.

★ **Govinda's** Kick off your shoes, stretch out and settle back on full-length pillows to watch the show. There are two screenings a day, at 7pm and around 8.45pm (plus 5pm on Saturday), and the releases are newish. But it's not so much what you see as *how* you see it that is the big deal here—watch while seated in super-comfy super-loungey seats. There's a great $28.60 movie-and-meal deal (to see a movie only, it's $12.80; p. 66).

112 Darlinghurst Rd., Darlinghurst. ✆ **(02) 9380 5155.** www.govindas.com.au. Train: Kings Cross. Map p. 204.

Japan Foundation `FREE` Japanese cinema fans and language students should head to the Japan Foundation for free Japanese movies on selected Wednesdays at 6.30pm. All films are in Japanese, but they do have English subtitles. Check the website for screening details and dates.

Shop 23, level 1, Chifley Plaza, 2 Chifley Sq., Sydney. ℭ **(02) 8239 0055.** www.jpf.org. au. Train: Martin Place. Map p. 204.

★ **Madame Fling Flong** Tuesday night's movie night at this great little cocktail bar. For $20 you can snag a meze plate for one, a glass of wine or beer and a movie (cult, classic or foreign). The place is tiny, so book a space on the couch before you arrive and be there at 7.30pm sharp.

Upstairs, 169 King St., Newtown. ℭ **(02) 9565 2471.** www.madameflingflong.com. au. Train: Newtown. Map p. 210.

Mu-Meson Archives Cult classics, music and other exotica are screened in this den of underground trash-culture. There's a lot of sci-fi fantasy, and the crowd has a tendency to oversubscribe to the latest conspiracy theories, but $10 will get you a flick and supper. Screenings happen whenever the staff feel like it, so check the website for details.

Cnr. Trafalgar St. and Parramatta Rd. (behind King Furniture Building), Annandale. www.mumeson.org. Bus: 412, 413, 436, 437, 438 or 440. Map p. 210.

Palace Cinemas This is the best place to go if you're looking for quality art-house and foreign-language movies. The Academy Twin is home to the annual French, Italian, Spanish and Mardi Gras film festivals, while the Verona screens edgy independents. Monday is discount day and all sessions are $9.50 (they're usually $16.50). You can become a movie club member for $19 and get tickets at a flat rate of $12 for you and one buddy every time you go.

Academy Twin: 3A Oxford St., Paddington; ℭ **(02) 9361 4453.** Verona: 17 Oxford St., Paddington. ℭ **(02) 9360 6099.** www.palacecinemas.com.au. Bus: 378 or 380. Map p. 204.

Randwick Ritz Catch the latest blockbuster in a grand Art Deco masterpiece. All tickets are $8 on Tuesday (they're normally $12).

43–47 St Pauls St., Randwick. ℭ **(02) 9399 5722.** www.ritzcinema.com.au. Bus: 372, 373, 376 or 377. Map p. 201.

State Library of New South Wales `FREE` The State Library has a great collection of historic Australian films and documentaries. You can catch one for free almost every Thursday at 12.10pm in the Metcalfe Auditorium in the Macquarie Street Wing.

Macquarie St., Sydney. ✆ **(02) 9273 1414.** www.sl.nsw.gov.au. Train: Martin Place. Map p. 204.

6 Cheap Laughs

The Fringe Bar   Monday night is comedy night in this ruby-red lushly decorated pub, where $10 lets you see three comics, or $25 buys you dinner, a drink and the show. Check the talent list because you'll often see some headliners as well as many of Australia's favourite TV and radio personalities. You'll need to book if you want the meal deal.

106 Oxford St., Paddington. ✆ **(02) 9360 5443.** www.thefringe.com.au. Bus: 378 or 380. Map p. 204.

Old Manly Boatshed   There are belly laughs aplenty when stand-up comics hit the stage in this basement bar on Monday nights. Tickets cost around $20, which includes dinner as well as the show.

Old Manly Boat Shed, Basement, 40 The Corso, Manly. ✆ **(02) 9977 4443.** Ferry: Manly. Map p. 202.

The Roxbury Hotel   There's comedy on stage here almost every night of the week, but for those who don't want to spend more than $10 to have their funny bone tickled, come here on Tuesday or Friday nights for some of the best improvised theatre and comedy around (it is more expensive on other nights).

182 St Johns Rd., Glebe. ✆ **(02) 9692 0822.** www.roxbury.com.au. Bus: 431 or 433. Map p. 210.

Popcorn Taxi

If you're a serious film buff, take yourself along to the next **Popcorn Taxi** event. Watch the movie, then meet the stars and director and listen to them chat about their craft. Previous guests have included Baz Luhrmann, George Miller and Dennis Hopper. Tickets cost $17 and it's on at Greater Union Cinema in Bondi Junction (Level 6, 500 Oxford St., Bondi Junction; ✆ **(02) 9212 7222;** map p. 201). Go to www.popcorn taxi.com.au for info on upcoming events.

7 Free (& Dirt-Cheap) Speech: Talks, Lectures & Readings

★ **Art Gallery of New South Wales** `FREE`   Wednesday night brings **Art After Hours** to the Art Gallery of New South Wales. It's a changing program of events from 5 until 9pm, featuring films, talks and performances.

Art Gallery Rd., The Domain. ℂ **(02) 9225 1700.** www.artafterhours.com.au. Train: Martin Place, then a 10-min. walk. There's a free bus to Martin Place every 15 min. from 7.15pm until after the last film. Map p. 204.

Brett Whiteley Studio `FREE`   On the fourth Sunday of each month, this tiny back-alley art space, the former studio of artist Brett Whiteley (p. 117), is host to a Poets Union poetry reading from 2 until 3.30pm.

2 Raper St. (near cnr. Devonshire and Crown sts.), Surry Hills. ℂ **(02) 9225 1881.** www.brettwhiteley.org. Bus: 301, 302 or 303 from Castlereagh St (near King St). Map p. 204.

COFA Talks `FREE`   Listen, learn and talk about art with the lecturers and visiting artists at the University of NSW's College of Fine Arts (COFA). There's a free talk at 6pm every Tuesday night during college semesters. Check the website for full program details.

College of Fine Arts, Greens Rd., Paddington. ℂ **(02) 9385 0684.** www.cofa.unsw. edu.au. Bus: 378 or 380. Map p. 204.

Gaelic Club `FREE`   There's no better place to talk politics than in the pub, so head to the (imaginatively named) Politics in the Pub session at 6pm on a Friday night for some lively debate and a discussion led by journalists, authors, academics and politicians. It's (theoretically) not aligned to a political party, but you'll find a definite lean to the left. It's free, although a donation of $7 to cover expenses is appreciated.

64 Devonshire St., Surry Hills. ℂ **(02) 9212 1587.** www.politicsinthepub.org.au. Train: Central. Map p. 204.

★ **Gleebooks** `FREE`   A book launch is a great way to meet a famous author, hear them read from their book and, quite possibly, score a free glass of cheap cask wine and a cube of cheddar cheese. Gleebooks, one of Sydney's best bookshops, holds regular launches and other literary events. Launches are free, but you'll hear more of what the writer has to say at one of the $10 events that usually include a panel discussion or hosted 'conversation'. Tickets to these events often sell out fast, so book a place online.

49 Glebe Point Rd., Glebe. ℂ **(02) 9660 2333.** www.gleebooks.com.au. Bus: 431 or 433. Map p. 210.

NSW Parliament `FREE` If you enjoy a bit of parliamentary debate, mudslinging, finger-pointing and name-calling, take a seat in the Legislative Assembly and see members of the state's lower house debate bills and trade insults. Visit the website for details of sitting dates.

Parliament House, Macquarie St., Sydney. ℂ **(02) 9230 2111.** www.parliament.nsw. gov.au. Train: Martin Place. Map p. 204.

Powerhouse Museum `FREE` Talks After Noon is a series of lectures on Wednesday (at 12.30pm) and Sunday (at 2pm) on a wide range of subjects relating to history, science, technology, design, industry, decorative arts, music, transport and space exploration, so expect anything from space travel to dolls' houses, delivered by experts in their field, and curators from the Powerhouse Museum. `FINE PRINT` The talks might well be free, but you'll still have to pay the $10 entry fee to get inside the museum (which is well worth the splurge).

500 Harris St., Ultimo. ℂ **(02) 9217 0111.** www.powerhousemuseum.com. Monorail: Paddy's Markets. Map p. 204.

Ravesi's `FREE` Forget the cheap and nasty wine you get at most literary events—at Zabriskie Book Club, you can sip a cocktail on the couch at Ravesi's while mixing with A-list authors. Held on the last Tuesday of each month, this book club attracts some of the country's best writers. It's free, but you need to book.

Cnr. Campbell Pde. and Hall St., Bondi. ℂ **(02) 9365 4422.** www.ravesis.com.au. Bus: 380 or 389. Map p. 201.

Stanton Library `FREE` National and international best-selling authors—and lesser-known authors who will hopefully one day be famous—talk about their books on Tuesday and Thursday at 1pm. Light refreshments are provided and there's no need to book. See the website for who's appearing when.

234 Miller St., North Sydney. ℂ **(02) 9936 8400.** www.northsydney.nsw.gov.au. Train: North Sydney. Map p. 202.

TED Talks `FREE` Want to know what Al Gore, Bill Gates, Bill Clinton and Jane Goodall think about science, arts and design, politics, education, culture, business, global issues, technology and development? The Young Entrepreneurs Society has a free screening of TED (technology, entertainment, design) Talks from some of the world's most profound thinkers, doers and leaders. They screen each Friday during university semester from 1 to 3pm, next door to Manning Bar at the University of Sydney.

Margaret Telfer Room, Level 2, Manning Building, University of Sydney. ℂ **(02) 9563 6000.** www.usu.usyd.edu.au. Bus: 412, 413, 435, 438, 440, 461, 480 or 483. Map p. 210.

The University of NSW `FREE`   The Faculty of Arts and Social Sciences at the University of New South Wales (UNSW) holds a series of public lectures called So, what? Topics range from nation building to human decency to gender equality. They're free, but you must book. See the website for details.

University of NSW, Kensington Campus. ℂ **(02) 9385 1000.** www.arts.unsw.edu.au/ news/publiclectures.html. Bus: 391, 392, 393, 395 or 399. Map p. 201.

A Friend in Hand is Worth Two in the Bush

Head to the **Friend in Hand Pub** (58 Cowper St., Glebe; ℂ **(02) 9660 2326;** www.friendinhand.com.au; map p. 210) to see up-and-coming comedians and poets every week.

- See the best up-and-coming comedians on stage at **Mic In Hand** for $10 every Thursday at 7.30pm. If you're really lucky, you might even catch some high-profile acts trying out their new material, a dirt-cheap preview to the next big comedy show. Visit www. amicinhand.com/sydney for upcoming line-ups.

- `FREE` You never know what—or who—you'll stumble across, but on the first Tuesday of month you can be sure it will a mad poet at the high-energy **Word in Hand** at 7.30pm. You can even test your own couplets on the open mic. Entry's free, but a $10 donation is suggested to prevent the poets from starving in their garrets.

The University of Sydney FREE Part of the Sydney Ideas lecture series organised by the University of Sydney, Thoughts and Thinkers is a free lecture series on those who have shaped our society's institutions and beliefs, delivered by University of Sydney academics from a range of disciplines. Each lecture is 45 minutes long, plus a Q & A session and kicks off at 6.30pm on Wednesday in the Law School. See the website for program details.

Lecture Theatre 101, New Law School, Eastern Ave., University of Sydney. ℂ **(02) 9351 2222.** www.usyd.edu.au/sydney_ideas. Bus: 412, 413, 435, 438, 440, 461, 480 or 483. Map p. 210.

8 Happy Hours

You can buy beer or house wine at a discount at most pubs and bars at some stage of the week. Some venues offer cut-price cocktails; others give a two-for-one deal. We've listed a few favourite happy hours below, but check out the pub nearest you to see if they have a happy-hour deal. However it works, happy hour, which is often much longer than 60 minutes, is a great way to drink on the cheap—you can't help but be happy about that!

A Pot of What?

You can always tell where an Aussie is from by the way they order their beer. Confusingly, each state in Australia has a different name for the same thing when it comes to the size of a glass of beer.

A schooner in South Australia is the same size as a middy in Sydney (where a schooner is the same as a pint)—but ask for a pint in Sydney and you'll get much more than would fit in the same glass in South Australia.

Ask for a pot in Melbourne or Brisbane and you'll get a middy, whereas a pot in Western Australia will get you a schooner. Ask for a pot in Sydney and you'll just get a strange look—or a saucepan.

Confused? Here's our easy guide: 200 millilitres (7 oz) is a seven, a pony or a glass; 285 millilitres (10 oz) is a middy; 425 millilitres (15 oz) is a schooner.

Bar Europa   Cocktails in this stylish and dimly lit subterranean bar are normally $12, but on Thursday the prices drop to a much more affordable $8 from about 5pm.

82–88 Elizabeth St., Sydney. (02) **9232 3377.** www.bareuropa.com.au. Train: Martin Place. Map p. 204.

The Bellevue Hotel   This pub harks back to the days when Paddo was a working-class suburb; it's one of the few pubs in the area that haven't been gussied up. And while the dining room prices certainly reflect the change in the neighbourhood's socioeconomic demographics, the Monday to Friday happy hour from 5.30 to 6.30pm offers beer at prices from the days of yore. For those with champagne tastes and a beer budget, don't despair, there's $3 bubbly all day on Friday.

159 Hargrave St., Paddington. (02) **9363 2293.** www.bellevuehotel.com.au. Bus: 389. Map p. 201.

★ **Bondi Social**   The sun may not actually set over Bondi Beach, but the balcony that overlooks the famous stretch of sand at this great little upstairs restaurant is the perfect place to be around sundown. It's even better if you go during happy hour when beers are $5 and cocktails are $8. Happy hour runs from 6 to 7pm Tuesday to Friday, 4 to 7pm Saturday and all night Sunday.

Level 1, 38 Campbell Pde., Bondi. (02) **9365 1788.** www.bondisocial.com. Bus: 380. Map p. 201.

The Bourbon   A Kings Cross landmark since 1967, The Bourbon tends to be more popular with visiting sailors and other tourists than locals, but is still worth a look in. There's a dance space, lounge and cocktail area and a meat-heavy restaurant where you can get $10 steaks for lunch and dinner daily. There's also a three-hour happy hour every day from 6 to 9pm, where you can get beer, wine and spirits for $3, or go up-market and head onto the terrace for $8 cocktails Monday through Thursday from 10pm to midnight.

24 Darlinghurst Rd., Kings Cross. (02) **9358 1144.** www.thebourbon.com.au. Train: Kings Cross. Map p. 204.

Brooklyn Hotel FREE   Not only is this a great pub for an after-work drink, but there's a free glass of wine on offer every Wednesday from 5 to 8pm, and at the same time on Thursday the cocktails are half-price and the sparkling is free.

Cnr. George and Grosvenor sts., Sydney. ☏ **(02) 9247 6744.** www.brooklynhotel. com.au. Train: Circular Quay. Map p. 204.

Charlie Chans   The schooners are $3.50 every day between noon and 6pm, as well as on Monday until midnight—but they're even cheaper during happy hour, when they are just $2.50 on Thursday from 6 to 7pm. There are also half-price cocktails between 5 and 9pm on Thursday and Friday. My favourite day to visit is teapot Tuesday, when cocktails are served in a teapot for $8. It's very mad hatter.

631–635 George St., Sydney. ☏ **(02) 9281 4299.** www.charliechans.com.au. Train: Central. Map p. 204.

The Clock Hotel   This is one of my favourite inner-city pubs, but I especially like the Balcony Bar, which has a happy hour from 6 to 7pm every day (except Sunday) with all cocktails just $9.

470 Crown St., Surry Hills. ☏ **(02) 9331 5333.** www.clockhotel.com.au. Bus: 310 or 302. Map p. 204.

The Coogee Bay Hotel   The beer garden is a great place to be on a summer Sunday afternoon (it's very popular with backpackers), but the best time to be here is during happy hour in the Sports Bar, Monday through Friday 5 to 7pm. Flirty Thursday has $4 sparkling wine, $6 cocktails and a DJ in the Arden Lounge from 9pm. There's the added bonus of free bar snacks at happy hour on Friday.

Cnr. Coogee Bay Rd. and Arden St., Coogee. ☏ **(02) 9665 0000.** Bus: 372 or 373. Map p. 201.

Edinburgh Castle Hotel   Ease yourself back into the working week with $3 schooners and $3 house bubbly Monday through Wednesday from 5 to 7pm.

294 Pitt St. (cnr. Bathurst St.), Sydney. ☏ **(02) 9264 8616.** www.ecastlehotel.com.au. Train: Town Hall. Map p. 204.

Great Southern Bar   A cut-price cocktail can be hard to find on Friday night, but not so at the Great Southern Bar, where all cocktails are half price (usually $12) on Friday and Sunday nights between 6pm and 9pm. Monday night is $5 night, when you can get $5 pints, $5 Breezers and $5 nachos.

Great Southern Hotel, 717 George St., Sydney. ☏ **(02) 9211 1337.** Mains $8–$16. Lunch and dinner daily. Train: Central. Map p. 204.

FREE Light up Your Life

Trip the light fantastic with these four fabulous free light shows.

- **Christmas lights:** Bigger and brighter is better, or so it seems in some Sydney suburbs, where competition is fierce to have the best set of Christmas lights on the street. Suburban streets to watch from late November include: Sorlie Road, Frenchs Forest; Hodge Street, Hurstville; and Franklin Street, Barwon Crescent and Flanders Avenue, Matraville. See map p. 201.

- **Fireworks:** Sydney has some of the best fireworks displays in the world. The big one is, of course, New Year's Eve, one of the largest free public events on the planet. It involves more than 3000kg of explosive devices; approximately 11,000 shells, 10,000 shooting comets, making a total of 100,000 individual pyrotechnic effects that explode above **Sydney Harbour Bridge** and around the harbour. There are usually two shows, one at 9pm for families, then the big one at midnight (p. 20). There are also fireworks over Darling Harbour on Australia Day (January 26; p. 16). See map p. 204.

- **Hyde Park:** Take a walk down the central avenue of figs in Hyde Park once the sun sets for a romantic stroll under a canopy of fairy lights. Not for loners; this is best done with a lover—or at least someone with the potential to be. See map p. 204.

- **Vivid Sydney:** This amazing music and light festival lit up the city like it had never been lit before during the inaugural event in mid-May to mid-June of 2009. Highlights included luminous art installations around the harbour foreshore and city streets, and stunning light projections that painted the sails of the Opera House in a kaleidoscope of colours. There are plans to make it an annual event—keep your fingers crossed it will get the funding and visit www.vividsydney.com for information. See map p. 204.

Kings Cross Hotel FREE The Kings Cross Hotel's rooftop bar offers great cocktails with a view, but, even better, when you buy two cocktails from Monday to Thursday, you get a free tapas plate.

248 William St., Kings Cross. ℂ **(02) 9331 9900.** www.kingscrosshotel.com.au. Train: Kings Cross. Map p. 204.

★ **Kuleto's**   You can buy one and get one of the same drinks for free at this popular little cocktail bar during happy hour on weekdays between 6pm and 7.30pm and on Saturday between 6 and 7pm.

157 King St., Newtown. ℂ **(02) 9519 6369.** www.kuletos.com.au. Train: Newtown. Map p. 210.

Martin Place Bar   This place is usually packed with office workers blowing off steam after a hard day being chained to their desks. Tuesday night is half-price cocktail night—cocktails are just $7.

51 Martin Pl., Sydney. ℂ **(02) 9231 5575.** www.martinplacebar.net.au. Train: Martin Place. Map p. 204.

Newtown's Cocina   This Mexican restaurant does a great deal on margaritas of all persuasions between 5.30 and 7.30pm every day. Order a plate of nachos to share (main meals are a bit pricey, but they're big enough to share, although it's not the best Mexican food in town) and you've got a lively start to the night.

403 King St., Newtown. ℂ **(02) 9519 8211.** Train: Newtown. Map p. 210.

Paddington Inn   With all the designer shopping to be had, they don't call Oxford Street the 'Style Mile' for nothing. But the best place to go shopping after dark has to be the Paddo Inn, where an extended happy hour, known as 'Late Night Shopping', offers cocktails for $10 (they're usually $16) and beer, wine and spirits for $4 every Thursday from 9pm to midnight.

338 Oxford St., Paddington. ℂ **(02) 9380 5913.** www.paddingtoninn.com.au. Bus: 378 or 380. Map p. 201.

★ **Scubar**   It seems there's always a dirt-cheap deal on offer at this lively backpackers' bar underneath the Sydney Central YHA. There's all-you-can-eat pizza for $10 between 7 and 9pm, happy hour on Wednesday and Saturday from 7 to 8.30pm, $6 cocktails on Friday and cheap jugs of beer most of the time.

Sydney Central YHA, cnr. George St. and Rawson Pl., Sydney. ℂ **(02) 9212 4244.** www.scubar.com.au. Train: Central. Map p. 204.

Slip Inn   This is a popular haunt for the after-work crowd, especially on Friday when it can get seriously packed. Don't let the suits turn you off, it's got a great atmosphere, and can be a good place to pick

FREE Take Your Cue

Pool sharks and wannabee hustlers can rack 'em up for free at countless pubs around Sydney. Here are our favourite 10 places to perfect your corner shot without dipping into our wallet.

- **3 Weeds.** There's free pool in the front bar at 3 Weeds (193 Evans St., Rozelle; ✆ **(02) 9818 2788;** www.3weeds.com.au; map p. 210) from 5pm each Thursday.

- **The Coogee Bay Hotel.** Enjoy free pool every Thursday from noon until closing time in the Sports Bar (Coogee Bay Rd., Coogee; ✆ **(02) 9665 0000**; www.coogeebayhotel.com.au; map p. 201). Plus, there are $1 burgers from 6pm—you can't get more dirt cheap than that!

- **Darlo Bar.** There's free pool on Sunday at the Darlo Bar (cnr. Liverpool St. and Darlinghurst Rd., Darlinghurst; ✆ **(02) 9331 3672;** www.darlobar.com.au; map p. 204), along with $10 jugs.

- **Golden Barley Hotel.** Play pool from 7pm until midnight for free every Tuesday at the Golden Barley Hotel (167 Edgeware Rd., Enmore; ✆ **(02) 9565 1166;** www.goldenbarleyhotel.com.au; map p. 210).

- **Old Fitzroy Hotel.** There's free pool all day Tuesday at 129 Dowling Street, Woolloomooloo (✆ **1300 438 849;** www.oldfitzroy. com.au; map p. 204).

- **Scubar.** The pool tables are free on Sunday from 3pm at Scubar (cnr. George St. and Rawson Pl., Sydney; ✆ **(02) 9212 4244;** www. scubar.com.au; map p. 204).

- **The Sly Fox.** Enjoy free pool all day every day at this lesbian-friendly pub (199 Enmore Rd., Enmore; ✆ **(02) 9557 1016;** map p. 210).

- **Union Hotel.** Head to 576 King St., Newtown (✆ **(02) 9557 2989;** map p. 210) for free pool from 6pm on Tuesday—it's only $1 on Thursday nights and all day Sunday.

- **Unity Hall Hotel.** The Unity Hall Hotel (292 Darling St., Balmain; ✆ **(02) 9810 1331;** www.unityhallhotel.com.au; map p. 210) has free pool all day Monday.

up—just ask Princess Mary. The underground Chinese Laundry night-club is worth a look just for the quirky decor and you can get $5 drinks on Friday from 5 until 7pm.

111 Sussex St. (cnr. King St.), Sydney. ℂ **(02) 8295 9999.** www.merrivale.com/#/slipinn/mainbar. Train: Wynyard. Map p. 204.

The Sugarmill   There's a nightly happy hour at this groovy pub, with $3 beer and $4 wine from 5pm (along with $10 steak and fries all day and all night). But if Sunday morning comes along and your memories of Saturday night are a bit sketchy, then perhaps a breakfast bevy is in order. On Sunday the Sugarmill offers $10 bloody mary jugs from 10am to 6pm, along with a $10 big breakfast all day. It could be just what the doctor ordered.

33–37 Darlinghurst Rd., Kings Cross. ℂ **(02) 9368 7333.** www.sugarmill.com.au. Train: Kings Cross. Map p. 204.

Tea Gardens Hotel   If you're desperate for a beer before breakfast, head to Tea Gardens Hotel at 7am for a $3 schooner in one of the earliest happy hours in town. For those who prefer to wait until the sun is over the yardarm, there's an $8 cocktail happy hour from 7 to 9pm every Wednesday, Thursday and Friday in the upstairs Circa bar.

2–4 Bronte Rd., Bondi Junction. ℂ **(02) 9389 3288.** www.teagardenshotel.com.au. Train: Bondi Junction. Map p. 201.

Just one of the spectacular (and free!) views you'll encounter on the Bronte to Bondi Coastal Walk (p. 250).

FREE & DIRT CHEAP DAYS

Sydney is happy to charge visitors and out-of-towners $40 for a hop-on-hop-off bus trip around the city, but with a little forward planning you can do the same circuit of sites using public transport for next to nothing. The same goes for those must-do harbour cruises that cost $50: you can see exactly the same things for just a few dollars on a ferry trip—all you are missing out on is a corny commentary and a cup of tea. But the really magic thing about spending a few days in Sydney is that if you are prepared to wear away a bit of shoe leather, you can get away without spending much money at all.

Itinerary 1: The Rocks & the Harbour

Start	Customs House.
Finish	Circular Quay.
Time	All day (at least 5 hours—more if you want to linger over dinner).
Best time	Any day is good as long as it's not bucketing down with rain.
Worst time	Walking across the bridge during peak hour can be a tad unpleasant with all the traffic roaring by.
Tips	There are no morning ferry services to Milsons Point, so you'll need to catch the train or walk across the bridge (it takes about 20 minutes each way).

You can turn this day upside-down and treat yourself to breakfast at Ripples (which is also half the price of dinner). The apple hotcakes make a sinfully divine breakfast and you can walk the calories off as you cross the bridge afterwards.

① Customs House

Take a quick bird's-eye view of Sydney by looking down in the centre of the lobby area in gorgeous old Customs House, which is now a library, and checking out the model of the city's central business district. The model is built to a precise 1:1500 scale, which means Sydney Tower is just 50cm high.

Take a stroll to Harrington Street, turn right and then left into Cumberland Place.

② Cumberland Place

You'll get a real sense of living history as you wander around The Rocks, Sydney's most historic and colourful suburb. Until the late 20th century, when it became a gentrified tourist destination full of museums, galleries and boutiques, it was a hotbed of vice, beginning life as an open-air gaol, before becoming renowned for its drunken debauchery, sailors, brothels and other unsavoury characters in the late 19th century. It reinvented itself as an overcrowded slum in the early 20th. The network of narrow streets and concave steps worn by the passing of countless feet in and around Cumberland Place dates back to before 1807.

Keep ambling along Argyle Street until you get to Kendall Lane.

③ The Argyle Cut

This tunnel through the sandstone ridge connects The Rocks to Millers Point and Darling Harbour and was one of the most impressive engineering feats in early Sydney. Work began in 1843 with convicts in chain gangs and was finally completed using explosives in 1859.

ITINERARY 1: THE ROCKS & THE HARBOUR

Customs House **1**
Cumberland Place **2**
The Argyle Cut **3**
Sydney Observatory **4**
The Rocks Discovery Museum **5**
Cadmans Cottage **6**
Sydney Harbour Bridge
   pedestrian walkway **7**
Pylon Lookout **8**
Ripples **9**
Ferry Back to Circular Quay **10**

C CityRail Stop
† Church
ⓘ Information
✉ Post Office
• • • Walking Path

Great views

There's a nice little secret park here

0 — 1/4 mi
0 — 0.25 km

Head up Cambridge Street to Argyle Street, turn left and walk until you get to the next stop.

4 Sydney Observatory

This is one observatory that is just as interesting during daylight hours as it is when the sun goes down—if anything, it's even better during the day because the exhibitions inside are free, whereas night-time tours come at a cost. Highlights include the Cadi Eora Birrung, which looks at Sydney's stars from an Aboriginal perspective and the Transit of Venus, which was one of the main reasons Cook set sail and ended up discovering Australia after observing the transit in Tahiti.

Walk back towards Circular Quay along Argyle Street.

5 The Rocks Discovery Museum

You can easily spend an hour or so in this great museum that focuses just on The Rocks—particularly if you get caught up watching the terrific archival films that play continuously throughout the day. Even if you don't like museums, this one is definitely worth a look into as it brings the tumultuous history of the very streets you have been walking to life (p. 113).

From here, turn left and walk along Argyle Street towards Circular Quay.

6 Cadmans Cottage

Built in 1816 this two-storey cottage is one of the oldest buildings in the city. It housed the Government Coxswain (the man responsible for government boats and their crews in the early days of the colony) and originally stood just metres from the harbour's edge, before sea walls were built enabling land reclamation. It's now the information centre for Sydney Harbour National Park, but is worth a quick peek inside.

Turn left into Cumberland Street and look out for the sign that says 'Bridge Stairs'.

7 Cross the Coathanger

It will cost you almost $300 to climb it, but crossing the Sydney Harbour Bridge via the pedestrian walkway is a free adventure with superb photo opportunities. Fondly known by the locals as the 'Coathanger', it is the world's largest (but not the longest) steel arch bridge with the top of the bridge standing 134m above the harbour.

As you approach the southeast pylon, stroll along the pedestrian walkway until you reach the Pylon Lookout.

8 Pylon Lookout

If you're feeling cashed up break your harbour bridge crossing to climb the 200 steps to the top of the southeast Pylon Lookout, for views almost as good as what you get from the top of the arch—but $290 cheaper. The Pylon Lookout also features exhibitions on the history and construction of the bridge, which was officially opened in 1932 (although the ribbon was cut by a dashing mounted guardsman who appeared out of nowhere brandishing a sword, much to the consternation of the premier and other officials).

When you've copped an eyeful, head down to the pedestrian walkway and cross the bridge. Take the stairs at the end and walk downhill along Alfred Street South to the water's edge, where you'll see Olympic Drive to your right.

9 Dinner with a View at Ripples

If there is one thing you should splurge on during your time in Sydney, it's a dinner with a view of the Opera House and Harbour Bridge. Most restaurants charge an arm and a leg for the privilege, but this great little alfresco

The Rocks & the Harbour Costs

Free	
Four museums, walking around The Rocks and across the Sydney Harbour Bridge	$0
Dirt Cheap	
Ferry ride across the harbour	$5.20
Add-Ons for Spendthrift Millionaires	
Pylon Lookout	$9.50
Two-course dinner with a view at Ripples	$40–$50
Breakfast and coffee at Ripples	$15–$20

restaurant next door to Luna Park at Milsons Point has fabulous food and more than reasonable prices (p. 81). It's licensed and is also BYO, which makes it even kinder on the wallet. Don't panic if it's raining: staff will pull out the clear PVC awnings to keep you dry.

From Ripples, it's a hop step and a jump to Milsons Point Wharf.

The Rocks & the Harbour Itinerary Index

Cadmans Cottage   111 George St., The Rocks. Mon–Fri 9.30am–4.30pm, Sat and Sun 10am–4.30pm.

Customs House   31 Alfred St., Sydney. ℂ **(02) 9242 8595.** Mon–Fri 10am–7pm, Sat and Sun 11am–4pm, closed public holidays.

Pedestrian Walkway   Access via Cumberland St., The Rocks. Daily 24 hr.

Pylon Lookout   Enter the southeast pylon via the pedestrian walkway. ℂ **(02) 9240 1100.** www.pylonlookout.com.au. Admission $9.50 adults and kids over 13, kids $4, kids under 7 free. Open daily 10am–5pm.

Ripples   Olympic Dr., Milsons Point. ℂ **(02) 9929 7722.** Breakfast, lunch and dinner daily.

Sydney Observatory   Watson Rd., Observatory Hill. ℂ **(02) 9241 3767.** www.sydneyobservatory.com.au. Daily 10am–5pm.

The Rocks Discovery Museum   Kendall Ln. (off Argyle St.), The Rocks. ℂ **(02) 9251 8804.** www.rocksdiscoverymuseum.com. Daily 10am–5pm.

⑩ Take a Ferry Back to Circular Quay

The five-minute ferry ride across the harbour from Milsons Point Wharf (right outside Ripples) back to Circular Quay might work out at about $1 a minute, but it's $5 well spent in my opinion. Cruising past the bridge and Opera House towards the city skyline—lit up in all its glory—is the perfect way to round off the evening. FINE PRINT There are no ferry services on Sunday evenings, so walk up the hill to Milsons Point Station and catch the train instead.

Itinerary 2: Art & About

Start	The Museum of Contemporary Art, Circular Quay.
Finish	Australian Centre for Photography.
Time	You'll want to spend anywhere from 45 minutes to 1 hour at each museum, so allow at least 5 hours.
Best time	Any day.
Worst time	The Australian Centre for Photography is closed on Monday.
Tips	If you're still hungry for more art, wander around the side streets of Paddington at the end of this tour. It's home to countless small commercial art galleries. The work on show might be expensive, but looking is free. See p. 182 for more gallery suggestions.

① Museum of Contemporary Art

I think it's kind of weird that one of Sydney's most conservative-looking buildings, the squat four-storey sandstone edifice that sits on the western shore of Circular Quay, is home to some of the country's weirdest—ahem—contemporary art. Actually, the art is very good, it's just that I don't always understand it, but I suspect I'm not alone in that regard. Beyond the permanent collection there are changing exhibitions featuring both Australian and international artists. Exhibitions are usually free, although the occasional blockbuster show may have a ticket price. It also has an excellent collection of Aboriginal art.

Cut across the Quay (keep an eye out for the Writers Walk plaques as you go; p. 127) and into the Botanic Gardens.

② Royal Botanic Gardens and The Domain

Slowly make your way to stop ③, taking time to seek out some of the 35 fountains, sculptures

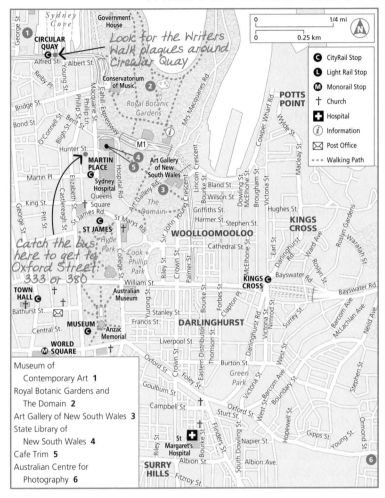

Look for the Writers Walk plaques around Circular Quay

Catch the bus here to get to Oxford Street: 333 or 380

C	CityRail Stop
L	Light Rail Stop
M	Monorail Stop
†	Church
✚	Hospital
ⓘ	Information
✉	Post Office
•••	Walking Path

Museum of
  Contemporary Art **1**
Royal Botanic Gardens and
  The Domain **2**
Art Gallery of New South Wales **3**
State Library of
  New South Wales **4**
Cafe Trim **5**
Australian Centre for
  Photography **6**

and memorials scattered throughout the parklands. Personal favourites include the soundscape installation by Nigel Helyer called **Dual Nature,** relating to the history of people and shipping in Woolloomooloo Bay with shell-like objects sitting on the seabed, held in place by crane sculptures mounted on the foreshore. The chambers create sounds from the ocean and mix with a solar-powered recording. Also worth finding is Janet Laurence's **Veil of Trees,** a meandering line of forest red gums with glass panels embedded with seeds, ash, honey, resin, and fragments of prose and poems by Australian writers, inspired by the landscape. You can't miss Brett Whiteley's famous 'redhead' matches, one live and one burnt, behind the Art Gallery of New South Wales. The sculpture's official name is ***Almost Once.***

③ Art Gallery of New South Wales

I never tire of this gallery; there's always something new to see. It presents a snapshot of the history and evolution of Australian art, from Aboriginal and colonial pieces through to modern works, as well as significant collections of European and Asian art and international exhibitions. If you just want to focus on art you can't see at home, head to the Australian collection and then the Yiribana Gallery, a permanent display of Aboriginal and Torres Strait Islander art.

Walk across The Domain to Macquarie Street to the next stop.

④ State Library of New South Wales

There are five galleries inside and the changing program of exhibitions means there's always something worth having a look at. Most are drawn from the collection of more than five million items; books, of course, but also pic-

tures, posters, sheet music, maps, newspapers, films and videos, sound recordings, photographs, architectural plans, coins, postage stamps and other objects and are curated in such a way as to give a fascinating snapshot of Australian history and culture.

⑤ Cafe Trim

Refuel with a light lunch at Cafe Trim, which was named after the ship's cat which accompanied explorer Matthew Flinders on his voyages to circumnavigate and map the coastline of Australia in 1801–03. Sadly, Trim came to a rather unfortunate end: having survived falling overboard off the Cape of Good Hope on one voyage (he managed to swim back to the vessel and climb aboard by scaling a rope) and a shipwreck off the Great Barrier Reef in 1803, he went missing when Flinders was accused of spying and imprisoned by the French in Mauritius between 1803–10. Flinders believed that Trim was stolen and eaten by hungry slaves. Don't let that put you off the sandwiches at the cafe, though, they are very good.

Catch the 333 or 380 bus from one block west of the Library (Elizabeth St) to Oxford Street and get off the stop after Victoria Barracks.

Art & About Costs

Free	
Four museums, walking around a walk around the Royal Botanic Gardens and The Domain	$0
Dirt Cheap	
Bus fare to Oxford Street	$3.20
Add-Ons for Spendthrift Millionaires	
Sandwich or pie and salad at Cafe Trim	$5–$10

6 Australian Centre for Photography

This is, hands down, my favourite photographic gallery in Sydney. There are two gallery spaces, a foyer display area and a Project Wall for emerging artists, many of whom are students at the centre. The exhibition program is a mix of Australian and international work from both established artists and fresh new talent.

Art & About Itinerary Index

Art Gallery of New South Wales   Art Gallery Rd., The Domain. ☎ **(02) 9225 1700.** www.artgallery.nsw.gov.au. Daily 10am–5pm.

Australian Centre for Photography   257 Oxford St., Paddington. ☎ **(02) 9332 1455.** www.acp.org.au. Tues–Fri noon–7pm, Sat and Sun 10am–6pm.

Cafe Trim   State Library of NSW, Macquarie St., Sydney. ☎ **(02) 9273 1235.** Morning tea, lunch and afternoon tea daily.

Museum of Contemporary Art   140 George St., The Rocks. ☎ **(02) 9245 2400.** www.mca.com.au. Daily 10am–5pm. Free tours Mon–Fri 11am and 1pm, Sat and Sun noon and 1.30pm.

Royal Botanic Gardens and The Domain   Mrs Macquaries Rd., Sydney. www.rbgsyd.nsw.gov.au. Daily 24 hr.

State Library of New South Wales   Macquarie St., Sydney. ☎ **(02) 9273 1414.** www.sl.nsw.gov.au. Mon–Thurs 9am–8pm, Fri 9am–5pm, Sat and Sun 10am–5pm.

Itinerary 3: Manly Scenic Walkway

Start	Manly Scenic Walkway.
Finish	Manly Wharf.
Time	All day. The walk itself takes 3 or 4 hours.
Best time	You'll be outside all day, so pick a sunny one. Any day of the week is good, but if you want to browse the markets at Manly, go on a weekend.
Worst time	This walk can be miserable on a rainy or blustery day.
Tips	There's more than 10km of walking on today's itinerary, so comfortable walking shoes are a must. Wear sunscreen (even if it's overcast), carry a couple of litres of water and take a light jacket just in case the weather turns. Take your swimmers in summer.

1 Manly Scenic Walkway

Take any northern beaches bus (140 to 144 or 168 to 190) from Carrington Street in Wynyard and get off at The Spit Bridge.

It's easy to believe you are miles away from anywhere on this terrific 10km bushwalk, one of my favourites, on the northern side of Sydney Harbour. In fact, most of it is in Sydney Harbour National Park, and even though you are rarely very far from the harbourside suburbs, you are in native bushland most of the time. During the walk, which hugs the harbour foreshore, you cross several pretty harbour beaches, walk though subtropical rainforest and past a number of Aboriginal sites, including a shell midden. Clontarf Beach was a popular 19th-century picnic ground and was the site of an assassination attempt on Prince Alfred in 1868 on his first royal visit to Australia. Disgruntled Irishman Henry O'Farrell shot the prince in the back while he was enjoying a picnic but, luckily for the prince, the bullet hit his rubber braces, which reduced its impact and undoubtedly saved his life. Stop and soak in the harbour views from Grotto Point Lighthouse.

2 The Corso

It's in need of a makeover but The Corso, designed in 1855 and modelled after the Via del Corso in Rome, was once one of Sydney's grand promenades. A warning: most of the cafes along it are overpriced and mediocre at best, so head to Wentworth Street to the south, which runs parallel to The Corso.

3 Fishmongers

You'll have well and truly earned lunch by the time you reach

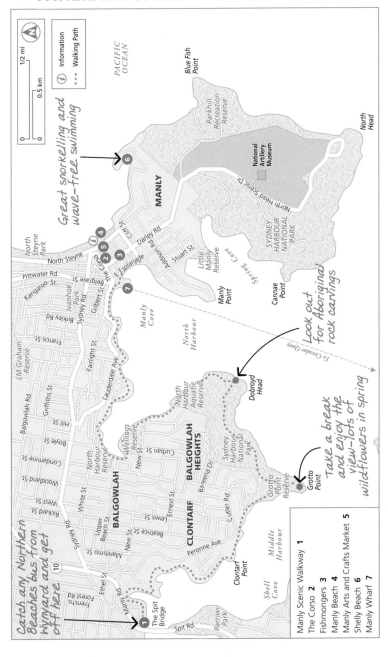

PACIFIC OCEAN

Blue Fish Point

Parkhill Recreation Reserve

North Head

National Artillery Museum

Great snorkelling and wave-free swimming

MANLY

North Head Scenic Dr.

SYDNEY HARBOUR NATIONAL PARK

North Steyne Park

Darley Rd.

Addison Rd.

Stuart St.

Little Manly Reserve

Spring Cove

North Steyne

The Corso

E. Esplanade

Cliff St.

Manly Point

Cannae Point

Pittwater Rd.

Kangaroo St.

Belgrave St.

Gilbert St.

Sydney Rd.

Ivanhoe Park

Manly Cove

North Harbour

Look out for Aboriginal rock carvings

Francis St.

Birkley Rd.

Fairlight St.

Lauderdale Ave.

North Harbour Aquatic Reserve

Dobroyd Head

To Circular Quay

LM Graham Reserve

Balgowalh Rd.

Griffiths St.

Hill St.

Boyle St.

Condamine St.

Woodland St.

West St.

Rickard St.

White St.

North Harbour Reserve

Wellings Reserve

New St.

Curban St.

Bareena Dr.

BALGOWLAH HEIGHTS

Sydney Harbour National Park

Take a break and enjoy the view—lots of wildflowers in spring

BALGOWLAH

CLONTARF

Ernest St.

Lewis St.

Cutler Rd.

Grotto Point

Grotto Point Reserve

Maretimo St.

Beatrice St.

New St.

Upper Beach St.

Peronne Ave.

Middle Harbour

Shell Cove

Clontarf Point

Catch any Northern Beaches bus from Wynyard and get off here

Sydney Rd.

Ethel St.

Frenchs Forest Rd.

Manly Rd.

The Spit Bridge

Spit Rd.

Parriwi Park

Manly Scenic Walkway **1**
The Corso **2**
Fishmongers **3**
Manly Beach **4**
Manly Arts and Crafts Market **5**
Shelly Beach **6**
Manly Wharf **7**

0 ——— 1/2 mi
0 ——— 0.5 km

(i) Information
··· Walking Path

Manly Scenic Walkway Costs

Free	
Manly Scenic Walkway, markets, Manly Beach and Shelly Beach	$0
Dirt Cheap	
Bus and ferry fares	$9.60
Add-Ons for Spendthrift Millionaires	
Fish and chips	$10

Manly, so grab some tasty barbecued prawns from Fishmongers—and some of the best hand-cut chips in Sydney—and eat them on the Manly Beach.

4 Manly Beach

Cool off with a swim at Manly Beach (recommended for summer only as the water is icy without a wetsuit in winter). Rivalling Bondi as the city's most popular beach, the one-mile-long stretch of sand is big enough that it never feels too crowded, although the safe swimming section between the red-and-yellow flags can be elbow-to-elbow on summer weekends. On weekdays, you'll have the water almost to yourself.

5 Manly Arts and Crafts Market

If you're here on a weekend take a wander around the market stalls on Sydney Road, down near Manly Beach, where you can pick up some great handmade souvenirs.

If you're not too footsore, turn right at the beach and head east along Marine Parade to Shelly Beach.

6 Shelly Beach

This tiny north-facing beach is much more sheltered than the surf beach at Manly, so it's a good option for those who want to swim without the waves. There's also Fairy Bower Pool, a nice rock-ledge swimming pool, around halfway along Marine Parade. Keep an eye out for the marine-inspired sculptures embedded in the sandstone along Cabbage Tree Bay.

When it's home time, retrace your steps to Manly Wharf at the other end of The Corso.

7 Ferry back to Circular Quay

The half-hour ferry trip between Manly and Circular Quay is one of the world's great ferry rides. If the weather is not too blowy or cold, grab a seat outside for fantastic views of the Harbour Bridge and Opera House. Be prepared for some rocking, rolling and lurching as you cruise through the heads, especially on a stormy day.

Manly Scenic Walkway Itinerary Index

Fishmongers 11 Wentworth St., Manly. ℂ (02) 9977 1777. www. mongers.com.au. Lunch and dinner daily.

Manly Arts and Crafts Market Sydney Rd. (beach end), Manly. Sat and Sun 10am–5pm.

Manly Ferry Manly Wharf, Manly. www.131500.info. Mon–Fri 6am–midnight, Sat and Sun 8am–midnight. Ferries depart approximately every 30 min. Admission $6.40 adults, $3.20 kids.

Manly Scenic Walkway Avona Cres. (under The Spit Bridge), Seaforth. Download a brochure and map from www.manly.nsw.gov.au. Daily 24 hr.

Itinerary 4: Coastal Cliff Walk

Start	Waverley Cemetery.
Finish	Fishermans Wharf.
Time	This is a full-day tour; the walk itself takes around 4 hours.
Best time	Another itinerary for a non-rainy day. Sunday is best if you want to hit the markets.
Worst time	Avoid early morning, late afternoon and weekends, when locals hit the track for their daily constitutional.
Tips	There's a lot of walking on this itinerary, so wear comfortable walking shoes. Sunscreen, water (and swimmers in summer) are other essential day-pack items.

1 Waverley Cemetery

It might seem like a strange place to start a fun day out, but this is one of the world's most scenic cemeteries with views to die for—literally! The oldest grave here dates back to 1877, and some of the more famous residents include writer Henry Lawson; poets Henry Kendall and Dorothea Mackellar (of '*I Love a Sunburnt Country*' fame); and aeronautical pioneer Sir Lawrence Hargrave. It is an operational cemetery, so please be respectful of any funerals in progress. Photography buffs can get some great 'arty' shots at sunrise.

Beyond the cemetery you'll find the new cliff-hugging Sesquicentenary Boardwalk, which links the headland to the beginning of the Bronte to Bondi Coastal Walk. Take time to savour the views at one of the five viewing platforms along the way.

2 Bronte to Bondi Coastal Walk

This spectacular 3.5km walkway links two of the city's most famous beaches and is a must-do. It's an easy-to-medium walk, mostly along the cliff edge that begins on the northern headland of Bronte Beach, traverses the tiny but perfectly formed Tamarama Beach and skirts the headland of Mackenzies Bay to the southern end of Bondi Beach. It's one sweeping view after another. Look out for Aboriginal rock carvings of sharks and whales in the rocks beside the path—and you may well see real whales in the winter months. For three weeks in late October and early November the section between Tamarama and Bondi is lined with more than 100 sculptures as part of the annual free Sculpture by the Sea exhibition (p. 20). The pathway is not fenced, so keep an eye on your kids.

3 Bondi Baths

Take a swim at this iconic ocean pool at the southern end of the Bondi Beach if you're game. It's home to the Bondi Icebergs, a group of dedicated wintertime swimmers that was founded in 1929, originally as a way for local surf lifesavers to keep fit during the winter months. To be a member you have to compete in the open-air ocean pool on three winter Sundays out of four, for a period of five years. If the water's not deemed cold enough, blocks of ice are added. You can watch the action on Sunday mornings (first weekend in May to the last weekend in September) from 10.15am (there's a spectator fee of $1).

When you've dried off, take the short walk to your next stop.

4 Bondi Beach

Swimming is free at Sydney's most famous beach. Even if you're here during winter, dip your toes in just for the brag factor back home. If you do decide to take the plunge, stay between the red-and-yellow surf lifesaving flags, as the water can be treacherous if you're not used to swimming in the surf.

5 Bondi Markets

Sunday is market day at the northern end of the beach, and Bondi Markets are a great place to pick up a vintage treasure or two.

ITINERARY 4: COASTAL CLIFF WALK

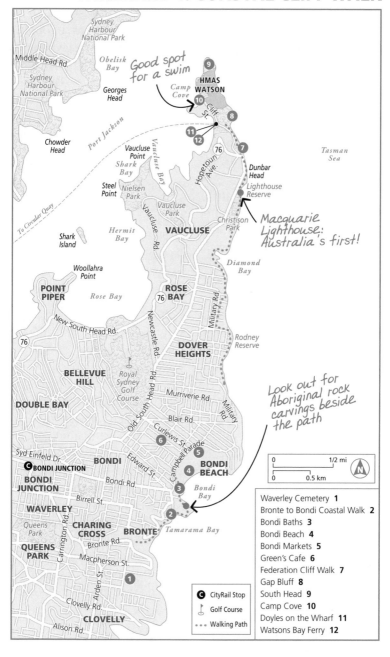

Good spot for a swim

Macquarie Lighthouse; Australia's first!

Look out for Aboriginal rock carvings beside the path

Waverley Cemetery	**1**
Bronte to Bondi Coastal Walk	**2**
Bondi Baths	**3**
Bondi Beach	**4**
Bondi Markets	**5**
Green's Cafe	**6**
Federation Cliff Walk	**7**
Gap Bluff	**8**
South Head	**9**
Camp Cove	**10**
Doyles on the Wharf	**11**
Watsons Bay Ferry	**12**

C CityRail Stop

Golf Course

· · · Walking Path

Now it's time to leave the main Bondi drag. Walk up Curlewis Street and turn left into Glenayr Avenue and you'll reach Green's Cafe.

6 Green's Cafe

If you feel the need for a snack to keep you going you'll find plenty of options in Bondi. Campbell Parade is lined with cafes and takeaway joints, but, sadly, many are best avoided unless you like to pay a lot of money for crappy coffee and bad service. Stay well clear of those in the centre of the strip and head instead for the far northern and southern ends, or a few blocks west. **Green's Cafe** is popular with locals in the know and it's a good place for coffee or a light snack and they serve a sensational breakfast all day. Go on—you've earned the calories!

From here, walk down Blair Street and turn left at Military Road. Keep going until you reach Lola Road, which is the start of the Federation Cliff Walk.

7 Federation Cliff Walk

This 5km walkway runs from Dover Heights on the northern side of Bondi to Diamond Bay (just south of Watsons Bay at the tip of South Head). It's not nearly as popular or as crowded as the Bronte to Bondi Coastal Walk, but it's just as scenic, if not more so. There are a couple of short sections through suburban streets, but it's pretty much cliff-edge the entire way. There are a number of staircases to negotiate, so it's not a good walk for those with dodgy knees. Just before you get to Watsons Bay you'll walk past the Macquarie Light-station, which has the distinction of being Australia's first lighthouse. The current lighthouse (1883) is an exact copy of an earlier one built on site in 1818 designed by convict architect Francis Greenway (p. 108).

8 Gap Bluff

Gap Bluff, along the Federation Cliff Walk, is one of the most popular cliff-top lookouts in Sydney—the sheer cliffs plunge more than 80m into roiling waves. Unfortunately, it was the site of Sydney's worst maritime tragedy when the *Dunbar* was shipwrecked in 1857, with the loss of 121 passengers and crew. The sole survivour was washed overboard and wedged into a crevice on the cliffs, 10m above the waves. The anchor is bolted into a sandstone ledge as part of a memorial at the northern end of the park.

Coastal Cliff Walk Costs

Free	
Waverley Cemetery, cliff-top walks, Bondi Beach	$0
Dirt Cheap	
Bus and ferry fares	$8.40
Add-Ons for Spendthrift Millionaires	
Swim at Bondi Baths	$4.50
Snack at Green's Cafe	$5–$15
Fish and chips and a beer	$20

9 South Head

South Head is part of Sydney Harbour National Park and the views across the harbour to North Head are nothing short of breathtaking. There is a short loop walk around the headland that takes in a number of glorious vantage points, old canons and gun emplacements of various 19th- and 20th-century vintages. The red-and-white Hornby Lighthouse is Australia's third-oldest.

Walk back along the path until you get to Cliff Street and Camp Cove.

10 Camp Cove

This charming little beach is a popular snorkelling spot. It marks the place where Captain Arthur Phillip first came ashore in Sydney Harbour in 1788, although you won't find much more than a plaque to commemorate the occasion.

Walk along the beach to Pacific Street, then follow Marine Parade until you reach Fishermans Wharf.

11 Fish and Chips and a Beer with a View

Grab some restaurant-quality fish and chips from **Doyles on the Wharf** (p. 74) and eat on the beach, or under the shade of a tree in Robertson Park, then head to the Watsons Bay Hotel for a beer at one of the city's best beer gardens. Don't be tempted by the menu; the last time I ate here the food was ordinary and over-priced, but the view is amazing. It's a very popular spot on Sunday afternoons.

12 Watsons Bay Ferry

Jump on the ferry at Watsons Bay for the 15-minute trip back to Circular Quay and watch all the little beaches and coves pass you by.

Coastal Cliff Walk Itinerary Index

Bondi Baths   1 Notts Ave., Bondi. ☏ (02) 9130 4804. The pool is closed for cleaning every Thursday. Mon–Fri 6am–6.30pm, Sat and Sun 6.30am–6.30pm.

Bondi Markets   Bondi Beach Public School, Campbell Pde., Bondi. Sun 10am–5pm.

Doyles on the Wharf   Fishermans Wharf, Watsons Bay. ☏ (02) 9337 6214. www.doyles.com.au. Lunch daily.

Federation Cliff Walk   Lola Rd., Dover Heights. Daily 24 hr.

Green's Cafe   140 Glenayr Ave., Bondi. ☏ (02) 9130 6181. Daily, 7am–3pm.

Watsons Bay Ferry   Fishermans Wharf, Watsons Bay. www.131500.info. Mon–Fri 10am–3.50pm, Sat and Sun 10am–7pm. Ferries depart approximately every 30 min. Admission $5.50 adults, $2.70 kids.

Watsons Bay Hotel   1 Military Rd., Watsons Bay. ☏ (02) 9337 5444.

Waverley Cemetery   St Thomas St., Bronte. www.waverley.nsw.gov.au/cemetery/. Daily 7am–dusk.

Itinerary 5: Keeping the Kids Amused

Start	Circular Quay.
Finish	Luna Park.
Time	This full-day tour is guaranteed to tire the kids out.
Best time	You could do this trip any day of the week. If you travel on 'Family Funday Sunday' you'll save a pile of money on public transport (p. 271).
Worst time	Luna Park is closed Tuesday to Thursday.
Tips	Bicycles are permitted on ferries free of charge and Sydney Olympic Park has some great bike paths. If you don't have a bike, hire them at the park, but be warned: they aren't cheap.

① RiverCat

It's a 40-minute ferry ride on the RiverCat to the wharf at Sydney Olympic Park. Kids (and adults) love sitting outside at the front of the boat (if it's not too breezy) because there's plenty to look at along the way. The ferry

ITINERARY 5: KEEPING THE KIDS AMUSED

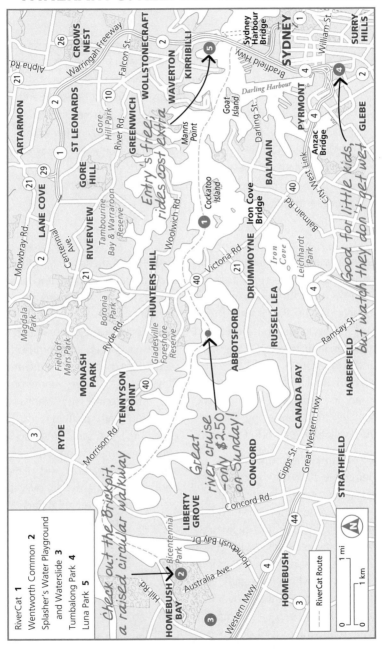

RiverCat **1**
Wentworth Common **2**
Splasher's Water Playground and Waterslide **3**
Tumbalong Park **4**
Luna Park **5**

Check out the Brickpit, a raised circular walkway

Great river cruise —only $2.50 on Sunday!

Entry's free; rides cost extra

Good for little kids, but watch they don't get wet

--- RiverCat Route

Sunday Saver

On Sunday $2.50 each gets you unlimited travel on all trains, buses and ferries if you are a family group. To qualify for the discount the travelling group must be related and include at least one child and one adult. If you're not travelling on a Sunday, get the DayTripper ticket, which gives you unlimited travel on buses, trains and ferries and will save you $6.20 per adult on today's tour. You only have to pay for two adults and one child—the rest of the family travels free.

You can also save up to 30% on return train fares when you travel after 9am Monday to Friday.

criss-crosses the harbour and cruises up the western reaches until the harbour finally narrows to become the Parramatta River, and harbourside mansions and marinas give way to mangroves and cormorants.

From the wharf, walk down Hill Road to Sydney Olympic Park, turn left into Bennelong Parkway and walk to Wentworth Common.

2 Wentworth Common

Before the 2000 Olympics, Homebush Bay was pretty much just a polluted industrial and urban wasteland, site of brickworks, armaments facilities, salt works, abattoirs, rubbish tips and goodness knows what else legally, and illegally, dumped there over the years. But it's quite amazing what many millions of dollars can do. The former Olympic Games venue is now one of the city's larg-est parkland areas, with wetlands and lots of open space and plenty of ways to keep active kids amused for not much cash (although be warned, there are plenty of expensive ways to keep them amused as well). Best bet is the Adventure Playground, a huge theme-park-like playground at Wentworth Common with a flying fox, an enormous sandpit, a slide, a climbing frame, swings and shade sails to keep parents and players cool, and a boardwalk over the wetlands in Bicentennial Park.

Keep strolling along Sarah Durack Drive to Olympic Boulevard, where you'll hit the Sydney Olympic Park Aquatic Centre.

3 Splasher's Water Playground and Waterslide

Cool the kids down at the water playground at the Sydney Olympic Park Aquatic Centre, where they can get wet and wild on the rapid river ride and play in bubbling beach fountains and spurting volcanoes. There's even a gigantic bucket that fills with water and splashes into the pool and water slides below.

When it's time for a change of scenery, retrace your steps and catch a RiverCat to Darling Harbour.

④ Tumbalong Park

A cheaper way to get the kids wet is at Tumbalong Park in Darling Harbour, where there is a large shallow spiral fountain that is perfect for kids to paddle in. There's also a large playground here, with slippery dips, climbing frames and other kid-friendly devices to climb on and run around. FINE PRINT It can get seriously crowded here on weekends and public holidays.

From here, you can catch a ferry to Milsons Point (or catch a train from Circular Quay) and Luna Park.

⑤ Luna Park

If the kids aren't already exhausted, round off the day with a trip to Luna Park. The iconic smiley-face gate at this Heritage-Listed amusement park on the harbour's edge has been a family favourite since the 1930s, and while some of the rides are quaint and nostalgic, many are definitely high-octane. Entry is free, but rides cost extra—but at least you can watch the kids without having forked out money just to stand there. Teenagers will find it all too tame and daggy and will want to spend money on the big thrill rides, but younger kids are best off at Coney Island, an authentic 1930s fun house (which just means it is still exactly the way it was when the park first opened!). For $10 they can have unlimited turns on all the rides.

Keeping the Kids Amused Costs

Free	
Sydney Olympic Park, Wentworth Common, Tumbalong Park, Luna Park (entry only)	$0
Dirt Cheap	
DayTripper ticket (Mon–Sat)	$17 adults, $8.60 kids
Ferry fares (Family Funday Sunday)	$2.50 each
Add-ons for Spendthrift Millionaires	
Bike hire at Sydney Olympic Park	$20 for 2 hr. ($15 kids)
Waterslide and Splasher's Water Playground	$6.80 adults, $5.50 kids ($3.30 if you don't want to get wet).
Coney Island Pass at Luna Park	$10

Keeping the Kids Amused Itinerary Index

Bike Hire @ Sydney Olympic Park ☏ (02) 9714 7517. Bicentennial Park (near Lilies on the Park Cafe): daily 8.30am–5.30pm. Blaxland Riverside Park (at the Information Booth on the wharf): Sat, Sun and public holidays 8.30am–5.30pm.

Luna Park 1 Olympic Dr., Milsons Point. ☏ (02) 9033 7676. www.lunaparksydney.com. Mon 11am–6pm, Fri 11am–11pm, Sat 10am–11pm, Sun 10am–6pm. Closed Tues–Thurs.

Sydney Olympic Park Aquatic Centre Olympic Blvd., Sydney Olympic Park. ☏ (02) 9752 3666. www.aquaticcentre.com.au. Splashers Water Playground: daily 10am–7pm. Waterslide: Mon–Thur 3–7pm, Fri 3–8pm, Sat, Sun and public holidays noon–6pm.

Sydney Olympic Park Visitor Centre Cnr. Showground Rd. and Murray Rose Ave., Sydney Olympic Park. ☏ (02) 9714 7888. www.sydneyolympicpark.com.au. Daily 9am–5pm.

Tumbalong Park Southern section of Darling Harbour. ☏ (02) 9281 0788. Daily 24 hr.

Wentworth Common Majorie Jackson Pkwy. (via Bennelong Pkwy.), Sydney Olympic Park. Daily sunrise–sunset.

Itinerary 6: Day Trip to Asia

Start	Freedom Plaza.
Finish	Advanced Chinese Herbs.
Time	5 hours.
Best time	Shops tend to close on Saturday afternoon and Sunday, so this is a good trip to do mid-week.
Worst time	Night. The area around the station can be a bit rough when the sun goes down.
Tips	Keep in mind that Cabramatta is an hour from Central Station.

Since the 1980s the outer western suburb of Cabramatta has been a centre for the Vietnamese community. According to the last census, Cabra, as the locals call it, has more residents born in Vietnam than in Australia (in fact, 75% of Cabra's residents were born outside Australia), and the number of people speaking Vietnamese at home is three times higher than the number that speak only English. This means that spending a day in Sydney's Little Saigon is like taking a day trip to Asia, complete with all the requisite sights, sounds and smells.

1 Freedom Plaza

Leave Cabramatta Station on the Railway Parade side (on the right of the platform if coming from Central) and walk two blocks west to Freedom Plaza, a pedestrian-only section of Park Road. You can't miss the massive red Pai Lau Gate, which is flanked by bronze, copper, marble and granite sculptures and statues. Both sides of the plaza are lined with hole-in-the wall food shops selling everything from fresh juices, bubble tea (also called Pearl Milk Tea; it's a sweet milky tea with tapioca and it's delicious) to moon cakes to dim sum. It's a great spot to sit with a glass of freshly squeezed sugar cane juice and people-watch.

When you're done here, wander down John Street and Park Road.

2 Shop 'til you Drop

Go on a unique shopping odyssey at bargain basement prices on **John Street** and **Park Road.** The best finds are dirt-cheap fabrics (mostly of the floaty, chintzy, synthetic kind), Chinese kitchenware and Asian fashions, including cheongsams and jade jewellery. See the index below for some best bets, but make sure you stop at 96B John Street.

3 New One Gift Shop

Despite my best intentions I always walk out of this crowded little shop with more than I had intended to buy, even when I promise to myself that I will 'just have a quick look'. It's a jumble sale of trash and treasure with a feng shui twist that's utterly irresistible.

Day Trip to Asia Costs

Free	
Freedom Plaza, window shopping, produce markets	$0
Dirt Cheap	
Off-peak return train fare from Central Station	$6.60
Add-ons for Spendthrift Millionaires	
Fresh sugar cane juice	$2.50
Bowl of pho	$7–$9.50
Bubble tea	$3
Consultation with herbalist	$20

ITINERARY 6: DAY TRIP TO ASIA

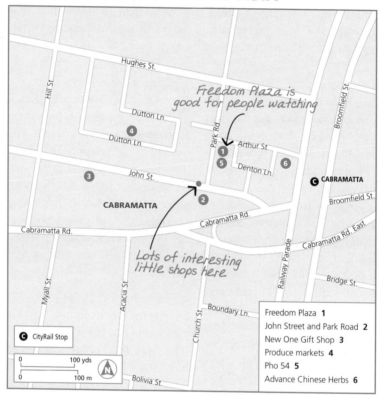

Freedom Plaza is good for people watching

Lots of interesting little shops here

C CityRail Stop

0   100 yds
0   100 m

Freedom Plaza **1**
John Street and Park Road **2**
New One Gift Shop **3**
Produce markets **4**
Pho 54 **5**
Advance Chinese Herbs **6**

From here, amble through the food market area in the tiny arcades leading off John Street towards Dutton Lane.

4 Produce Markets

You won't find lots of plastic packages and neatly stacked produce here. Fresh fish are piled outside doorways, ruby-red barbecued ducks hang in shop windows, and great crates of evil-smelling durian, perfect purple banana flowers, mangosteens, spiky dragon fruit and bunches of lychees (as well as plenty of stuff that I don't recognise) overflow everywhere while wizened women in baggy silk pyjamas haggle furiously over price. You might be in suburban Sydney, but it sure doesn't look— or smell—like it.

When you've had your fill of sights and sounds, head to 54 Park Road to fill your belly.

5 Pho 54

It's all about the divine noodle soup at this tiny little cafe. Don't expect any fancy decor; it's strictly no-frills laminated tables, plastic chairs, cutlery plunked in a bucket in the middle of the table and the occasional soup splatter on the wall. But with eight types of beef pho on offer and an always-packed room of silent people slurping happily, you know they take their pho (pronounced 'fur', not 'foe' or 'po') very seriously here.

When you're full, turn right down Arthur Street and prepare to be prodded.

6 Advance Chinese Herbs

It never fails to amaze me how someone can look at your eyes and your tongue and feel your pulse, then come up with a correct diagnosis of what ails you. A consultation with a traditional Chinese herbalist will cost around $20 (the herbs cost extra), but if all you want is a tea to help you detox after too many big nights on the town, you'll get what you need for just a few dollars. As for the intoxicating aroma as you walk in the door, that's priceless!

Day Trip to Asia Itinerary Index

Advance Chinese Herbs 2 Arthur St., Cabramatta. ℂ (02) 9723 9139. Daily 9.30am–7pm.

Danielle Fashion 95 John St., Cabramatta. ℂ (02) 9725 6403. Daily 9am–5.30pm.

Du Thanh Fabric 95 John St., Cabramatta. ℂ (02) 9727 2917. Daily 9am–5pm.

Freedom Plaza Park Road, Cabramatta.

Hong Thai Fabric 94 John St., Cabramatta. ℂ (02) 9794 9211. Daily 9am–5pm.

Hung Thanh Material 46 Park Rd., Cabramatta. ℂ (02) 9726 7527. Daily 9am–5pm.

KT Jewellery 85 John St., Cabramatta. ℂ (02) 9724 0562. Daily 9am–5pm.

New One Gift Shop 96B John St., Cabramatta. ℂ (02) 9723 6238. Daily 8am–7pm.

Pho 54 54 Park Rd., Cabramatta. ℂ (02) 9726 1992. Daily 8am–7pm.

Itinerary 7: The Blue Mountains

Start	Katoomba.
Finish	Scenic World.
Time	All day. The train trip from Central Station is 2 hours each way. Allow at least 4 hours once you're there if you want to do a bushwalk.
Best time	Mid-week. The Blue Mountains is a popular weekend destination for Sydneysiders so it can get quite busy.
Worst time	Weirdly, much of the public transport does not operate on weekends.
Tips	Always be prepared for cold and wet weather if you're bushwalking in the Blue Mountains. Carry lots of water, basic supplies, a first aid kit, a good map and a mobile phone. Do *not* stray off the track; it's very easy to become lost—people have died here.

❶ Katoomba Station

The massive ridge of mountainous wilderness is known as The Blue Mountains because of the blue haze produced by the oil of the eucalypt trees. It's around 2 hours by train from the centre of Sydney. Impenetrable for the first 25 years of the colony, the mountains were finally crossed in 1813 by the trio of Blaxland, Wentworth, and Lawson, who finally opened up the western hinterland to settlement. It's an area of dramatic mountain scenery and a great place to do some bushwalking or curl up in front of an open fire in winter when snowfalls are not uncommon. There are lots of art galleries, historic houses, wonderful gardens and many delightful coffee shops specialising in home-made scones and Devonshire teas—but the real reason to come here,

particularly if you are keen to spend time rather than money in this World-Heritage-Listed wonderland, is to go bushwalking.

From the train station at Katoomba walk down Katoomba Street to Echo Point, around 2km. (Take local bus 686 if you don't feel like walking, but the service runs every 40 to 50 minutes, so it may be quicker to walk.)

❷ Echo Point

Echo Point has the best view of the mountain's most famous icons—and one of the most photographed spots in the state—the Three Sisters. These three sandstone towers, 922, 918 and 906m tall respectively, are, according to local legend, three Aboriginal sisters, Meehni, Wimlah and Gunnedoo, who were turned into stone by a witchdoctor to keep them safe during a tribal battle. The witchdoctor was

ITINERARY 7: THE BLUE MOUNTAINS

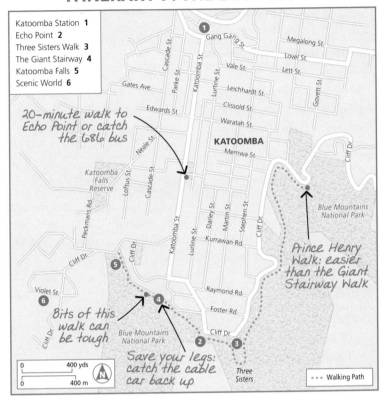

Katoomba Station **1**
Echo Point **2**
Three Sisters Walk **3**
The Giant Stairway **4**
Katoomba Falls **5**
Scenic World **6**

20-minute walk to Echo Point or catch the 686 bus

KATOOMBA

Blue Mountains National Park

Prince Henry Walk: easier than the Giant Stairway Walk

Bits of this walk can be tough

Blue Mountains National Park

Save your legs: catch the cable car back up

Three Sisters

• • • Walking Path

killed, and so they remained in stone.

Collect a map of the Three Sisters Walk and off you go.

3 Three Sisters Walk

This terrific 45-minute walk starts behind the visitor information centre and will give you great views of Mount Solitary, the Jamison Valley and, of course, the Three Sisters themselves. At the end of the track you walk across 'Honeymoon Bridge' to stand on one of the Sisters. It's an easy walk, although it can get crowded.

4 The Giant Stairway

One of the most popular (and challenging) short walks in the mountains starts at Echo Point. The track, which takes around 3 hours to complete, descends some 900-odd steps into the valley and along the base of the cliffs. But remember: what goes down must come up. It's a tough climb out of the valley, so you will need to be fit; however, there is an

The Blue Mountains Costs

Free	
The Three Sisters and three bushwalks	$0
Dirt Cheap	
Return train fare from Central Station	$24.40
Add-ons for Spendthrift Millionaires	
Bus fares	$1.90–$3.80
Scenic World	$10

easier way if you don't mind spending a bit of cash (see ❻). Even so, this is a tough walk, and the National Parks advises that 'visitors with heart or breathing difficulties are advised not to attempt this descent'.

If you don't fancy the hard slog of the Giant Stairway, follow Prince Henry Cliff Walk along the cliff-tops to Katoomba Falls.

❺ Katoomba Falls

This is where the Kedumba River falls about 150m over the edge of the escarpment in two main stages. Some of the best views of the falls themselves are from just underneath Scenic World (see ❻). You can also follow **Prince Henry Cliff Walk** in the other direction from Echo Point, west to Gordon Falls to the west of Leura. If you like lookouts, you'll love this walk and you can catch the 695 bus back to Katoomba or walk to Leura Station at the end.

❻ Scenic World

Yes, it's a tourist attraction and yes, at around $1.40 a minute, it's not exactly the cheapest ride in town, but when you're on the valley floor facing a 45-minute lung-busting muscle-melting climb up, a $10 one-way ride is well worth it (and the views are pretty amazing). There are two options: the **Scenic Railway,** the steepest incline railway in the world, was originally part of a network of tramlines built to bring coal and kerosene shale from mines up to the main railway. It's probably a bit more thrilling going down than up. The second option is the the **Scenic Cableway,** which is the steepest aerial cable car in the Southern Hemisphere. It's a 545m cable car ride out of the rainforest of the Jamison Valley back up to cliff-tops just west of Echo Point. You can pay for your ticket on arrival up the top.

The Blue Mountains Itinerary Index

Echo Point Visitor Information Centre   Echo Point Rd., Katoomba. © 1300 653 408 (toll free in Australia). Pick up maps of the Three Sisters Walk, The Giant Stairway and Katoomba Falls, or download them from www.visitbluemountains.com.au.

Katoomba Falls Reserve   Cliff Dr., Katoomba.

Katoomba Station   Goldsmith Pl., Katoomba. First train to Katoomba leaves Central Station at 3.57am; last train to Central Station leaves Katoomba at 11.16pm.

Scenic World   Cnr. Violet St. and Cliff Dr., Katoomba. © (02) 4780 0200. www.scenicworld.com.au. Daily 9am–5pm.

ENDANGERED

BANDICOOTS

SLOW
DOWN

Sydney is wild at heart.

SYDNEY BASICS

1 Information Central

Internet Access for Free (or Cheap)   There's no shortage of cheap Internet cafes and e-mail centres in Sydney. You'll find many clustered around Central Station, Kings Cross, Bondi and Manly. Many cafes and pubs also offer free wireless for paying customers and will usually advertise the fact with a poster on the window—if you see lots of people inside bent over laptops it's a sure sign that access is free. If you get really desperate, almost all McDonald's and Starbucks offer free Wi-Fi. Public libraries also offer inexpensive (sometimes free) internet access (see p. 154).

Manly Visitors Information Centre   Get all the info you need about Manly at the Manly Visitors Information Centre (Manly Wharf; ℂ **(02) 9976 1430;** www.manlyaustralia.com.au), plus friendly advice. It's open Monday through Friday 9am to 5pm and weekends 10am to 4pm.

Sydney Visitor Centre   Go to the first floor of The Rocks Centre (cnr. Argyle and Playfair sts.; ℂ **(02) 9240 8788;** www.sydneyvisitorcentre. com) to pick up maps, brochures and general tourist information about Sydney as well as towns in New South Wales. It's open daily from 9am to 5pm.

Tourism Australia   This is another good source of information. Visit www.australia.com.

Tourism NSW   This is the best source of information on Sydney and surrounding areas. The website (www.visitnsw.com) has details on attractions, hotels, events, transport and more.

2 Getting To & Around Town

Getting into Town from the Airport   **Sydney International Airport** is 8km from the city centre. There are three terminals: **T1** is the international terminal; **T2** is home to a number of domestic and regional airlines including OzJet, Jetstar, Virgin Blue, Tiger Airways, Rex Regional Express, Aeropelican, Air Link, Big Sky Express and Qantas flights QF1600 and above; **T3** is the terminal for domestic Qantas flights QF0400 to QF1599.

The **Airport Link** train connects the international and domestic airports to the city stations of Central, Museum, St James, Circular Quay, Wynyard and Town Hall. You'll need to change trains for other Sydney stations. Trains run approximately every 10 minutes. The journey into the city takes 15 minutes; a single fare from T1 to Central costs $14.80 for adults, $10 for kids. It can get crowded during peak hour (approximately 7 to 9am and 4 to 6.30pm) and the trains do not have dedicated luggage racks. If you have lots of luggage and you're travelling into the city at these times, it's probably best to take an airport bus (see below) or a taxi.

Sydney Airporter shuttle buses (ℂ **(02) 9666 9988;** www.kst.com. au) operate to the city centre from bus stops outside the terminals every 15 minutes from 5am to 8pm. This service will drop you off (and pick you up) at hotels in the city, Kings Cross and Darling Harbour. Pick-ups from hotels require at least three hours' advance notice, and you can book online. Tickets cost $14 one-way and $23 round-trip (slightly cheaper if you buy online). The return portion can be used any time in the future.

A **taxi** from the airport to the city centre costs $30 to $35 depending on traffic conditions, so if there are three or four of you it can be a cheaper option than a shuttle bus or train.

BY BUS

Buses cover a wide area of metropolitan Sydney and are usually frequent and reliable. The minimum fare is $1.90 for adults and 90¢ for children for a 4km 'section' (which covers most short hops in the city). A trip from the city, say, to Bondi Beach costs $3.20 ($1.60 for kids). Sections are marked on bus-stand signs, but if in doubt, just say your destination and the driver will tell you the fare. More and more bus routes are being converted to prepay only, which means you can't buy your ticket on the bus. Tickets are available from newsagents, convenience stores, CityRail stations and Sydney Ferries wharves.

A **TravelTen** ticket offers 10 bus rides for a discounted price. A **Blue TravelTen** covers two sections on the bus route and costs $15.20 for adults and $7.60 for children; a **Brown TravelTen** covers up to five sections and costs $25.60 for adults and $12.80 for children. TravelTen tickets are transferable, so if two or more people travel together, you can use the same one.

Most buses bound for the northern suburbs, including night buses to Manly and the bus to Taronga Zoo, leave from **Wynyard Park** on Carrington Street, behind Wynyard Station. Buses to the southern beaches, such as Bondi and Bronte, and the western and eastern suburbs leave from **Circular Quay.**

If you need help planning your trip call the **Transport Info Line** (© **13 15 00**) for information, visit www.131500.info or ask the staff at the bus information kiosk on the corner of Alfred and Loftus streets, behind Circular Quay Station (© **(02) 9219 1680**).

FREE 555 Bus

The free **555 city shuttle** runs in a loop from Central Station down Elizabeth Street to Circular Quay and back up George Street to Chinatown and Central. It operates every 10 minutes in both directions between 9.30am and 3.30pm on weekdays (until 9pm on Thursday nights) and between 9.30am and 6pm on weekends.

BY FERRY

Ferries are a great way to get around Sydney, and they're fun. Almost all ferries leave from **Circular Quay.** For ferry information, call ✆ **13 15 00** or visit the ferry information office opposite Wharf 4. Timetables are available for all routes. One-way journeys within the inner harbour (virtually everywhere except Manly and Parramatta) cost $5.20 for adults and $2.60 for children ages 4 to 15 (kids under 4 travel free). The ferry to Manly leaves from Wharf 3 and takes 30 minutes and costs $6.40 for adults and $3.20 for children. Ferries run from 6am to midnight. Bicycles are permitted on all ferries free of charge.

If you plan on doing a lot of ferry travel, the **FerryTen** ticket costs $33.50 for adults and $16.70 for kids and is good for 10 trips within the inner harbour (excluding Manly). Buy TravelTen and FerryTen tickets at newsagents, bus depots or the Circular Quay ferry terminal. Tickets are transferable, so if two or more people travel together, you can use the same ticket.

BY TRAIN

Sydney's subway and train system is a quick way to get around, though timetable information should be used as a guide rather than gospel and it's not the safest option late at night, particularly if travelling to the outer suburbs. The main station is **Central**, although you can also pick up most trains at **Town Hall** and **Redfern** as well. Single tickets within the city centre cost $3.20 for adults and $1.60 for children; return tickets are double. All return-trip train tickets are 30% cheaper if you buy them off-peak (after 9am Monday through Friday).

The **City Hopper** allows unlimited all-day train travel around the city centre (Central, Town Hall, Wynyard, Circular Quay, St James, Museum, Martin Place and Kings Cross stations). Tickets cost $8 for adults and $4 for kids if bought before 9am, and $5.60 for adults and $2.80 for kids if bought after 9am.

Information is available from **Transport Info;** call ✆ **13 15 00.**

BY LIGHT RAIL & MONORAIL

Metro Light Rail runs between Central Station and Wentworth Park in Pyrmont and Glebe, providing good access to Chinatown, Paddy's Markets, Darling Harbour, Star City casino and the Sydney Fish Markets.

Discount Travel Passes

- **Day Tripper:** This ticket allows unlimited bus, train, and ferry travel for 1 full day and is good value if you are doing even a moderate amount of travel on public transport, particularly if your day includes a return trip on one of the longer ferry routes. Tickets cost $17 for adults and $8.60 for the first child (other children travel free). The pass is available at all bus, train, and ferry ticket outlets.

- **Family Funday Sunday:** It's almost too good to be true, and you can't help but think that when the cash-strapped State Government realises what a good deal this is it'll jack the prices up. Until they wise up, $2.50 gets you unlimited travel on all trains, buses and ferries each and every Sunday. FINE PRINT To qualify for the discount the travelling group must be related and include at least one child and one adult.

- **TravelTen and FerryTen passes:** See p. 269.

- **Weekly Travel Pass:** This seven-day pass allows unlimited travel on buses, trains, and ferries. There are six different passes (each is a different colour) depending on the distance you need to travel. The passes visitors most commonly use are the **Red Pass** and the **Green Pass**. The Red Pass costs $38 for adults and $19 for kids and covers all transportation within the city centre and near surroundings. This pass will get you aboard inner-harbour ferries, but not the ferry to Manly. The Green Pass, which costs $46 for adults and $23 for kids, will take you to more distant destinations, including Manly. You can buy either pass at newsagents or bus, train and ferry ticket outlets.

They run every 10 minutes and a one-way fare is $3.20 to $4.20 for adults and $2 to $3.20 for children (aged 5 to 15 years; kids under 5 years are free, depending on the distance).

Seldom used by Sydneysiders, the monorail connects the CBD to Darling Harbour. The trip takes around 12 minutes; to walk it takes around 15 from Town Hall, which explains why it's not very well used by locals. Tickets are $4.80, free for children under 5. Look for the grey overhead line and the tube-like structures that are the stations. Call ✆ **(02) 8584 5288** or visit www.metrotransport.com.au for more information.

BY CAR

Unless you're planning on heading out of town or exploring the outer suburbs, you can get around Sydney pretty well just by using public transport (and perhaps the occasional late-night taxi).

If you do want to get around by car, be aware that all of the major freeways in and out of the city, as well as the Sydney Harbour Bridge, Harbour Tunnel and Cross City Tunnel, are tolled roads and most are not payable with cash. You can get an **E-Toll pass** at www.rta.nsw. gov.au or call ✆ **13 18 65** before you travel (or up to 48 hours after you have travelled). Be mindful of T2 and T3 transit lanes; you must have two or three people in the car, respectively, in order to travel in these lanes. Check signs for times.

Parking   There is virtually no free parking in the city centre; parking meter rates vary depending on the time and location. All meters accept coins and some will accept credit card or payment via your mobile phone. Peak hours are 8am to 6pm and off-peak hours are 6 to 10pm. City Rangers keep an eagle eye on the few metered spots and will issue a fine to anyone who parks over time or illegally and the minimum fine is around $80. Many hotels offer parking, but at a fee—expect to pay upwards of $25 per day. There are a number of parking stations throughout the city centre and most offer good early bird rates for full-day weekday parking (around $20 to $30) if you enter between 6.30 and 9.30am and exit between 3.30 and 7.30pm. Otherwise, expect to pay around $12 to $15 per hour; rates are much cheaper on weekends and in the evenings.

BY TAXI

All **taxi** journeys are metered, although some trips attract a surcharge, including a trip across the Sydney Harbour Bridge or through the Harbour Tunnel and the Eastern Distributor from the airport. All fares are 20% more expensive between 10pm and 6am and an extra 10% will be added to your fare if you pay by credit card. Taxis line up at stands

Taxi Scam

One scam to watch out for is at busy taxi queues, when drivers may try to cash in by insisting you share a cab with other passengers in line at the airport. After dropping off the other passengers, the driver will attempt to charge you the full price of the journey—despite the fact that the other passengers paid for their sections—and you will have had a longer ride in the process. If you are first in line in the taxi stand, the law states that you can refuse to share a cab.

in the city, such as those opposite Circular Quay and Central Station. They are also frequently found in front of hotels. You can also hail a taxi in the street: a yellow light on top of the cab means it's vacant. Cabs can be hard to get on Friday and Saturday nights and around 3pm every day, when cabbies are changing shifts. All passengers must wear seatbelts and taxis are licensed to carry four people.

The **Taxi Complaints Hotline** (✆ **1800 648 478**; free in Australia) deals with problem taxi drivers. The main cab companies are **Taxis Combined** (✆ **13 33 00**); **RSL Taxis** (✆ **(02) 9581 1111**); **Legion Cabs** (✆ **13 14 51**); and **Premier Cabs** (✆ **13 10 17**).

3 Sydney Resources A to Z

ATMs/Cashpoints   ATMs are everywhere and most use global networks, such as Cirrus and PLUS. Australian ATMs use a four-digit PIN code, so check with your bank and make sure you change yours before you leave home. Many banks impose a fee every time you use a card at another bank's ATM, and that fee can be higher for international transactions (up to $5 or more) than for domestic ones (where they're rarely more than $2).

Credit Cards   Visa and MasterCard are universally accepted in Australia; American Express and Diners Club are less common and usually attract a 1 to 3% surcharge on top of the price of your purchases; Discover is not used. Always carry a little cash, because many merchants will not take cards for purchases under $15.

Disability Services Most hotels, major stores, attractions, and public toilets in Australia have wheelchair access, although the entrance or access may not be obvious and it may pay to call ahead. Some (but not all) buses and taxis (it's a good idea to book 24 hours in advance for taxis) have wheelchair access facilities, but many suburban train stations outside the city centre have stair access only. You can check access facilities on your intended public transport route at www. 131500.info, or ☎ **131 500**.

Holders of Vision Impaired Person Passes are entitled to free travel on CityRail, Sydney Buses and Sydney Ferries, and guide and hearing dogs registered as assistance animals are also permitted on these services and in all shops and restaurants. If you wish to visit Australia with your guide dog, remember that animals must satisfy certain health requirements and may need to undergo quarantine after arrival (visit www.daff.gov.au for more information). TTY facilities are still limited largely to government services.

Emergencies Dial ☎ **000** to call the police, the fire service or an ambulance.

Call the Emergency Prescription Service (☎ **(02) 9235 0333**) for emergency drug prescriptions, and the NRMA for car breakdowns (☎ **131 111**). If you are not a member of an auto club at home that has a reciprocal agreement with the NRMA, you'll have to join on the spot before they will tow or repair your car. This usually costs around $80.

GLBT Resources Sydney is one of the most gay-friendly cities in the world; the gay community has a high profile and lots of support services and there are plenty of gay and lesbian bars, particularly in Oxford Street in Darlinghurst and in Newtown, although overt demonstrations of gay affection are not always tolerated on the street. The annual **Gay and Lesbian Mardi Gras** festival and parade in February (p. 17) is one of the biggest events on Sydney's calendar.

The Gay and Lesbian Counselling Line (☎ **(02) 8594 9596**) is open 5.30 to 10.30pm daily.

Holidays Almost everything is closed on **Christmas Day** and **Good Friday.** On all other major public holidays—**New Year's Day, Australia Day** (January 26), **Easter Sunday, Easter Monday, Anzac Day** (April 25), the **Queen's Birthday** (the second Monday in June), **Labour Day** (first Monday in October) and **Boxing Day** (December 26) banks and businesses are closed, but larger stores and some tourist attractions may remain open.

Liquor Laws   It is illegal to supply alcohol to anyone under the age of 18. It is also illegal for a hotel or restaurant to serve alcohol to anyone who appears intoxicated.

Lost and Found   Call credit card companies the minute you discover your wallet has been lost or stolen and file a report at the nearest police station. Your credit card company or insurer may require a police report number or record. For items lost on trains, contact the **Lost Property Office** (494 Pitt St., near Central Station, ℂ **(02) 9379 3000**). The office is open Monday through Friday 8.30am to 4.30pm. For items left behind on planes or at the airport, go to the **Federal Airport Corporation's administration office** on the top floor of T1 at Sydney International Airport (ℂ **(02) 9667 9583**). For stuff left behind on buses or ferries, call ℂ **(02) 9245 5777**. Each taxi company has its own lost property office.

Pharmacies   Most suburbs have at least one pharmacy (often called 'chemists') that is open late. You can also buy common over-the-counter medications such as headache tablets and cough syrups at supermarkets. Australian pharmacists may only fill prescriptions written by Australian doctors, so it's best if you carry enough medication for your trip.

Post Offices   Stamps for standard-sized mail inside Australia are 55¢; to send a postcard outside Australia will cost $1.30 and will usually take between 5 and 7 working days to reach its destination. Stamps are only available from post offices, although you can post a stamped letter or postcard at any of the red post boxes that are plentiful around the city. The **General Post Office (GPO)** is at 130 Pitt Street, near Martin Place (ℂ **13 13 18**; open Monday to Friday 8.30am to 5.30pm and Saturday 10am to 2pm). General delivery letters can be sent c/o Poste Restante, GPO, Sydney, NSW 2000, Australia (ℂ **(02) 9244 3733**), and collected at 310 George Street, on the third floor of

Surfin' Safely

For most visitors, the most dangerous thing they encounter in Sydney is the surf. Always swim or surf at patrolled beaches between the red-and-yellow flags, which mark the safest area for swimming.

the Hunter Connection shopping centre. It's open Monday to Friday 8.15am to 5.30pm.

Safety Sydney is generally safe, but just like in any big city, it pays to be careful and use common sense. Keep your wallet hidden, don't wear money belts, 'bum packs' or 'fanny packs' outside your clothing.

Areas to be careful in, especially at night, include Kings Cross, Redfern, around Central Station, the cinema strip on George Street near Town Hall Station and the southern end of King Street in Newtown. Inner-city back lanes should also be avoided. The eastern suburbs of Bondi and Coogee can also be rough in the early hours of the morning when pubs and clubs close. If travelling by train at night (not recommended for solo women), travel in the carriages next to the guard's van—they're marked with a blue light on the outside.

Smoking Laws Smoking is banned in all enclosed public places, including public transport, offices, hospitals, hotels, bars and restaurants. Some hotels have outdoor sections where smoking is permitted. Some local councils have also banned smoking in outdoor areas, such as Manly Beach. It is also illegal to smoke in cars carrying children under the age of 16.

Tipping Tipping is not expected anywhere, but it's certainly appreciated. Most Australians leave tips for good restaurant service, but usually only in expensive restaurants. The usual figure is 10%, with more for exemplary service. In hotels, if you want to tip luggage porters, $1 or $2 is plenty, as is a small gratuity of $2 to $5 for those delivering room service, but no more than 10% of the bill. Most people also tip taxi drivers any small change left over from the fare and $5 to $10 for tour guides.

Toilets You rarely have to pay to use a public toilet in Sydney, but the cleanliness of those at parks and train stations often leave a lot to be desired. Be warned that some, especially those in and around popular gay areas, are better known for their liaisons than their facilities, so make sure your intentions are clear. The toilets at Circular Quay Station are usually okay, and you don't need to have a train ticket to use them; ditto for those on the country platform of Central Station. Generally, toilets at beaches tend to be okay and they often have cold showers. I always find libraries and free museums a good option and they are always spotless, as are those in most shopping centres.

The best pub loos (toilets) without a doubt are the subterranean mirror-tiled show ponies at The Beresford (p. 68)—worth a visit just so you can use the extraordinary hand dryers.

Useful Websites

- **www.131500.info.** You'll find everything you need to plan your trip on Sydney's public transport system on this site.

- **www.eatability.com.au/au/sydney/.** This is another good site with restaurant reviews and tips and comments from diners.

- **www.mynrma.com.au.** Everything you need to know about motoring in NSW.

- **www.sydney.citysearch.com.au.** For events, entertainment, dining, and shopping.

- **www.sydneyairport.com.au.** This site gives you information about your flights to and from Sydney International Airport.

- **www.sydneyaustralia.com.** More information from Tourism New South Wales, but this site focuses on Sydney.

- **www.timeoutsydney.com.au.** A well-known independent entertainment bible, focused on Sydney.

- **www.visitnsw.com.au.** Learn where to go and what to see with information from Tourism New South Wales.

- **www.whereis.com.** Go here for online maps and driving directions.

- **www.yourrestaurants.com.au.** Restaurant and bar reviews.

INDEX

ACCOMMODATION